NO ART WITHOUT CRAFT

The Life of Theodore Low De Vinne, Printer

Theodore Low De Vinne

No Art Without Craft

THE LIFE OF
THEODORE LOW DE VINNE,
PRINTER

BY

Irene Tichenor

David R. Godine · Publisher
BOSTON

First published in 2005 by

DAVID R. GODINE, PUBLISHER

Post Office Box 450
Jaffrey, New Hampshire 03452
www.godine.com

LIBRARY OF CONGRESS CATALOGING-IN-PUBLICATION DATA

Tichenor, Irene, 1942–
No art without craft : the life of Theodore Low De Vinne, printer /
by Irene Tichenor.— 1st ed.
Gift 8/09   p.   cm.
Includes bibliographical references and index.
ISBN 1-56792-286-4 (alk. paper)
1. De Vinne, Theodore Low, 1828–1914.   2. Printers—United States—Biography.
3. Printing—New York (State)—New York—History—19th century.
4. Printing—History—Bibliography.   5. De Vinne Press—History.   I. Title.
Z232.D52T53   2005
686.2'092—dc22
2004029102

FIRST EDITION
PRINTED IN THE UNITED STATES OF AMERICA

To

Randal Robert Craft Jr.

MY HUSBAND

who sustains me in many ways
and whose name lends my title
a felicitous irony

Contents

ILLUSTRATIONS

ACKNOWLEDGMENTS

I AM BEHOLDEN to the numerous colleagues and friends who have assisted me in this effort. Rather than thank them on this page, however, I shall name only the four who started me down this path in the first place. Susan Otis Thompson's course at Columbia University in the history of books and printing was an epiphany from which, happily, I never recovered. Terry Belanger – from the early days of the Book Arts Press at Columbia to the full flowering of the Rare Book School at the University of Virginia – continues to make printing history real and vital. G. Thomas Tanselle, through example and generous encouragement, inspires us all to aim for higher levels of scholarship. Kenneth T. Jackson's enthusiasm for history and unabashed love for the city of New York reaffirmed long ago that in both academic discipline and domicile I made the right choices.

I am grateful to David Godine for the care with which he has undertaken the production of this volume. And nothing could please me more than to have Jerry Kelly design it.

Context

O N T H E A F T E R N O O N of 16 February 1914 the officers of the De Vinne Press traveled uptown to hold the firm's annual meeting at the home of the patriarch and president, Theodore Low De Vinne, then two months past his eighty-fifth birthday. The officers consisted of his son and only child, sixty-two-year-old Theodore Brockbank De Vinne, vice president; his one grandson, Charles DeWitt De Vinne, secretary at age thirty; and James W. Bothwell, the forty-nine-year-old treasurer. Neither of the younger De Vinnes had any practical experience at composition or presswork; they confined themselves to the "counting room." Bothwell, on the other hand, had entered the shop as a boy, learned every aspect of the business, and distinguished himself enough to be taken under Theodore De Vinne's wing. Blood relations or not, they represented a family business with Bothwell as the heir apparent.

The two buildings between which these men traveled were both impressive brick structures in New York City. The 1886 De Vinne Press Building at Lafayette and Fourth Streets, in its heyday known as "The Fortress," was an architectural monument to the period after the introduction of the elevator but before the use of structural steel. That circumstance allowed it to rise seven and one-half stories above street level but required masonry load-bearing walls – six feet thick at the base – for support. Even in twenty-first-century New York, this landmark building, with its three-story Roman arches and terra cotta ornaments, remains notable. Four miles to the north by straight-line measure, the 1889 residence stood at the southwest corner of Seventy-sixth Street and West End Avenue. Houses on corner lots were typically more sumptuous than those with a narrow frontage, and De Vinne's was no exception.

The house was filled with an eclectic assortment of decorative porcelains, busts, statues, and vases – typical Victorian fare for a person of De Vinne's circumstances. More important to the elder De Vinne, no doubt, was his library of some six thousand volumes, mostly treatises concerning the history of typography or examples of early printing.

At this time the reputation of the De Vinne Press was quite secure – or so it would have appeared to the casual observer. When Francis Hart took De Vinne on as a twenty-year-old compositor, the firm was a modest job-printing shop that catered to the transportation trade: tickets, timetables, and the like. Over the next six decades, with De Vinne's nurturing persistence, it grew to a book printing house of grand proportions. One should say "book and periodical" house, for it was *Century Illustrated Magazine* (né *Scribner's Monthly*) that inspired his technical innovation and gave De Vinne much of his visibility. There were also ambitious books printed for notable bibliophiles and their organizations as well as many trade books for the Century Company and other publishers. Not to be overlooked was the *Century Dictionary*, whose production required an addition to the De Vinne Press Building in 1890. More often than not, the printer of these works was named only on the verso of the title page in tiny 4-point sans-serif capitals. Understated and chaste though this imprint was, it conveyed a great deal.

While the reputation was sound, the ledger was faltering. The press had posted a loss for both 1912 and 1913, so the men had much to discuss on this February afternoon in 1914. Although he had retired from day-to-day involvement when Theodore L. De Vinne & Co. incorporated as the De Vinne Press, the founder held veto power over any significant changes. Two years before this meeting he had squelched an offer of outside capital, saying that he would rather keep the firm in the family, come what may.

Theodore Low De Vinne's personal status was at least as secure as that of his press, despite his declining energy in recent years. Within the printing trade, he was a living monument. He had earned the respect of his peers, local and national, through his heroic efforts: negotiating wages on behalf of employers, advocating cost-accounting techniques, writing instructional treatises, volubly holding a conservative position on typographic aesthetics, educating printers on the history of their craft. In his maturity he was often paired with the printers' patron saint Ben Franklin at trade celebrations, and medals were struck bearing their two likenesses. At the annual Franklin Day dinner (a tradition that dated back at least to 1825), the assembled printers rose when De Vinne entered the room. He was a founder and perennial officer of the New York printing proprietors' organization, the Typothetae, and was elected the first president of the national body. At the 1899 national convention, held in New Haven, the attendees had given the governor of Connecticut and the mayor of New Haven polite welcomes. But when De Vinne stepped onto the podium the printers broke into such a raucous response that it was some time before he could be heard. In 1910 these colleagues had commissioned a bronze bust of him – an unusual tribute during a person's lifetime.

Among workmen, too, De Vinne was held in awe. There was no doubt concerning the old gentleman's aversion to the unions' wage-and-hour demands or the preposterous notion of the closed shop, but it remained a badge of distinction to be a De Vinne employee.

It was not only within the printing trade that De Vinne was widely known and respected. With the 1876 publication of *The Invention of Printing*, his writings had burst out of their restricted trade-journal environment to encounter a wider audience. Further articles for *Century* and other general-interest periodicals gave him increasing visibility. The books he subsequently wrote were widely reviewed and distributed. Yale and Columbia Universities awarded him honorary degrees. Add to these personal accomplishments the prominence of his press in an era when print was *the* medium, and you have as close to a household name as any tradesman ever registered.

By 1914 his sight was nearly gone, but with clerical assistance he still carried on correspondence on the one topic that had sustained him since his youth: the history of typography. He now had plenty of time to reflect upon his life as a printer, and much upon which to reflect.

Earlier in February he had related to Bothwell, with some amusement, the following dream: He had been wandering on the bank of a river, apparently the Styx, when Charon tapped him on the shoulder and said, "De Vinne, you have been here about five years too long. Don't you think you had better come across?"

When the officers arrived at 3:30 on the sixteenth for that annual meeting, they learned that Mr. De Vinne was ill. They postponed the meeting. That evening he died.

What follows is a study of his life and work.

Origins

Omissis aliis, hoc legamus ["Laying aside other books, let us read this" or, more loosely, "Forget other books; just read this one"]

Inscribed by the Rev. Daniel De Vinné in the Bible he gave his seventeen-year-old son, Theodore, in 1846

THEODORE DE VINNE had a dual family heritage. On his father's side, he was an ambitious first-generation American; on his mother's, he was the confident product of a founding family. Many of the characteristics Theodore De Vinne exhibited throughout his life – determination, individualism, a love of learning, and a bent toward history – must have come from his father, Daniel. Born in 1793, the elder De Vinné was brought from the north of Ireland to upstate New York as an infant. There are conflicting traditions as to the origins of the family. Daniel (who used an accent on the surname, a practice dropped in the next generation) said there was a shadowy report that his paternal line came from France but that his mother's family were "Celts of the Celts" and had inhabited the north of Ireland from time immemorial.[1] Theodore said family tradition held that the paternal line descended from the Van der Vinne family of Holland, their branch having left during the religious wars of the seventeenth century to settle in the north of Ireland, shortening their name to De Vinne. Theodore and his siblings also had Dutch as well as Huguenot ancestry through their mother. Theodore's younger brother, Daniel S., gladly claimed all three strains:

> In speaking of bloods, it reminds me when going to Florida some years past, in a smoking-room were a number of men "half seas over" who demanded from each occupant, "Who in hell are you?" When it came my turn to speak, I said: I am a New Yorker by

birth, having lived there all my life, that whatever patience I had was owing to Holland-Dutch; whatever politeness, to French; whatever pugilistic, to the Irish – three fighting bloods; when fully aroused, all Irish, lick or be licked.[2]

Although the De Vinnés were Roman Catholic, the religious instruction Daniel received from his mother had no particular Catholic content. When she died, Daniel was sent at age eleven to live with his grandparents in Albany where his grandmother and aunt were both devout Catholics. Nevertheless, Daniel sampled numerous churches before finding the right one, and just before his seventeenth birthday, after some internal struggle, he converted to the Methodist Episcopal Church.

This denomination had been an ecclesiastical body only twenty-six years, having originated in the eighteenth century within the Church of England from small societies that stressed faith rather than works and established methodical habits of prayer and Bible study. Transplanted to the American colonies, the Methodist movement had been spread and nurtured by itinerant lay preachers. At periodic "conferences" (a term used both for meetings and for geographical divisions), circuits were reassigned. After the Revolution, seeing that there were too few Anglican clergy left in America to provide sacraments for the Methodists, founder John Wesley had provided for ordination of these lay ministers, in effect making Methodism a denomination all its own. The sect had claimed most of its adherents from the middle and lower classes. Daniel said Methodists were then a despised people, that they were "the fewest, the poorest, and the most inconsiderable of all the Christians in Albany."

When Daniel joined the church in the heat of the Second Great Awakening, Francis Asbury – prototype of the itinerant minister on horseback – still had six more years of service in the saddle ahead of him. Daniel caught the prevailing enthusiasm for the itinerancy and felt his destiny was to preach. Postponing this urge for several years, he became a junior partner in establishing a school in Brooklyn. In 1818, however, at the age of twenty-five, he sold his interest in the school to travel to Louisiana where he began a Sunday school for slaves, which was soon dispersed by opposition. He made his way upriver to the Natchez Circuit and was received into the Conference of 1819 as an itinerant minister assigned to the Opelousas Circuit where he preached to whites by day and to slaves by night. He traveled "thirty to forty miles a day over prairies without roads or bridges; fording the bayous, or when they were high, swimming them, or passing over by floats of decayed logs, tied together by grapevines."[3]

This close view of slavery "without its holiday dress" appalled Daniel De Vinné, and he found himself in a series of disagreements with the church establishment – both local and national – that placed him at a repeated disadvantage. In 1824 he succeeded in obtaining a transfer to the North only by convincing the bishop that he would cause more trouble for both slaveholders and the church if he was left in slave territory. Back in New York, in March of 1826 the penniless thirty-three-year-old married Joanna Augusta Low (rhymes with "now"), known as Augusta. Like Daniel, she had converted to Methodism while in her teens, against the wishes of her Reformed Dutch family. One wonders whether her well-established family welcomed her marriage to a man without any obvious prospects.

Augusta's Dutch and Huguenot ancestors had settled in New Amsterdam in 1668.[4] Her father, Samuel Low, wrote two volumes of poems published in New York in 1800 by T. & J. Swords. The family was proud of its heritage in the new world. When Augusta willed to her two daughters "every article in the house . . . from the attic to the kitchen," the inventory included numerous pieces of furniture and other household items of venerable lineage. When daughter Emma mentioned them later in her will, they included a "looking glass saved from destruction by the British," a "dressing table . . . stolen by the British and left on Broadway Road, later recovered," and other pieces with Revolutionary War connections. Emma bequeathed many items to the Society of Colonial Dames and to the Washington Headquarters Association. She left to the Metropolitan

Museum of Art for their early American art collection a portrait of her mother painted in 1821 or 1822 by John Paradise and a miniature portrait of her uncle, the Rev. Samuel Low, painted by William Dunlap in about 1820. Daniel De Vinné had apparently married a woman who was not without resources.

For the next eight years De Vinné served two-year appointments in the New York towns of Hempstead, Mount Pleasant, and New Rochelle and in Stamford, Connecticut, where Theodore Low, the second of eight children, was born on Christmas Day in 1828. After arguing in vain against a proslavery resolution at the 1836 New York Conference, De Vinné was appointed to a location on Long Island where local Methodists claimed they could not provide adequate financial support for a minister. Either family or friends within Mrs. De Vinné's circle protested to a presiding elder and the bishop. As a result, the appointment was changed to the Harlem Mission, but at a single man's salary even though the De Vinnés were by now a family of nine. Not yet eight years old, by observing his father the young Theodore was getting an early lesson in determination and adherence to one's principles.

When the slavery debate resumed at the 1838 New York Conference, De Vinné told two proslavery bishops that Methodism was as much his as theirs. For this breach he was sent to a remote circuit in the Catskill Mountains to occupy a dilapidated house, and there, in the village schools, Theodore completed his formal education. Daniel continued to make known his antislavery sentiments, writing articles in the Methodist *Zion's Herald* in 1843 and 1844, arguing against slaveholding on the part of Methodist ministers, an issue that split the church into two bodies in 1845.

In his memoirs the Reverend De Vinné said that his salary as a circuit rider began at $12.75 per year and averaged only $327 annually throughout his career. In addition, he probably received food and other goods his congregants could spare. Augusta may have brought to the marriage resources beyond the furniture mentioned above, but the family seems to have lived in rather humble circumstances throughout Theodore's childhood. De Vinné retired from the ministry in the late 1850s. When he died in 1883 at age ninety, he was the owner of two houses in Morrisania, Westchester County, New York, and left an estate totaling $5,125. When Augusta died four years later, her estate amounted to $5,250.[5]

Daniel De Vinné not only left a legacy of sturdy moral conviction and modest lifestyle; he also exhibited a strong respect for learning. In addition to some 8,440 sermons preached during his lifetime, he wrote a history of the Methodist Church's stand on slavery and a history of early Irish Christianity.[6] Both books involved a careful examination of earlier documents. The former analyzed the wording of John Wesley's tract against slaveholding and other seminal documents of the church, arguing that slaveholding had never been condoned by the Methodist Episcopal Church. In the latter work, De Vinné sifted through countless historical documents to support his contention that Christianity in Ireland had been founded on the basis of scripture, not orders from Rome. Daniel De Vinné's style was logical and exceptionally lucid, skills he may have acquired through preparing many sermons. It was a fine model for any son with the slightest inclination for studying historical documents and distilling them for readers.

Having learned Latin, Greek, Hebrew, and French himself, the erstwhile schoolmaster taught Latin to his sons. It was Theodore, rather than the eldest son, John Augustus, who proved most susceptible to his father's pedagogy.

According to Theodore's own recollection, he first set foot in a printing office in 1835, before his seventh birthday, when he accompanied his father to the Harper Brothers' establishment on Cliff Street in New York. The Reverend De Vinné was an old friend of Methodist James Harper, a fact commonly thought to have led the six De Vinne sons into the book trades: four into printing and two into binding. On that day Harper presented young Theodore with a copy of *The Life of Captain John Smith*, a treasure that remained in his library throughout his life.

After attending school in the New York villages of Catskill, Amenia, and White Plains, Theodore did some temporary work in

1843 in a printing shop in Fishkill, a small town east of the Hudson River in Dutchess County, and was soon an earnest apprentice in the office of the *Newburgh Gazette* operated by S. T. Callahan. (Callahan printed the *Gazette* from 1838 to 1852 and then apparently tried his hand as a book and job printer in New York City; he is listed as such in Rode's 1853 *New York City Directory*.) An article based upon an interview with Theodore four decades later described the *Gazette* office in these terms:

> It was a small office, frugally furnished with one hand press and a few fonts of type, but the owner and his foreman were men of ability and gave sound teachings to the three boys who made up the working force. All had to take turns in work, to roll behind and pull before the press, to wet paper, to help at mailing and roller-making, to set type and make up the paper, to do odd jobs, and even read proof. Some of the work exacted was sad drudgery, but it had its compensations for those who could take them. Mr. De Vinne thinks that he learned rather more of practical printing in this small printing-office, where he had to do so many things, than he could have done in a finely equipped office in which he would not have been obliged to exercise as much of forethought and ingenuity.[7]

In addition to the newspaper, this small shop did some book and job printing. De Vinne had his first experience at book printing when he did composition, including the title page, and presswork on Samuel W. Eager's *An Outline History of Orange County* (1846–47). In later years he sought a copy for his own library; it would become item No. 558 in the 1920 auction of his collection.

A town of about fifty-eight hundred inhabitants, Newburgh was situated high on the west bank of the Hudson River in Orange County. It was ideally situated as a shipping point for produce from northern New Jersey and Pennsylvania to Albany ninety-five miles north and, more significantly, to New York City sixty miles south. But the construction of the Delaware and Hudson canal and the subsequent building of the New York and Erie Railroad robbed it of its natural advantages as a commercial center, and by the 1850s it was struggling to maintain its position. There was a daily passenger steamboat running to New York City and various regular steamers and other craft carrying produce and goods on different days of the week.

A town the size of Newburgh was a good stepping-stone for the young De Vinne as he made the transition from the upstate villages of his boyhood to New York City. After completing his apprenticeship, he was ready to take the steamboat downriver and ply his new trade in the nation's printing capital.

PRINTING OFFICE FOR SALE,

IN THE CITY OF NEW-YORK.

On account of continued ill health, the result of a life-time of confinement and sedentary employment, the subscriber wishes to dispose of his Printing Establishment, and engage in some active, health-promoting business —in order that, before he dies, he may enjoy the pleasure of eating and drinking in moderation, without suffering the pangs of Dyspepsia—and that he may know what it is to have elastic spirits and a clear head, if, indeed, it be not too late.

The following Catalogue shows of what his office principally consists, though it does not embrace every thing; and he believes that no materials of the like kind were ever kept in better order, or less abused in being used. There are no accumulations of old rubbish. The proprietor has been in the habit of buying the new and fashionable styles of Type, and of discontinuing the use of such as were too much blemished to produce handsome work. Every thing is in fine order, and exactly adapted to the business attached to the Establishment, for which, indeed, it has been purchased, and by which it has been paid for.

The custom which is offered with the Office is as permanent as any custom can be, not guaranteed in writing, and can be retained by any skilful printer possessing good business talents. It is of the best and most desirable character, and will enable any prudent man to live handsomely, enhance the value of the office, and lay by something yearly.

This Establishment does not belong to the superannuated class, which are going to the grave with their decrepit owners, but is as valuable in proportion to its extent as any printing office whatever. No one can doubt this, when assured that it has cost upwards of $8000, and has paid for itself in the last six years. The patronage is constantly increasing.

Price $7000.   —:1849:—   **FRANCIS HART,**

No. 4 THAMES ST., N.Y.

CATALOGUE.

This Catalogue embraces but few articles not purchased within the last three or four years. Many of them were new within one and two years, and all are in excellent condition. The Nos. and Prices refer to Bruce's Specimen.

COUNTING ROOM FURNITURE.

1 Desk—mahogany	$24.00
2 Easy Chairs	6.00
1 Sofa	15.00
1 painted pine Rack, 40 drawers	30.00
Ink Stand 1.50, &c., &c.	3.00
1 Desk	5.00
1 Dictionary—$5.00, Typography—$1.00	6.00
2 large Frames with Glass	2.00

PRESSES, &c.

1 large Cylinder Printing Press, made by Hoe & Co., 23x24½ inches with the appurtenances complete..........$1200.00
(This Press is in perfect order. The proprietor would hardly thank Hoe & Co. to put a new one in its place gratuitously.)
1 Super Royal "Washington" Hand Press, 26x32½, including a Self-Inking Machine, Bank, &c. 290.00
(This Press is as good as new.)
1 Super Royal "Washington" Hand Press, including Self Inking Machine, and valuable Bank with drawers......... 250.00
1 Foolscap "Boston Press," including Distributors, Rollers, Bank, &c. 100.00
1 Card Press—Gillman's Patent—new...... 140.00
1 Proof Press—Hoe's Cylinder......... 65.00
1 Standing Press—4 inch screw—Austin's make......... 200.00
7 gross Pasteboards, used with do......... 63.00
1 Cherry Boards   do......... 12.00
2 thick black walnut Boards   do......... 4.00
Lot of blocking for do......... 4.00
1 Cutting Machine—Ruggles'......... 63.00
1 Card and Lead Cutter......... 10.00
Roller and Furnace for making Rollers... 4.00
Mallets, Planers, &c. 3.00

IMPOSING STONES.

1 Imposing Stone, 4 ft. 15 in. by 2 ft. 2 in., with Table, Drawer, and Form Rack......... $20.00
2 Imposing Stones, 7 ft. by 2 ft. 2 in. each, with Table and Drawers......... 20.00
1 Imposing Stone, 4 ft. 7½ in. by 2 ft. 3 in., and Table with Drawers and Form Rack... 30.00
1 Imposing Stone, 6 ft. by 2 ft. 3½ in., and Table with Drawers......... 25.00
2 Imposing Stones, 3 ft. 3½ in. by 2 ft. 3 in., and 2 ft. by 2 ft. 3 in., and Table with Drawer......... 20.00

CHASES.

1 pair Dbl Medium Chases, wrought-iron, with cross bars......... cost $25.00
1 Double Medium, with crosses......... 2.00
1 Imperial Chases, do......... 12.00
2 Super Royal Chases, do......... 12.00
16 cast iron Cap Chases......... 16.00
3 wrought iron ..   with cross bars... 12.00
3 long and narrow Chases for headings.. 3.50

25 Job Chases—various sizes—smaller than Cap	15.00
2 medium cast iron Chases	5.00
3 .. wrought iron Chases with cross bars	25.00
4 Demy cast iron Chases	10.00

MISCELLANEOUS ARTICLES.

1 Counter Table	10.00
1 (with draws)	15.00
1 Counter, with draws,	5.00
1 Cut Rack	4.00
1 Rack for Leads	1.00
2 Galley Racks	6.00
1 Case of Draws for Leads, &c.	3.00
Iron Pipes for heating office	24.00
2 Stoves and Pipe	24.00
1 Sink, Lead and Iron Pipe	25.00
1 Wetting Trough	3.50
1 Paper Cutting Table	3.00
1 Long Pine Table	1.50
1 Mahogany Cabinet for Paper, &c.	8.00
1 Clock	8.00
1 Riglet Rack	2.00
1 Ink Rack	1.50
1 Book Rack	2.50
12 Super Royal Paper Boards }	8.00
6 Super Royal Letter Boards }	
1 Ley Kettle	1.50
5 Camphene Lamps	4.00
1 Oil Can	.50
2 Camphene Cans }	
2 Camphene Fillers	.25
1 Pair Large Shears	.75
1 Pair Small do.	.25
2 Straight Edges	3.00
2 Saws	1.00
20 Candlesticks	1.50

STANDS, CASES, AND RACKS.

1 Standing Galley, with Form Rack and 10 draws	22.50
2 Double Stands with Case Racks and Draws, $6 50 each	45 50
11 Double Stands with Racks, $5 50 each	60.50
1 Double Stand with Case and Board Rack and Boards	8.50
1 Single Stand with Rack	3.50
72 Upper Cases, (best quality),	52.50
63 Lower Cases, (best quality)	47.25
17 Job Cases, (best quality)	17.00
25 Case Frames	12.50
1 Cabinet, 10 cases	4.00
1 Cabinet, 9 cases	7.00
1 Cabinet, 12 cases	7.00
1 Cabinet, 36 cases	18.00

GALLEYS.

13 Double Brass-bottom Galleys	35.75
1 Single Brass-bottom	3.50
26 Common	9.00
1 Standing Galley	1.00

COMPOSING STICKS.

1 wood,	24 inches	1.50
1 iron,	15 ..	1.50
2 ..	12 ..	3.00
1 ..	10 ..	1.25
2 ..	9 ..	3.00
9 ..	8 ..	16.00

LEADS—VARIOUS LENGTHS.

	Lbs.
10 4 to Pica	2.50
20 3 to Pica	5.00
4 6 to Pica	1.00
25 3 to Pica	6.25
4 6 to Pica	1.00
7 3 to Pica	1.75
4 6 to Pica	1.00
7 5 to Pica	1.75
6 6 to Pica	1.50
6 6 to Pica	1.50
4 6 to Pica	1.00
9 4 to Pica	2.25
9 6 to Pica	2.25
12 6 to Pica	3.00
12 9 to Pica (Pathfinder)	6.34
12 6 to Pica (Gazette)	3.00
8 6 to Pica	2.00
10 6 to Pica (Churchman)	2.50
62 6 to Pica (M. Times)	15.50
7 Foot Leads	1.75
63 6 to Pica (Evergreen)	15.75
6 3 to Small Pica	1.50
8 of other leads, used on Evergreen	2.00
3 6 to Pica	.75
15 leads, (broken)	2.00

BRASS RULE.

192 Newspaper Dashes, 10 cents each	19.20
246 Newspaper Advertising Rules, 6 cents each	14.36
1 Set Parallel Rules, 17 feet, mitred, No. 8,	5.72
1 Set Parallel Rules, 18 feet, mitred, No. 8,	7.63
2 feet No. 1 Rule, for do	.16
5 Rule, 19 feet, cut for Lower corner	7.80
No. 11	15 .. mitred	11.35
No. 14	2 ..	1.15
No. 14	1 ..	.50
No. 30	14 ..	1.35
No. 14	1 ..	1.25
No. 11	20 ..	7.87
No. 27	2 .. Plain	1.30
No. 9	32 ..	5.12
No. 11 Rule 45 feet, Plain	9.00
No. 11 ..	1.60
No. 24	4 ..	.80
No. 30	2½ ..	1.00
No. 13	2½ ..	.75
A large quantity of Brass Rule of various Numbers and Prices	20.00
Column and Head Rules for Newspaper	12.00
16 Column Rules, and 8 Head Rules	3.00

FIG. 1. First page of a three-page circular in which Francis Hart offered his printing establishment for sale, 1849.

Journeyman's Journey (1850–1857)

*I among the workmen pulled the stroke oar – I was
there earliest and last – nights and Sundays – endeav-
oring by presence and example to give greater efficiency
to my fellow workmen.*

TLD to Francis Hart, 1855

HAVING LEARNED the rudiments of both composition and
presswork, young Theodore embarked upon a career in
New York City in 1848 before his twentieth birthday. A lively seaport and commercial hub of half a million population, New
York nevertheless was still primitive in many ways. Some sixty years
later he remembered

a city of small houses of brick, and occasionally of wood, mostly
of two or three stories, and rarely exceeding five stories even in
the most crowded business quarters; of badly paved cobblestone
streets, which, during a rainy season, were often foul with mud;
without street cars, and not many lines of omnibuses; with
Croton water just introduced, but not yet supplied even to the
basements of all houses; without baths or water-closets; without
gas lighting, telegraphs or telephones, and other conveniences of
modern life.[1]

The built part of the city stopped at Fourteenth Street. The 1811
street-grid plan did not apply to the old portion of the city where
short streets at various angles, cut through by alleys, were the rule.
It was in this southern portion of Manhattan Island that printing
and all other business activity took place, dovetailing a community
of mixed commercial and residential activity.

In New York City Theodore held several temporary positions,
reportedly including newspaper composing and stereotype founding.[2] In 1850 the foreman of Francis Hart's printing shop on

Thames Street engaged De Vinne as a compositor. Francis Hart had come to New York City from New England, where he was born in New Bedford, Massachusetts, in 1815. Hart first appeared in New York City directories in 1841 as a partner of William H. Thompson, printer, of No. 1 Pine Street. (Thompson's bill-heads called his business "Printing, Paper Ruling and Book Binding.") After 1842 Thompson ceased to be listed, giving support to the presumption that Hart bought him out in 1843. Thompson, in turn, had succeeded William Plows, who established himself as a printer in 1836. The De Vinne Press in later years would print on its letterhead "established 1836." The rationale for this is indicated in a scrapbook assembled by long-time De Vinne employee James W. Bothwell and now in the Grolier Club Library. On the back of a Thompson bill-head Bothwell wrote: "William H. Thompson was the successor of Samuel [i.e., William] Plows [here the date 1836 is inserted as an afterthought] who occupied the second floor of an old building on Broadway Cor. Pine St. Francis Hart bought him (Wm. H. Thompson) out. Thus was Samuel [*sic*] Plows' office the potential beginning of the De Vinne Press. JWB." William Plows is actually listed as early as 1834 in city directories as a printer, but apparently as a journeyman, not a proprietor.

Shortly before De Vinne joined the Hart shop, the owner had advertised the business for sale at $7,000[3]:

> On account of continued ill health, the result of a life-time of confinement and sedentary employment, the subscriber wishes to dispose of his Printing Establishment, and engage in some active, health-promoting business – in order that, before he dies, he may enjoy the pleasure of eating and drinking in moderation, without suffering the pangs of Dyspepsia – and that he may know what it is to have elastic spirits and a clear head, if, indeed, it be not too late.[4]

The circular stated that the plant had cost upwards of $8,000 and had paid for itself in the six years Hart had owned it (fig. 1).

Francis Hart's equipment included a hand-powered Hoe cylinder press, two Washington handpresses, a Gillman card press, and a proof press. It included the appropriate imposing stones, chases, galleys, leads, brass rules, etc. The three-page circular listed in detail the engravings and stereotype plates, which ran largely to steamboats plus a few canal boats, packets, and other vessels, express ponies, express wagons, railroad trains, and other transportation apparatus. All of these would have been useful in printing the timetables and tickets that were the shop's mainstay at that time. Type consisted of about three thousand pounds of newspaper and book fonts, two thousand pounds of job display type, four hundred pounds of German (i.e., black letter) type, three hundred fifty pounds of flowers and borders, and sixty pounds of Greek. In the inventory were five camphene lamps and twenty candlesticks, a reminder of the rigors of setting and distributing type in ten-hour days without electric lights.

In addition to the plant, the purchaser would acquire a profitable patronage that could be "retained by any skillful printer possessing good business talents." The circular continued, "The business of the office will be prosecuted with the same vigor as if no sale were contemplated and will be turned over in the most flourishing condition possible. If not sold for the sum designated, the proprietor will continue in business as heretofore." This is precisely what happened; Hart had found no buyer, had continued the business, and had moved it to Nos. 2 and 4 Thames Street. The sale circular did not mention the stationery side of the business, but that was continued as well.

De Vinne had been with Hart less than a year when he was made foreman upon the retirement of a Mr. Simpson, who had presumably held that position long enough to have hired De Vinne himself. The foreman of the compositors customarily also managed the shop if it was too small to justify the hiring of a separate manager. This seems to have been the case with De Vinne, who was overseeing the work of the house while still working regularly at the type case.

After his experience with a platen press upstate, De Vinne became well acquainted with the early "type smashing" cylinder press in Hart's shop.[5] (This machine "received its power from the efforts of a laborer who, for a dollar a day, toiled unflaggingly at a separately rigged up crank.") In the mid-nineteenth century the cylinder was considered fit only for posters and newspapers, but the Hart firm proved that the cylinder press could be successfully used on fine book work, although other printers remained skeptical about it "for a long time." According to De Vinne, the cylinder did not catch on firmly with non-newspaper printers before 1855, and as late as 1860 many book publishers would not allow their stereo-type plates to be printed on a cylinder.[6] Clearly, he was overseeing the work of the shop while the use of the cylinder press for books and high-quality job work was still a novelty.

The best evidence we have concerning De Vinne's early management skills comes from a letter he wrote Hart in about 1855.[7] The first two years of De Vinne's foremanship were spent at new quarters at 117 Liberty Street where the shop received "large accessions of business, which had to be done under great disadvantage with insufficient presses – with an unorganized body of quarrelsome and ignorant workmen – and a deficiency of type and materials." All this required "economy of time and labor and great skill, perseverance and faithfulness in management." De Vinne continued,

> Without wishing to arrogate any undue share of honor, I think you will agree with me in saying that during these two years I among the workmen, pulled the stroke oar – I was there earliest and last – nights and Sundays – endeavoring by presence and example to give greater efficiency to my fellow workmen. I believe I succeeded. I had good control over the office and yet retained the respect and good will of all hands – (one excepted).

In 1853 the firm moved to the corner of Washington and Cortlandt streets. Building up steam, De Vinne said,

> I felt great satisfaction in finding myself in charge of so large an office – and an honest pride in seeing your indebtedness going down – for your business and profits increased though you contended against heavy odds – against heavy rent and grasping landlords – against embezzling rogues and defaulting customers. Despite all, you grew and flourished – your business and material had more than doubled in three years.

By De Vinne's estimate, Hart's printing shop had done $12,000 worth of business in 1850 under Hart's management as compared with $30,000 in 1854 under his own. Profits for those years, he said, had been $2,000 and $5,000 respectively (or 16 ²/₃ percent of business volume in both years). His own salary, meanwhile, had gone from $600 to $775. In the former year, before his management duties had commenced, his salary represented 30 percent of profits and 4 percent of volume of business. In the latter year both percentages had decreased by half. This, in fact, was the point of his twenty-page letter to Hart.

De Vinne had been hired initially at piece rates of twenty-five cents per thousand ems, the "em" being equivalent to a square piece of type, a unit used for both paying compositors and charging customers for set type. He had moved from piece rates to time rates at $9.00 and then $10.00 per week. He was receiving $12.00[8] a week when he took full charge of the office in 1851. At the time, this sum had seemed adequate to him, since he was more ambitious to learn management of the business than to make money. Further, he was still basking in the glow of his marriage on his twenty-second birthday (Christmas Day 1850) to Grace Brockbank.[9] That alone, he said, waxing both romantic and biblical, "was enough to make a new heaven and a new earth."

His labors had increased with the growth of the business, but his salary had lagged behind. Gradually, lack of appreciation of his services had chilled his ardor. Both his business and his personal responsibilities had grown – his only child, Theodore Brockbank De Vinne, was born in 1852 – but his salary stood at only $15.00 per week. He had been forced to move across the Hudson River to Jersey City, New Jersey, adding two hours to his traveling time, because he "could not afford to pay rent for a decent house in New York or Brooklyn." Indeed, he lived in Jersey City for some three decades. Hart lived in Brooklyn (which also meant a ferry ride for him at least until the Brooklyn Bridge opened in 1883).

To show how far out of line his salary was, De Vinne listed a number of men in the printing business whose responsibilities were less than his but who earned more. He concluded his letter, "On Monday next I will give you a plan for our future connection which I trust will meet with your approbation."

Composing this lengthy letter was obviously an arduous exercise judging from its several drafts. It was a traumatic episode in his life that De Vinne kept to himself, unknown to contemporaries and historians alike until his great-grandson told this author that he had given family papers to his own boarding-school alma mater, now Choate Rosemary Hall.

At any rate, partnership did eventually follow. Several accounts say that an offer to De Vinne to take over a business in Ogdensburg, New York, was countered by a partnership proposal from Hart. This letter, however, suggests a somewhat different set of facts. Hart had sent De Vinne off to the Ogdensburg interview with his blessing. De Vinne had rejected the new opportunity because that proprietor had a son who would no doubt take over the business after De Vinne had built it up. De Vinne had resumed his duties with Hart but not with any increased salary or promise of advancement. He would have to wait until 1858 for the partnership he desired.

Meanwhile, under De Vinne's guidance, the Francis Hart job printing establishment advertised aggressively for customers:

> This is one of the oldest, best organized, and most thoroughly equipped Printing Establishments in the city. It is provided with all the ingenious and efficient machinery, and is enriched with a profusion of the many beautiful styles of Types, Borders and Ornaments which have been conferred of late years upon the Typographical Art with such noble rapidity, and more to the advantage of patrons than proprietors.
>
> Adopting, from taste and habit, a high standard of excellence, and retaining only the ablest class of workmen, we claim for our productions an average skill, judgment and beauty, almost unparalleled among the craft.

This extensive advertisement, headed "Francis Hart, Printer, 63 Courtlandt Street," must have appeared in the 1853–57 interval – after they moved to that location and before the firm became Francis Hart & Co. It went on to emphasize "mercantile printing":

This is a department in which we excel, turning out every species of Printing used by the Business Community judiciously arranged and carefully elaborated in styles, corresponding to the price charged, viz: Bill Heads, Shipping Receipts, Bills of Lading, Checks, Notes, Drafts, Bills of Exchange, Catalogues, Prices Current, Circulars, Labels, Cards, &c. &c.

It further highlighted the shop's experience at printing for the "steamboat, railroad, and express" trade, banks, and insurance companies. It also mentioned the stationery department, which dispensed such items as custom-ruled-and-bound account books. "The location is easily found," claimed the ad. "Travelers are invited to call and examine [specimens of printed work] for themselves, and this invitation is not only extended to those who wish to leave orders, but to all who desire to see the machinery and operations of a well-appointed Printing Office." [10] Hart and De Vinne were clearly feeling confident about the firm's prospects (fig. 2).

At least by the time he became Hart's foreman, if not earlier, De Vinne was somehow finding time to study printing history. As early as July 1851 he was a dues-paying member of the Printers' Library and Reading Room of the New York Typographical Society. (De Vinne would join the Typographical Society itself in 1863, become a life member in 1871, and serve as president from 1893 through 1898). The Society, founded in 1809, had incorporated in 1818 as a self-improvement and benevolent organization, devoting its funds to "the relief of sick and superannuated members, their widows and children." All acquisitions for its library, begun in 1823, came as direct gifts from members or donations the society was able to arrange from printers and publishers. In 1852 the library owned about eighteen hundred titles; in addition, it received twelve daily and seventeen weekly New York newspapers and eleven other periodicals. More than five hundred titles were added between 1852 and 1855, mostly newly published works. [11]

It was a good resource for an autodidact like De Vinne. The library was for the use of "printers, type-founders, stereotypers, engravers, bookbinders, and all others connected with the newspaper and book business," but it was not a typographical library, as such. Rather, it was a general collection, as would befit a self-help organization, containing history, classics, poetry, travel, theology, modern fiction, and scientific works. It was not devoid of typographic titles; the 1852 catalogue listed Isaiah Thomas's *History of Printing in America*, John Johnson's *Typographia*, and Caleb Stower's *Printer's Grammar*, among others. It is almost inconceivable that De Vinne would not devour such books first. It is probable that he visited the library often, as it was only a few blocks from Hart's shop and was open from 6:00 to 10:00 p.m. every working day.

De Vinne may have also been a subscriber to the New York Mercantile Library, which in 1859 was the sixth largest library in the United States and in 1875 the fourth, following only the Boston Public and Harvard University Libraries and the Library of Congress.[12]

As other collections became available to him, De Vinne would take advantage of them. Henry Lewis Bullen says that *Printer's Miscellany* (1859), which De Vinne edited and to which he contributed, indicates that De Vinne "was a careful user of the Astor Library at that time." In 1848 John Jacob Astor had left $400,000 for the establishment of this free public library, to be accessible "at all reasonable hours and times for general use." It opened to the public in 1854.[13]

Although James Lenox did not welcome visitors to his exquisite private library until it was incorporated for public use in 1870, he willingly deposited books in the Astor Library for study. De Vinne may have been able to peruse examples of early printing as well as bibliographical works through this arrangement. (The Lenox and Astor Libraries would become the New York Public Library in 1895.) From at least 1871 onward De Vinne would have access to David Wolfe Bruce's superb collection of early printed books.[14] To be sure, he also began building a collection of his own.

FRANCIS HART,

PRINTER,

63 COURTLANDT STREET, NEW YORK,

(CORNER OF WASHINGTON STREET.)

This is one of the oldest, best organized, and most thoroughly equipped Printing Establishments in the city. It is provided with all the ingenious and efficient machinery, and is enriched with a profusion of the many beautiful styles of Types, Borders and Ornaments which have been conferred of late years upon the Typographical Art with such notable rapidity, and more to the advantage of patrons than proprietors.

Adopting, from taste and habit, a high standard of excellence, and retaining only the ablest class of workmen, we claim for our productions an average skill, judgment and beauty, almost unparalleled among the craft.

MERCANTILE PRINTING.

This is a department in which we excel, turning out every species of Printing used by the Business Community judiciously arranged and carefully elaborated in styles, corresponding to the prices charged, viz: Bill Heads, Shipping Receipts, Bills of Lading, Checks, Notes, Drafts, Bills of Exchange, Catalogues, Prices Current, Circulars, Labels, Cards, &c. &c.

CARD PRINTING.

Having an infinite variety of Ornamental Type, and ever aiming at elegance and propriety, our Cards are very superior. Our emission for the last 12 months has been 2,500,000. We have three Card Presses, the fastest and most perfect in use.

Steamboat, Railroad and Express Printing.

We have been familiar for many years with all the various and difficult styles of Jobs required by Railroad, Steamboat and Express Companies, and have acquired an experience, and accumulated an amount of materials specially adapted to their execution, in which we are unrivalled. Companies at a distance would secure a beauty and perfection of Typography by corresponding with us, which are impossible to provincial establishments, and would, at the same time, obtain the superior articles at less than local prices.

Illustrated Show Cards designed and printed in the most elegant style, for the execution of which this office affords superior facilities.

Banks, Insurance Companies, and Joint Stock Associations supplied with new and tasteful designs for Stock Certificates, Checks, &c.

Specimens of every variety of work always open for the inspection of visitors, from which may be selected patterns for any kind of Letter Press or Lithographic work.

The Location is easily found—being on one of the highways of Southern and Western travel, (near the People's Line of Steamers and the Jersey City Ferry.) Travelers are invited to call and examine for themselves, and this invitation is not only extended to those who wish to leave orders, but to all who desire to see the machinery and operations of a well-appointed Printing Office.

STATIONERY SUPPLIED AT MODERATE PRICES.

RULING AND BINDING,

Of every description, performed in connection with printed Headings, Checks, &c.

ACCOUNT BOOKS

Made to order, of the first quality, and marked and paged.

FIG. 2. Advertisement in which Francis Hart & Co. enumerated their services, ca. 1853–57.

Partnership (1858–1877)

De Vinne was, at the age of 48 years, still at school in typography, eager to advance.

Henry Lewis Bullen, 1922

FRANCIS HART announced to the trade on 1 January 1858, "I have this day admitted to a Co-partnership in the Printing and Stationery Business Theodore L. De Vinne, who, as foreman, has long been connected with this office." The firm offered its services as follows:

> Possessing an Office inferior to none in this City, either in the quality of its workmanship or in the amplitude of its materials, we feel confident of our ability to satisfy every demand for Fine Letter Press Printing. This department will still remain under the constant superintendence of the Junior Partner, who will aim to maintain the reputation of the Office for promptness and accuracy.[1]

The announcement also noted that the blank book and stationery department had been "entrusted to a thoroughly competent stationer." With its printing business thriving, stationery became less important to the firm and eventually was dropped, although in later years De Vinne would reminisce about the sights and smells of old-fashioned blank-book binderies.

The articles of copartnership declared the capital stock of the new firm, called Francis Hart & Co., to be $15,000.[2] De Vinne was to own one-third of the firm, for which, over time, he would pay Hart $5,000 with interest out of his share of the profits. De Vinne was allowed to draw $1,000 a year and Hart $2,000 for living expenses. Any profits due De Vinne above $1,000 were to be applied to satisfy his $5,000 obligation until it was extinguished. The articles charged Hart with the responsibility of managing the financial business of the firm, including balancing the books "at least once in each year" and dividing the profits.[3]

Becoming a partner – a proprietor – opened a wholly new phase of De Vinne's career. His day-to-day labor at the printing office probably did not change significantly, but the fact that he was partial owner of a business, rather than a hired hand, gave him a new status. His name appeared on the firm's elaborately "jobbish" business cards (plate 1A). De Vinne was now worthy of a listing in the New York City directory, even though his residence was in New Jersey. He immediately began his writing career and took up a leadership role in New York's book-and-job printing trade.[4]

Thus, at age thirty, De Vinne began to make his voice heard on a great variety of subjects related to printing, some of which would engage his attention for the remainder of his life. (Appendix A lists his published writings.) His first writing effort was as editor of and contributor to *The Printers' Miscellany*, a short-lived trade journal (April, July, and December 1859) "published" by Francis Hart & Co. but essentially an eight-page advertising circular for press manufacturer R. Hoe & Co. and typefounder George Bruce, whose wares it featured and who undoubtedly underwrote it. In one very substantive article in the July issue, De Vinne turned a discussion of the virtues of Scotch-face type into a four-page treatise on the history of typefaces – a portent of writings to come.[5]

Even in his first decade as a writer De Vinne covered a wide range of topics. There was the instructional pamphlet, *The Practice of Lithography for the Use of Novices*. Two historical articles appeared in *The Printer*: "Fust and Gutenberg" and "Mediaeval Printing," the latter addressing aesthetics as well. Several pieces had to do with business management: "The Profits of Book Composition," a series of five articles and letters also in *The Printer* on strikes and trade unions, and the 1869 *The Printers' Price List*. In the 1870s he would take up technical matters, most notably the printing of wood engravings. For the next thirty years he would cover ever more varied topics and then, after the fourth volume of *The Practice of Typography* was published in 1904, concentrate most of his remaining efforts on historical and aesthetic subjects.

In addition to publishing his thoughts, De Vinne reached out beyond the Hart & Co. printing shop in another way – by facilitating better communication among master printers. The destabilization of values and prices brought on by the Civil War inspired De Vinne and Peter C. Baker of the printing firm Baker and Godwin to hold luncheon meetings to discuss business matters. By late 1862 they decided to try to interest other printers in some formal association. As De Vinne would describe it later, "In this great upheaval of everything that had been stable, all our trade landmarks and guide posts disappeared. We were at our wits' end and called together a general council of the trade."[6] Their efforts finally bore fruit in March 1865 with the election of officers and the selection of the name Typothetae, a word of Greek derivation having to do with typesetting. The name was suggested by Baker, perhaps from an entry in T. C. Hansard's 1825 *Typographia.* They pronounced Typothetae to rhyme with "apostrophe," as the following bit of verse reveals:

> Some make it rhyme with all things sweet,
> And bold pronounce it Ty-po-<u>thetae</u>.
>
> On classic grounds some others try
> To make the word Ty-poth-e-<u>tae</u>.
>
> Others still, for reasons meaty,
> Insist on saying Ty-po-<u>the</u>-tae.
>
> A few will make a sip o' the tea,
> And timidly venture <u>Typ</u>-o-the-tae.
>
> But most of us are wroth at he
> Who will not say Ty-<u>poth</u>-e-tae.[7]

Although the youngest of the group, De Vinne accepted the position of secretary, the most active and demanding post. He called the meetings, handled correspondence, kept minutes, wrote annual reports, and generally marshaled support. After arriving at a new price scale and holding quarterly meetings for a few years and annual dinners for several more, the Typothetae as such would have a low profile for several years before being revived in earnest. De

Vinne served as spokesman for the employing printers on a number of occasions during this interval.

One of the most serious business problems in the book-and-job printing trade at this time was underbidding by printers who had little idea of what prices would actually yield a profit. In 1864, a time when cost accounting was in its infancy, De Vinne made his first argument for more sophistication in the methods printers used to calculate costs and, hence, what prices to offer their customers. It came as a six-column letter to the editor of *The Printer*, headed "The Profits of Book Composition" and signed "Brevier."[8] It analyzed the costs of a hypothetical twenty-seven-employee book composition office, demonstrating that if labor at prevailing rates plus rent, light, heat, insurance, taxes, depreciation, loss, and damage were taken into account, the prevailing price of sixty cents per thousand ems was inadequate to make any profit. If one added interest for the capital invested and the management services of the proprietor, the financial loss would be even more severe. This piece was welcomed by De Vinne's colleagues and was reprinted in pamphlet form for the Associated Employing Printers of New York, a name the Typothetae used intermittently in this period.

So strongly did De Vinne feel the need for cost analysis in the printing trade that five years later, in 1869, he published a more elaborate treatment of the subject as the 164-page *The Printers' Price List*. He said in the preface that "friends in the trade . . . advised" him to make his own experience at cost figuring available to his colleagues. This was called the "proof copy" on its title page and reportedly had an edition of only six hundred, for De Vinne wanted to circulate copies for correction and emendation by other printers. In 1871 he issued a revised version. Its prospectus announced that a medium duodecimo "on fine calendered paper" had been electrotyped and was in the press. Available for $4.00 bound in cloth or $5.00 in morocco, it was said to have had a sale of five thousand copies.[9]

The Typothetae members began to educate themselves and then other printers on the newly developed cost-accounting techniques.

They made estimate blanks available to anyone in the trade. Isaac Blanchard gave lantern-slide lectures and blackboard talks to the group on the methods he had developed; De Vinne offered to underwrite further dissemination of those methods to other interested printers. This activity would generate at least two books at the turn of the century by members of the New York Typothetae: *How to Make Money in the Printing Business* by Paul Nathan (1900) and *Actual Costs in Printing* by Isaac Blanchard (1901). The former was dedicated "to Theodore Low De Vinne, The Dean of American Printers, who gave me my first lessons in the making of prices." In addition, *The Printer and Bookmaker* and the United Typothetae took up the cost-accounting cause and gave it national prominence among printers. Early in the twentieth century English printers adapted a cost-finding system based on American models.

Although others developed more formalized procedures for figuring costs and making price estimates based on more sophisticated information, De Vinne deserves much of the credit for the growing awareness among printers of the need to take all manufacturing costs into account.

Improved knowledge of the components that make up operating costs did not solve the problem of underbidding. Cutthroat competition was always a problem in the book-and-job branch of the industry. There was a long-standing tradition in New York of standard prices for composition and presswork, but not every printer adhered to it. Beginners whose zeal was "not always accompanied with proper knowledge" frequently underbid to get a foothold in the business – often not surviving but depressing prices nevertheless. Moreover, as De Vinne noted in his 1872 *The State of the Trade*, experienced but unscrupulous printers knowingly violated the informal price code. The mere existence of the Typothetae, with its dinners, meetings, and increased social intercourse among printers, was supposed to reduce underbidding; it never did so to De Vinne's satisfaction. Late in the century, while the 1890 Sherman Antitrust Act was yet to be tested, there would be considerable sentiment favoring a printing "combination." De Vinne would oppose any such effort on the grounds that the New York printing industry was too diverse to allow for success.

If underbidding among fellow printers was one business problem, the uncertainties wrought by growing unionization of workers was another.

De Vinne's earliest public pronouncements on the subject of trade unions came in a series of articles in 1864 and 1865 in *The Printer*, one of the very few contemporary organs of the printing trade – and one in obvious sympathy with the unions.[10] First was a letter in the September 1864 issue, again signed "Brevier." The editor of *The Printer* found it necessary at the end of this piece, headed "The Strike, from an Employer's Point of View," to print a brief rebuttal. Then came a three-part article – signed "Theo. L. De Vinne" – in October, November, and December 1864 titled "Trade Unions. 'Strike! but hear,'" which inspired a debate in that journal's pages between De Vinne and representatives of the Typographical Union.[11]

In these articles De Vinne's principal theme was that capital and labor were not in opposition in America. Modern trade unions in this country were taking inappropriate inspiration from those in England and Europe where social history had been quite different from America's experience. "The capitalists of Europe," he said, "are seldom of the people. The money they use is mostly that of inheritance. They have little acquaintance, and little sympathy with workmen." In England where "master" meant both master of one's business and master of men, trade unions had arisen out of a tradition of privilege and class. After the decline of the guilds, workmen found it natural to form combinations, albeit covertly, as they were no longer protected from the power of wealth. When the laws against worker combinations were repealed, it was natural for workmen who had suffered injustice to form unions in direct opposition to the interests of the master.

In America, De Vinne maintained, the assumption of a natural hostility between the two classes was inappropriate. Indeed, in the printing business even the existence of two distinct classes was debatable, the categories of employer and employee being so fluid. "In this country," he said, "there is no real hostility between employer and employed. The journeyman of this year may be the employer of the next, in which position he may give wages and work to his old master."

The "capitalists" in the American printing business, he reminded his readers, had all been journeymen, working at case or press for existing wages: "There is not one who does not know, through experience, all the ills of a journeyman's life. There is scarcely one who feels so rich as to scout [i.e., dismiss] the possibility of a reverse of fortune that would compel him to ask work, in future years, of the apprentice he is now instructing."

Finally, the union member's depiction of capital as "a remorseless vulture preying on his vitals" was absurd when one considered the profits being made in the printing business. Although there were some very prosperous publishing houses of books or newspapers, their money had been earned from publishing, not printing. And even "these worthy gentlemen would cut a sorry figure in Wall Street" next to the Astors and Vanderbilts.

De Vinne's second theme was that association and combination were – far from an evil – quite laudatory. They were "a trusty index of civilization." If unions concentrated on self-improvement and the maintenance of high skill levels for their ranks, then superior wages would be a natural consequence of membership. Instead, De Vinne claimed, they took in any workman they could induce to join and put the last first by giving all their energies toward wages: "Their claims for regulating wages appear to be based not on the fact that their members are more skillful, useful, or intelligent than they would have been, but that through association, they have become more powerful, and can dictate terms."

As a third theme, De Vinne protested on several grounds the unions' unilateral declaration of wage rates. To admit the mechanic's right to fix the price of his own labor was a barren concession. The employer had an equal right not to buy that labor. "Each party has the right to name its own terms, but neither can *fix* them for the other." The adjustment of wages for labor requires two parties, the seller and the purchaser of that labor.

Partnership

De Vinne depicted the contracting printer and to some extent the publisher as middlemen between the "operative producer" and the public. "If books were like beef, or flour, or coal – if they were necessities of life, instead of luxuries," he said, wage advances could be secured even in times of economic distress. Workmen who considered only their own needs (and not how well their wage increases could be passed along ultimately in the form of more expensive printed material) were simply unrealistic.

The proposition that workmen are entitled to a certain standard of living, said De Vinne, at first seems reasonable. But journeymen printers themselves do not follow this principle; they do not buy goods and services on the basis of the neediness of the seller. Nor would they agree that an employee with a family to support should receive higher wages than single men. "Necessity of the workman is not a true standard for the adjustment of wages," he declared. When business is depressed, "with what right can the operative claim that his prices [i.e., wages] must be held sacred – that he, alone, of all the parties interested, should lose nothing by the stagnation of business?" Men who are thrown out of work do "exactly what all merchants, manufacturers, and even professional men and artists, are doing daily – they are trying to sell their labor for as much as it will command."

> The fair price of labor is, then, not a definite sum, nor even a definite proportion, that can be fixed upon without regard to the receipts of the employer or to the employment of all the workmen. To be fair it must be just to both of these interests – so proportioned that it will yield a profit to the master as well as invite the buyer to purchase so largely as to give employment to everyone in the trade.

In other words, the conditions of the marketplace, including the exigencies of supply and demand, determine the value of labor.

Two further themes concerned De Vinne in these essays. He argued against strikes on grounds of their inexpediency, claiming that few of them in England or America had been successful and that they further removed any spirit of compromise in employers.

Finally, he deplored the unions' bid for uniform time wages as "a definite sum for an indefinite amount of work," a reward to poor and a punishment to superior workmen.

In these essays for *The Printer*, De Vinne was expressing his own views, leavened, no doubt, by discussions with his colleagues. He was not representing any formal organization of master printers, for there was none. The Typothetae would shy away from addressing labor questions for two decades.

It did become necessary, however, for "employing printers" to meet from time to time with representatives of the journeymen. As a result of such meetings, De Vinne took on the mantle of representing his colleagues when he wrote *The State of the Trade: Observations on Eight Hours and Higher Prices, Suggested by Recent Conferences Between the New-York Typographical Union and the Employing Book and Job Printers of that City*, published by De Vinne's own Francis Hart & Co. in 1872. This forty-four-page analysis of the economics of New York City book and job printing was mandated on 21 June 1872 as a "necessary preliminary" to the deliberations of the Joint Committee of the Employers and Employed in the Trade of Book and Job Printing. Whether it was the entire committee or only the employers who requested this report is not clear. Ostensibly, it was based in part on a questionnaire sent to every known book-and-job office in the city. Given De Vinne's previously expressed opinions, it could well have been written without input from other employers.

At issue was whether the printing trade could establish an eight-hour day (instead of the existing ten-hour day) at the prevailing rate of $20 per week. Predictably, De Vinne's report argued against it on economic grounds. First, to shorten the hours of work would increase costs and drive work out of the city. Second, the inevitable delays caused by shorter hours were "contrary to the spirit of the age and the habits of business men." Many customers would simply not tolerate delays.

De Vinne's pitch was as much moral as economic, however. "There never was greater need for work than there is today," he said.

Partnership

"There never was a time when men were more judged by their work. There is no greater stigma, short of criminality, than that of idler or loafer. It is the fashion to work."

His argument also had its political component:

This movement for eight hours and higher prices [i.e., wages] did not originate with the printers of the city. It is an epidemic. There is strike in the air. It is one of the many plans for embittering the relations of American employers and employed for which we are indebted to the old world. It is by foreign workmen that the strikes and the agitations in other trades of our city have been fomented. . . . It is from the apostles of the International and the Commune that American mechanics have been unwittingly receiving teachings and orders.

Not only was the movement foreign inspired; it was also undemocratic. "The majority of the compositors do not favor the movement. They have joined it with faint heart, if not with spoken protest, and only from a mistaken sense of fraternal obligation." There was only one way to improve the conditions of the workman, De Vinne maintained, and that solution was in his own hands. "If he desires better 'wages', he must sell a better quality of labor. . . . The reform that the workman desires in the trade must begin with himself." To support this creed, De Vinne closed by quoting that representative of Puritan virtue, Charles Francis Adams Jr.:

[T]he industrial and social reorganization essential to our future, like all far-reaching social movements, can only result from the combined and quiet action of an intelligent and determined people, attending in their own way to their daily work, and coldly disregarding all short cuts and royal roads to their promised land. It must be the result of the deep groundswell of a steady purpose. . . .[12]

Publicly De Vinne insisted that the decision to join societies was a workman's own business. Since his clear sentiments against the tactics and priorities of the Typographical Union were on record from the 1860s forward, however, it seems safe to assume that as he built up his business he avoided hiring union members when possible. Indeed, as early as September 1872 he expressed approval privately of a printer "thrusting out every union man" from his shop.[13]

Moreover, that same month he wrote Hart the following report about their own operations:

> We commence work on McKillop [and Sprague, a credit-reporting firm] on 16th October. We shall have no difficulty in getting hands – have already over 100 applicants. I have decided to put on an entirely new set of workers. The men who have worked on this work for years . . . are quietly trying to control the management in the interest of the Union. It is time they were upset, and I am ready for it.[14]

Meanwhile, under De Vinne's management, his firm continued to branch out into more ambitious printing projects. From a business that was largely commercial job printing, Hart & Co. had expanded in quantity and type of product. When collecting imprint data one never can be sure how representative the known imprints are or what percentage of the total output they comprise. And it is virtually impossible to find examples of the more ephemeral sort of job printing, which typically did not bear the printer's name and often simply did not survive beyond immediate use. From the imprints collected thus far it appears that most of Hart & Co.'s early "books" were little larger than pamphlets. They did print the book-length works of De Vinne: *The Printers' Price List* (1869 and 1871), *The State of the Trade* (1872), and *The Invention of Printing* (1876, 1877, and 1878). They also printed the books of Theodore's father, the Rev. Daniel De Vinné: *The Methodist Episcopal Church and Slavery* (1857) and *A History of the Irish Primitive Church* (1870). But much of the early Hart & Co. book-printing business consisted of insurance, legal, medical (homeopathic), or religious pamphlets, most of which would have to be classified as job printing.

As part of its business expansion, the Hart shop undertook work in a new category: catalogues and other works illustrated with line-cuts and wood engravings. The firm received a silver medal for its excellence in 1865 from the American Institute, a trade and agricultural fair held annually in New York City from about 1828.[15] It was, in fact, this class of work that would allow De Vinne to break out of job printing into the book-and-periodical trade. Among the illustrat-

FIG. 3.

Title page of an illustrated Hoe catalogue, 1860. Printed in red, black, and gold on a gray moiré background.

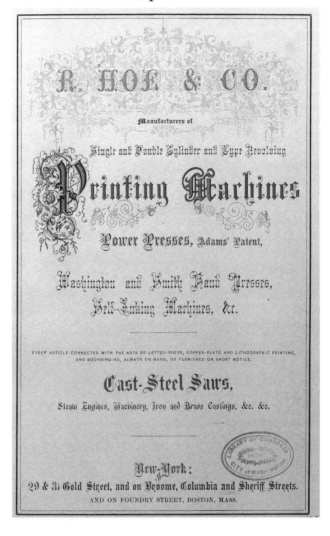

ed items were several catalogues of R. Hoe & Co.'s printing presses and other equipment, their title pages displaying the cluttered, eye-catching style of the day via a dozen ornate type faces (fig. 3).

In 1866 De Vinne and Hart attempted to diversify their business further by purchasing from J. M. Kronheim a process for printing illustrations in colors by metal relief plates. They agreed to buy out

Kronheim's partner for $10,000 and to pay Kronheim $15,000 for his printing plant and the rights to his invention. Kronheim was to instruct Hart and De Vinne in the process for five years, during which term the inventor would receive one-fourth of the profits. An 1883 account tells it thus:

> In 1866 Francis Hart & Co. were induced to buy the process and the plant of an adventurer who undertook to reproduce in the form of relief plates of etched zinc all the delicacy and beauty of crayon lithography. The purchase money was large, and taxed their resources. This enterprise proved impracticable, and the process had to be abandoned, after serious loss, but all liabilities incurred for it were promptly paid.[16]

Writing about this episode at the turn of the century, De Vinne said the makeready for printing these shallow zinc plates was "horribly expensive," and he was not sad to give up the competition brought on by the steam lithographic press in 1870. In fact, the agreement dated 19 November 1866 was canceled by mutual consent on 28 September 1867 with signatures of Hart, De Vinne, and Kronheim.[17] As we shall see, De Vinne retained an interest in relief color processes and adopted less problematic techniques in subsequent years.

Searching for new ways to expand business, Hart & Co. launched itself into the field of illustrated periodicals with *The New-York News-Letter: a Journal of Instructive and Entertaining Literature* of which it was publisher and copyright holder beginning in 1868 and running at least through 1872. Judging from the advertisements, the newsletter was funded substantially by insurance companies, particularly the New York Life Insurance Company. Each issue was eight pages (13" x 9"). It was edited by Julius Wilcox and James M. Hudnut. Although there was a decided insurance theme, there were also poems and stories. And there were often sketchlike, line-block illustrations that occupied a full page.[18]

In October 1869 a notice from the publishers, Francis Hart & Co., said that in 1870 they would begin producing *The New York Almanac* "elegantly illustrated with an illuminated cover in eight colors." Indeed, they did publish the almanac from 1870 through 1883. The first one ran fifty-three pages plus fourteen more that advertised salves, extracts, sewing machines, watches, pianos, etc. It was again edited by Wilcox and had a decided insurance presence. In addition to the traditional almanac fare, there was poetry, prose, and many illustrations, now including wood engravings, often covering the whole 9" x 6½" page.

In *The New-York News-Letter*, Hart & Co. also announced a new illustrated weekly they planned to publish:

> Without indulging in the extravagant promises so common in Publisher's announcements, the Proprietors will content themselves with pointing out some few of the general features of the New Serial, leaving it to speak for itself when it shall make its appearance.
>
> It will consist of Sixteen Large Quarto pages, printed on very superior Paper, and Illustrated by the Best Artists in this country and Europe. Fiction, of powerful interest, will form one of its prominent features, but with this will be associated Popular Articles on Current Topics, Striking Sketches, Domestic Narratives, and Papers on Social Subjects, which, it is believed, will be of interest to every family circle. It will specially address itself to the family, but while it will aim to instruct, it will also hope to be Amusing and Entertaining; in short, it will aspire to be a Cheerful Fireside Companion, whose coming shall be looked for with pleasure, and whose welcome shall be warmer and warmer as, week by week, and month by month, it grows in the acquaintance of its readers.[19]

This periodical, *At Home and Abroad: An Illustrated Journal for Family Reading*, was apparently fleeting. A later issue of *The New-York News-Letter* refers to the first issue of *At Home and Abroad* as having appeared on 4 July 1868, but no other record of it has been found at this writing. At any rate, the advertisements for it, alone, are evidence of De Vinne's and Hart's ambitions to solidify their gains in the promising illustrated periodical field.

In the next decade De Vinne acquired a customer that would be the most important of his career. According to tradition, De Vinne made the decision to print for Scribner and Company during Hart's absence in Europe. One account says that De Vinne made a unilateral decision to print Scribner's children's periodical, *St. Nicholas*; another says that it was the senior magazine, *Scribner's Monthly*.[20] Letters by De Vinne, however, indicate that some kind of work for Scribner's began before Hart left for his trip. Bringing his partner up to date shortly after his departure, De Vinne wrote on 22 September 1872, "Not much has transpired since you left that deserves notice. . . . Was offered yesterday the presswork and binding of a book of

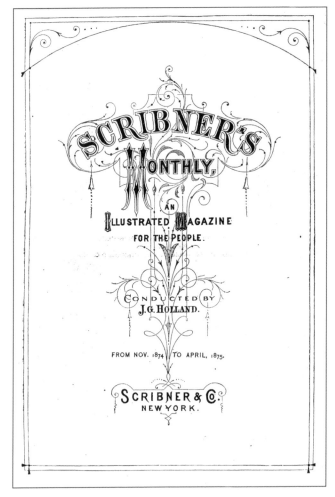

FIG. 4.

Title page of the first volume of *Scribner's Monthly* to bear the imprint of Francis Hart & Co., November 1874–April 1875.

wood cuts, wanted in a hurry, which I had to decline, as Scribners was in the way." A week later he wrote, "We have not yet finished Scribner's cut forms [i.e., printed sheets containing illustrations]. All that we have done pleases Mr. Smith highly. He says that we print them better than they have ever been printed before."[21] While work could conceivably have begun this far in advance on the first issue of *St. Nicholas*, dated November 1873, the last sentence could only be a reference to *Scribner's Monthly*, for which Scribner's had retained the services of at least four printers before Hart & Co. took over printing the entire publication. (Poole & Maclauchlan were the printers of attribution at this time; Volumes 2 through 5, covering November 1871 through April 1873, bear their imprint. They were preceded by New York Printing Co. and followed by the firm of Pelletreau & Raynor and then that of William H. Caldwell. Volume 9, which begins with the November 1874 issue, was the first to show the imprint of Francis Hart & Co. (fig. 4).

De Vinne's letters to Hart indicate that the senior partner was available and apparently a participant when the relationship with Scribner's began and that it commenced a year earlier than is commonly believed. Clearly, Hart & Co. started printing at least some *Scribner's Monthly* illustrations in 1872, two years before they took it on entirely and one year before *St. Nicholas* appeared.

Still, that Hart was in the country from the beginning does not conflict with evidence that De Vinne was already, for all practical purposes, at the helm of the firm. It was De Vinne who met with customers, saw their work through production, and collected the bills. As editor Robert Underwood Johnson said, when Francis Hart & Co. began producing work for Scribner's "We soon found that [De Vinne] was the active administrator."[22]

Some contemporary accounts say that De Vinne had misgivings about his shop's ability to meet art director Alexander Drake's exacting standards of printing wood engravings. As we have seen, De Vinne was no stranger to printing this kind of illustration. It is certain that De Vinne doubted the profitability of such work. Writing to Hart in Europe, he said that although the president,

Roswell Smith, was very pleased with the quality, "the cost is frightful." De Vinne gave some detail of the labor costs involved and concluded, "I don't believe we can get this price. It is not desirable work. We had better stick to . . . Brown and to McKillop at fifty cents per token." (The token, a common unit for pricing presswork, was half a ream of paper or 250 impressions.)

Despite initial reservations, something – perhaps the magazine publisher's willingness to pay top dollar or possibly the opportunity to print both illustrations and text for the forthcoming children's periodical – changed De Vinne's mind. Before Hart returned in the summer of 1873, a commitment very likely had been made to print *St. Nicholas*, the first issue of which appeared in November. De Vinne was the first printer of *St. Nicholas*, in an arrangement that lasted forty-four years.

A solid relationship of mutual respect developed between him and the staff of Scribner & Co. The care he took was exactly what the publisher had been searching for. Drake was fond of telling how he and De Vinne labored over the press, experimenting with materials and techniques, until both were satisfied with the resulting wood-engraved illustrations. Henry Lewis Bullen of the American Type Founders Company had no doubts about why the Scribner Company chose De Vinne:

> The contract to print *Scribner's* was given to De Vinne because in 1876 [*sic*] he was not only the best printer in America, but also because he was, at the age of 48 years, still at school in typography, eager to advance. He was, it would seem, the only printer in America at that time who knew that there was an art of printing which had its earlier masters and masterpieces.[23]

Indeed, as we shall see, the "earlier masters" of the art of printing were already absorbing any spare time De Vinne could find to study them. Meanwhile, in the summer of 1872 a crisis occurred in De Vinne's business relationship with Hart that, again, De Vinne kept private and is only revealed in the family papers at Choate. It became apparent to De Vinne that he and Hart lacked a common understanding of their partnership arrangements. The younger partner was so upset at Hart's view of the matter that the normally composed younger partner could not discuss it "without passion" and avoided any confrontation as Hart left for his year's tour of Europe. Although their 1858 agreement had called for an annual accounting, Hart had not made – and De Vinne had not insisted upon – a balance sheet for fourteen years, in fact not until Hart was tidying up his affairs before the trip. Both men had drawn out more than the $1,000 and $2,000 per year anticipated in the agreement. Hart held that since he had *not* drawn out *twice* as much as De Vinne, the younger partner owed him interest on Hart's excess capital left in the business. Moreover, since profits had been used for additional machinery and materials, and no formal division of profits had ever been made, Hart contended that De Vinne had paid off none of the $5,000 purchase price and therefore still owed him that plus fourteen years' interest on it.

In September, De Vinne discovered that before departing Hart had adjusted their interests on the ledger in a manner suiting himself and without any consultation. The entry took into account all the interest Hart claimed for himself and concluded that he now owned seven-eighths of the business, to De Vinne's one-eighth. Unable to suppress his anger and dismay, De Vinne drafted a series of letters to Hart protesting the older man's usurious stance and putting forth a number of arguments on his own behalf. The drafts of these letters show that in this instance De Vinne achieved restraint only with great effort.

De Vinne claimed that their contract compelled Hart to apply all undrawn profits due De Vinne toward the payment of the $5,000 until the obligation plus its interest was satisfied, a state of affairs that he calculated had been reached in 1865. He had never demanded an adjustment of the ledger because he trusted that delay would not injure his interests. De Vinne freely admitted that of the profits drawn from the firm over the fourteen years he had drawn more than one-third; he conceded that he owned Hart that excess, plus interest. But he objected to paying interest on the excess capital Hart had allowed to remain in the business. The 1858 contract, which De Vinne had drawn up at Hart's request, had not anticipated any such "unconscious borrowing." Even a calculation made by one Mr. Halstead, presumably an accountant retained by Hart & Co., placed De Vinne's portion at nearly 20 percent, but Hart was not disposed to accept that version. The matter would remain unresolved until Hart returned from his year's tour.

Back from his voyage in September 1873, Hart summarized his position on the partnership dispute. Since 1858 Hart and De Vinne had drawn out and used $95,339.64, of which De Vinne had used $5,300 more than one-third. De Vinne therefore owed him $5,300 with interest plus the original $5,000 with interest. Only when De Vinne paid that amount, said Hart, would he own one-third of the business.

Ultimately the men sought legal advice. One George W. Wingate submitted a legal opinion on 1 October 1873. He said De Vinne could not be charged interest upon his "overdrafts upon the profits," by which he presumably meant the $5,300. Regarding the original purchase price, if De Vinne's undrawn profits had gone to meet that obligation, then he owned just that much less of the firm's capital. But since Hart had not been paid in his private capacity in cash – both parties being equally to blame for the failure to issue regular profit statements – De Vinne still owed $5,000 plus interest.

Extant records do not show precisely on what financial terms the matter was settled, but Hart and De Vinne began again with a new partnership agreement dated 1 January 1874. The capital (unstated but agreed to be in excess of $83,000[24]) was owned in the proportions one-third to two-thirds. Hart and De Vinne were allowed to draw $6,000 and $3,000 respectively each year, any excess withdrawals to be agreed upon in writing and bearing interest.

Confirming the existing practice, De Vinne agreed to "devote his time and give his best services to the business of the said firm and at all reasonable hours by night and by day as the exigencies of the business may require to give his personal attention to the affairs of the office, continuing also to act as heretofore as manager in the same." Hart was to have the "general management of the financial business" of the firm when "not absent or disabled"; but he had "the right to absent himself at discretion," and at such times De Vinne was to assume management of the firm's financial affairs as well. There is every reason to believe that Hart, whose health continued to deteriorate, "absented" himself regularly.

Throughout this partnership turmoil and his preoccupation with other business matters, De Vinne continued to write and publish his own work. The origin of the printing art, not surprisingly, was a consuming interest. Through several early articles we can see him leading up to his monograph, *The Invention of Printing*. One of his first substantial pieces on any subject was a paper read before the New York Typographical Society in February 1864 titled "Mediæval Printing." In it he established his authority as an investigator, bolstered by his experience as a practical printer:

> I find that very few of the many persons who have written on printing were printers; and not one out of a hundred of those who speak confidently and authoritatively on the appearance of books have the necessary education to qualify them as competent judges. For there are certain kinds of knowledge useful and necessary in a comparison of books that cannot be learned outside of a printing office. There . . . is a knowledge of the mechanics of printing that can be acquired only before the case or behind the roller stand.[25]

The speech itself was somewhat rambling, but the theme to which he kept returning was that "typographic amateurs" had given early printing a reputation higher than it deserved. He mentioned crowding of type to save paper or vellum, rudely cut fonts, and unorganized title pages as problems common to many books produced during the first two centuries of movable type. It was misleading, he said, to bring forward a sumptuous folio or quarto as a specimen representing the average workmanship of that day; there were miserable printed products then as now. Despite his lifelong reverence for his forebears and his respect for the conditions under which they labored, he did not accept early printed examples uncritically.

At the second annual Typothetae dinner (1864) he was asked to respond to the toast, "Our fathers in the art: they builded wiser than they knew." Although he mentioned many fathers (Gutenberg, Schoeffer, Plantin, the Elzevirs, Baskerville, Bodoni, etc.) he decided to focus on the Dutch – the fact that New York was once New Netherland and that so many men seated around the tables had Dutch surnames. This inspired him to salute Laurens Janszoon Koster as the patriarch, the inventor of printing. Whether his mind was actually satisfied that Koster (or "Coster") deserved this citation or whether he was just keeping to his Dutch theme, it is a conclusion he would reevaluate as he examined the sources (particularly Van der Linde's 1869–70 work that put the Coster legend to rest).

That same year, 1864, De Vinne also clarified the orthographic confusion surrounding certain fifteenth-century printers. The name of Johann Fust (Gutenberg's "business partner and plunderer" reputed by some to have made Bibles with assistance from the devil) had been confused with that of Dr. Johann Faust, subject of Goethe's tragedy, who was actually born fourteen years after Fust died. De Vinne then set straight the matter of Gutenberg vs. Gensfleisch. Johann Gutenberg's family name was Gensfleisch, but he adopted the name of his mother's home, Gutenberg. (Although his imprint does not appear on any printed works attributed to him, that is how his name appears in court documents.) There had been confusion between him and his uncle, Johann Gensfleisch, who could not possibly, as some alleged, have stolen the invention from Coster. De Vinne sorted out this confusion that had been passed along by such American authorities as Isaiah Thomas (1810) and Joel Munsell (1839). For this article, De Vinne said he had consulted "all the leading French and German typographical historians."[26]

While the invention of printing had become a consuming interest to De Vinne, he was also studying other significant historical events and figures. In 1871 he wrote for *Printers' Circular* of Philadelphia a brief appreciation of Giambattista Bodoni, the late-eighteenth and early-nineteenth-century printer who restored Italy to the annals of fine printing after a century and a half of decline.

Forty years later in one of the last products from De Vinne's pen, it would become obvious that this earlier piece was inspired by the erection of a statue of Bodoni in Saluzzo in 1871 to help celebrate the reunification of Italy. The president of the United Typographical Societies of Italy had asked De Vinne to organize some American participation in the celebration, and De Vinne had arranged through the offices of the New York Typographical Society to send an exhibition of American printing to Italy for the occasion.[27]

The following year De Vinne contributed to *Printers' Circular* a four-part biographical sketch of England's first printer, William Caxton. On the surface, it was a compilation of the facts of Caxton's life; but it was much more than that. He gave Caxton only "honorable mention" as a practical printer, noting that he had his composition and presswork done "by such mechanics as he could find." De Vinne felt that critics had compared Caxton unfairly to the continental scholar-printers of the next century, not taking into account the limitations of fifteenth-century English culture under which Caxton worked. De Vinne was especially taken with the notion that Caxton was smitten by typography at the age of sixty and gave up a life of relative ease to embrace the "drudgery of learning a mechanical occupation." De Vinne may have identified with the modesty and determination of the first English printer:

> If we carefully read his writings, we cannot fail to perceive that he always acted from strong convictions of duty. It was an age in which people had not yet begun to prate of self-imposed "missions," but for all that the work of missions was done. There can be no doubt that Caxton was irresistibly drawn to printing. It was his work. Necessity was laid on him. . . . He had found his place, and he accepted it promptly and cheerfully.[28]

These articles appeared four hundred years after Caxton's decision to become a printer. When England celebrated the quadricentennial of the first work printed in that country, De Vinne was not among the dozen Americans on the General Committee (which included representatives of the leading American libraries as well as press manufacturer Richard Hoe, publisher H. O. Houghton, and

Albany printer-historian Joel Munsell). Although De Vinne was not personally involved, an example of his printing, *Scribner's Monthly*, was among the "Specimens Noticeable for Beauty and Excellence of Typography" exhibited at the celebration.[29]

His piece on Caxton reveals De Vinne's approach to printing history scholarship. He assembled whatever sources he could obtain, compared their assertions, and tested their conclusions against the evidence they presented. He began with John Lewis's *The Life of Master Wyllyam Caxton . . .* (London, 1737) and proceeded through other eighteenth-century writers and into the nineteenth, observing the prevailing convention of referring to his sources only by the author's surname. Curiously, he did not mention his English contemporary, William Blades, even though he must have had Blades's 1861–63 *Life and Typography of William Caxton* at his disposal. He did admire Blades and would review some of his works. For instance, in his 1882 review of the second edition of Blades's condensed version, *The Biography and Typography of William Caxton* (the first of which had appeared in 1877), De Vinne praised Blades's scholarship and his presentation of such meager facts of Caxton's life as could be found without "piecing out fact with fancy as earlier writers did."

> Blades's great merit was his thoroughness. A practical printer and a trained bibliographer, he was at all points fitted for his work. He searched records in Holland and England for details about Caxton's life; he hunted up and diligently compared copies and editions; he studied and described Caxton's types with rare intelligence; he told his story candidly, simply, and without eulogy of Caxton.[30]

In his 1892 review of Blades's *Pentateuch of Printing*, De Vinne would say, "His 'William Caxton' of 1861 was a model of intelligent research and of candid criticism, in which nothing of value was left unsaid."[31]

In his *Printers' Circular* piece on Caxton, De Vinne was not writing, as he sometimes did, for the neophyte printer. Instead, he assumed a significant level of sophistication on the part of the reader. Although this effort was printed in a trade journal, it was a dress rehearsal for his first historical monograph, which would be titled, infelicitously, *The Invention of Printing: A Collection of Facts and Opinions Descriptive of Early Prints and Playing Cards, the Block-Books of the Fifteenth Century, the Legend of Lourens Janszoon Coster, of Haarlem, and the work of John Gutenberg and his Associates* (Francis Hart, 1876, 1877, and 1878).

The invention of movable type has inspired much interest and investigation, but never had the debate over its inventor been hotter than in the mid-nineteenth century. There were two main schools of thought: one favoring Gutenberg and the other supporting Coster, although there had been arguments and legends favoring half a dozen others. Much of the existing scholarship was not available in English. Indeed, De Vinne's original intention was simply to translate August Bernard's 1853 *De l'Origine et des Debuts de l'Imprimerie en Europe*, the first book that considered the rival claims for the invention from a typographic point of view. When De Vinne discovered how much of Bernard's work was superseded by later investigations – particularly Van der Linde's *The Haarlem Legend of the Invention of Printing by Laurens Janszoon Coster, Critically Examined* (translated into English in 1871 by J. A. Hessels) – he decided to produce a new work.

We do not know exactly when De Vinne began drafting his text of *The Invention of Printing*, but it was apparently taking shape at least by late 1874. For in June of 1875 the editor of *The Quadrat*, a Pittsburgh typographic monthly, was able to say, "At intervals during the past six months we have had the privilege and pleasure of reading some three hundred pages of the work entitled [*The Invention of Printing*] from the pen of Mr. Theo. L. De Vinne, the well-known printer and author." [32]

In the fall of 1875 a four-page prospectus appeared, giving a statement of intent, the table of contents, and samples of the proposed 140 illustrations. He made it a point to say these were mostly photoengraved facsimiles, "carefully selected from scarce books, or from originals." It said the work was for "printers and general readers" and would be a distillation of "modern knowledge of early printing," taking into account the relevant scholarship of the previous two decades. The book was to come out in five parts at six-week intervals beginning December 1875. The parts could be purchased at $1.00 per part from typefounders and dealers in printing materials or from the publishers, Francis Hart & Co.

Rather than leave marketing to chance, De Vinne astutely promoted the book by sending Part 1 to a variety of general and typographical periodicals. This enabled him to quote on the paper wrappers of Part 2 some twenty-five favorable "notices of the press" including two from trade periodicals in Germany, two from France, and one from England. The twenty American periodicals included the *Chicago Tribune*, the *Boston Globe*, the *New-York Tribune*, and *Scientific American*. This price list also appeared with the parts:

Each part	$1.00
Cloth case for the 5 parts	1.00
Complete work in cloth	6.00
Complete work in half morocco	9.00

A second prospectus, designed for the Boston market, indicated where copies could be purchased in that city and said that a "canvasser" would call to show the book if requested. This leaflet contained a more tightly edited version of the statement of intent, allowing room for six of the press reviews.

The book was priced to encourage sales. De Vinne wrote Albany printer and antiquarian Joel Munsell, "Thanks for your prompt remittance. I put the price of my book low, with a view to influence larger sale, which some of my friends say I can get, if I try. I am not over sanguine, for I know that sales of books of this nature drag over a long time. But I have had this notion of a new book on the invention ever since I bought your copy of Bernard's *De l'origine* etc, and I suppose it must be gratified, whether I make or lose by it." [33]

The physical design of the book was obviously meant to evoke the past, in keeping with the subject matter. De Vinne chose a "laid" paper, whose thickness, rough texture, and ersatz chain lines all suggested handmade paper. [34] The format, as indicated by the

prospectus, was "broad octavo," causing the chain lines to be perpendicular to the spine as in a quarto rather than parallel to the
spine as in the usual octavo. Moreover, the book was to be bound so
the gatherings of this fairly thick paper would have four leaves, not
eight. All these design choices must have been calculated to make
this machine-made book seem closer to its handmade progenitors
and slightly more sumptuous than the standard octavo.

Likewise, the design of the original wrappers, carried over to the
cloth case binding of the completed work, was meant to put the
book in period dress. There are four medallion portraits on the
cover: Gutenberg, Fust, Schoeffer, and Coster. The men look out
from black backgrounds surrounded with flourishes. The typeface
on the cover is a pseudo-gothic. All stamping on the cloth is in black
except for "The Invention of Printing," which is in gold (plate 2).
The device of printers Fust and Schoeffer appears on the spine.

The cover typeface of the cloth binding and some of the faces
used inside are precisely the kinds of decorated faces De Vinne
would excoriate in his later writings. The chapter titles, in a face
called Chapel Text, are meant to convey the angularity of the gothic types used in the earliest printed books. But what they resemble
most is a picket fence with occasional protrusions. There is a quoted passage at the head of each chapter in a slightly more legible
angular face, Bold-Faced Black Letter No. 1, shown in *Specimens of
Pointed Texts and Black Letters in the Printing Office of Francis
Hart & Co.* (1878). In this type specimen De Vinne said of these
pointed faces, "Judiciously used for Texts or Mottoes they make an
effective relief to the colorless monotony of Roman Types." The
main text relies on one of the round old-style romans that De Vinne
would praise all his life.

If the overlong subtitle suggests a table of contents, the opening
pages of the chapters do so even more by following the old fashion
of listing the topics to be covered in a run-on paragraph.

De Vinne claimed that he had "no original discoveries to
announce, no speculative theories to uphold" in this book. Yet in at
least three respects his work was unique. First, he argued that the

real reason for the invention of printing was not the genius of a man (be he Dutch or German):

> The condition of society at the close of the middle ages; the growth of commerce and manufactures; the enlarged sense of personal liberty; . . . the revolt of the people against the authority of church and state; . . . the unsatisfied religious appetite which hungered for image prints and devotional books; the facilities for self-education afforded by the introduction of paper, – these were among the influences which produced the invention of printing.[35]

Second, as an early proponent of "internal evidence" as a key to understanding typographic history, he noted how inadequate the investigations of literary antiquarians had proven until they were augmented by typefounders' and practical printers' examinations of the printed artifacts. As he said in his preface, this new school of criticism "claims that the internal evidences of old books are of higher authority than legends, and that these evidences are conclusive, not to be ignored nor accommodated to the statements of the early chroniclers." [36] Conversely, as a reviewer noted, De Vinne "might have been a very good printer, but unless he had also had the mental furnishing which gives one judicial character, the patience of an investigator, and the orderly system of a scholar," he could not have produced this monumental analytical and historical offering.[37] He had been able to examine both the forty-two-line and the thirty-six-line Bibles, as well as other pertinent works, in David Bruce's significant collection, inspiring this heartfelt and poetic dedication: "To David Wolfe Bruce, in acknowledgement of instruction about types, not to be had by reading, of assistance in studies, not to be found in public libraries, of companionship more pleasant than books, this work is dedicated by his friend, Theo. L. De Vinne." Later De Vinne would say that he had known Bruce, son of type-founder George Bruce, since 1848. This would certainly make Bruce one of De Vinne's earliest typographic soul mates.[38]

Third, he elaborated upon his contention that the adjustable type mold was the real turning point in the history of printing. Block printing and perhaps typecasting in sand or by some other method may indeed have produced real and earlier relief printing, but type-mold technology was a prerequisite for printing on any large scale. Hence, it was really immaterial whether Coster or anyone else had printed before Gutenberg with types created by some less sophisticated method.

De Vinne's was indeed a respectable scholarly effort. His list of authorities consulted numbered some sixty-eight works (twenty-nine written in or translated into English, twenty-eight in French, four in German, and seven in Latin). Among other sources, he pored over transcriptions and translations of documents concerning some litigation in Strasbourg. This was the source of his belief that Gutenberg had been the one to create the key invention: the adjustable type mold. One Andrew Dritzehen had gone into debt to invest in a partnership with Gutenberg. When Andrew died, his brother sued Gutenberg to recover money or gain participation in the partnership. The testimony of this 1439 trial discussed secrets known only among the partners. Obscure references in the transcript made it obvious that the activities went beyond making mirrors, polishing gems, and other activities in which Gutenberg, a goldsmith, might logically have involved himself. De Vinne interpreted certain parts of the testimony in a new way. What particularly caught his attention were the sworn statements that Gutenberg had asked individuals to go to Dritzehen's and disassemble "the four pieces" so others would not perceive *its* function. In those four pieces that formed a single "it," De Vinne saw an adjustable mold for the making of metal types. De Vinne's focus on the casting instrument as the crux of the invention of printing eventually gained wide acceptance, although at the time his book was published, it apparently did not have a great impact among the European scholars at work on the subject.[39] Indeed, he had not written it for them; it was, he said, for the [English-speaking] printer and general reader.

The completed work of 566 pages bore the imprint "New York: / Francis Hart & Co. 12 & 14 College Place / 1876." In 1877, a "second edition" appeared with the imprint "London / Trübner & Co. 57 Ludgate Hill. / New-York: Francis Hart & Co. 63 & 65 Murray

Street." Nicholas Trübner was a German bookseller-scholar who established himself in London as a publisher of works in philology, philosophy, and oriental literature. He became involved with the book trade between England and the United States and published his own *Bibliographical Guide to American Literature* in 1855. Soon thereafter, he began paying visits to America, a practice that apparently continued until his death in 1884. It is not clear how he and De Vinne determined that he would copublish *The Invention of Printing*, but they do seem to have had opportunities to speak in person about it.[40]

In this 1877 printing, corrections to the text were made corresponding to those listed at the end of the original 1876 printing (with some rewording so that changes would not affect the electrotyped plates for subsequent pages), and some further comments were added to the notes. In 1878 another "second edition" appeared with no changes other than the title page, on which the London and New York publishers are reversed, with Francis Hart given first. The typefounding firm of George Bruce's Son & Co. used the text, set in various type faces and sizes, as part of its specimen books in 1878 and 1882. (fig. 5) (See Appendix B for a further discussion of the publication history of *The Invention of Printing*.)

The same year *The Invention* was first published De Vinne created a version of his Gutenberg story for *Scribner's Monthly*.[41] Three years earlier, he had the occasion of discussing a copy of the forty-two-line Bible that had recently sold for $21,000. He presented his analysis, atypically in first person: "I will add some conclusions which I have formed about the method of making the types, that may be of interest." Those conclusions were that the types of the two Bibles could have been made only by some precision instrument that created types that were uniform in two dimensions and variable in the third, and such an instrument, he suggested, was the adjustable mold of hard metal with an interchangeable matrix bearing the shape of the letter in reverse. He summarized: "Gutenberg's claims as an inventor should be based more on his skill as a typefounder than on his achievements as a printer."[42]

JOHN GUTENBERG AT MENTZ.

intimates that Gutenberg was really a trickster, who would have defrauded Fust if he had not resorted to summary proceedings. The defenders of Fust, who are few, have to admit that he here attempts a keen man of business, destitute of sentiment, and of ungenerous disposition. Sympathizers with Gutenberg denounce Fust as a cunning schemer, who had made the terms of the partnership rigorous with the secret determination to get possession of the invention through Gutenberg's inability to keep his contract.

This is the record of the proceedings before the court:

"INSTRUMENT of a certain day, when Fust produced an account and confirmed it by an oath. In the name of God, Amen. Be it known to all who shall see this public document or hear it read, that in the year of our Lord 1455, on Thursday, the fifth of November, between eleven and twelve at noon, at Mentz, in the large dining-hall (*refectorium*) of the convent of bare-footed friars, appeared before me, notary, and the witnesses to be mentioned hereafter, the honorable and prudent man Jacob Fust, citizen of Mentz, and has, in behalf of Johan Fust his brother, also present, shewn, said and exposed, that to the said Johan Fust on the one side and Johan Gutenberg on the other, should be administered the oath, according to judgment passed on both the parties, and for which this day and this hour had been fixed and the hall of the convent assigned. In order that the friars of the said convent, who were still assembled in the hall, should not be disturbed, the said Jacob Fust did ask through his messenger, whether Johan Gutenberg, or any one for him, were present in the convent, in order to finish the matter. At this message came into the said refectorium the reverend Heinrich Günther, pastor of St. Christopher's at Mentz, Heinrich Keffer, and Bertolf von Hanau, a servant of Johan Gutenberg, and when they had been asked by Johan Fust whether they had been authorized by Johan Gutenberg, they answered that they had been sent by Junker Johan Gutenberg to hear and see what should happen in this case. Thereupon Johan Fust begged leave to conform to the stipulations of the verdict, after he had waited for Johan Gutenberg till twelve o'clock, and was still waiting for him. He reads the sentence passed on the first article of his claim, from word to word, with its pretension and response, which runs as follows: First, that he, according to the written agreement, should lend Johan Gutenberg about 800 florins in gold, *with which he was to finish the work, and whether it would cost more or less was no matter to Fust;*

and that Johan Gutenberg was to pay six per cent. interest for this money. He had indeed lent him these 800 guilders on a bond, but Gutenberg was not satisfied, but complained that he had not yet received the 800 guilders. For that reason, Fust, being desirous of doing him some service, lent him 800 guilders more than he was bound by his contract to do, for which 800 guilders Fust had to pay forty guilders as interest. And, although Gutenberg had bound himself by contract to pay six per cent. interest on the first 800 guilders, yet he had not done so for a single year, but Fust had to pay this interest himself to the amount of 250 guilders. For, at present, Gutenberg having never paid interest, and Fust having been obliged to borrow this interest from Christians and Jews, for which he had paid about thirty-six florins, his payments, together with the capital, amount to about 2,020 guilders, of which he demands reimbursement. Thereupon, Johan Gutenberg answered that Johan Fust had agreed to lend him 800 guilders, *with which money he was to arrange and make his tools,* and that these tools should remain as security for Fust. But Fust had moreover agreed to give him every year 300 guilders for ex-*pences,* and to advance also *wages, house-rent,* VELLUM, PAPER, INK, etc. If, afterward, they did not agree, Gutenberg should then pay the 800 guilders back, and the tools should be free from mortgage; it should be understood, that with the 800 guilders he had to make the *machine,* which was to be used to spend these 800 guilders on the *work of the books* (i. e., on vellum, paper, etc.) And, although it is said in the contract that Gutenberg was to pay six per cent. interest, Fust had told him that he had no intention of accepting this interest from him. Moreover, he had not received the 800 guilders in full and at once according to agreement, as Fust had pretended in the first article of his claim; and as for the second 800 guilders, he is ready to give an account of them, but declines to give him interest or usury for them, and hopes he is not bound by law to pay them. We pass, therefore, sentence according to pretension and response: When Johan Gutenberg has submitted an account of all receipts and disbursements spent *on the work to their common profit* (i. e., printing), this work shall be added to the 800 guilders; if he has spent more than the 800 guilders, which did not belong to their common profit, he should pay it back; if Fust is able to prove, on oath or by witnesses, that he has borrowed the money on interest, and did not lend it out of his own resources, then Gutenberg is bound by contract to pay it.

"Now, after this sentence had been read in presence of the aforesaid witnesses,

JOHN GUTENBERG AT MENTZ.

Johan Fust has, with raised fingers, in the hands of me, public notary, taken the oath by all the saints, that everything was comprised according to truth and sentence, in an act which he placed in my hands. He confirmed it on oath, as truly as God and the saints may help him; and the contents of this document were as follows:

"I, Johan Fust, have borrowed 1,550 guilders, which have been received by Johan Gutenberg, and spent on our common work, for which I have paid an annual interest, and still owe a part of it. Therefore, I count for every hundred guilders which I have borrowed in this way, six guilders per annum; and for the money spent on our common work, I demand the interest according to judgment passed.

"The said Johan Fust demands from me, public notary, one or more public acts of this matter, as many and as often as he should want them; and all these matters recorded here, happened in the year, indiction, day, hour, papacy, month, and town aforesaid, in the presence of the honest men, Peter Grauss, Johan Kist, Johan Knoff, Johan Yecseck, Jacob Fust, citizens of Mentz, Peter Gernsheim and Johan Bone, clerks of the city and diocese of Mentz, asked and summoned as witnesses. And I, Ulrich Helmasperger, clerk of the diocese of Bamberg, by imperial authority, public clerk of the Holy See at Mentz, sworn notary, have been present at all the aforesaid transactions and articles with the witnesses mentioned. Therefore, being requested to do so, I have signed with my hand, and sealed with my common seal, this public act, written by another, as testimony and true record of all the aforesaid matters.[1]

"ULRICUS HELMASPERGER, *Notary.*"

The suit brought by Fust was, apparently, a surprise, for it cannot be supposed that Gutenberg would have been so completely unprepared to meet

[1] Hessels' translation, as printed in the *Haarlem Legend,* pp. 24 and 25.

his obligation if he had not been led to believe that Fust would postpone the collection of his claim. The enforcement of this claim before the book was published, or at least before money had been derived from its sale—taken in connection with the facts that the delay in the publication of the book, and Gutenberg's inability to pay his debt, were largely due to the delay of Fust in furnishing the money as he had promised—seems to warrant the charge that Fust meditated the despoilment of Gutenberg at the formation of the partnership. Gutenberg's defense before the court was very feeble: it is that of a man who knew he had no hope of success. He did not appear in person, but trusted his case to his workmen. Fust was more adroit; he was volatile and positive, and his relative, Jacob Fust was one of the judges. But the fates were against Gutenberg: the hard terms of the contract he had signed compelled an adverse decision.

That Fust did Gutenberg a grievous wrong is very plain; that Gutenberg had managed the business of the partnership with economy and intelligence is not so clear. At no period of his life did the great inventor show any talent for financial administration. He was certainly deficient in many qualities that should be possessed by a man of business, and Fust may have thought that he was fully justified in placing his money interests in the hands of a more careful manager. This, a copy of the oldest engraving known of Gutenberg, presents him to us as a man of decided character, not to be cajoled or managed by a partner in business. The thin curving lip and pointed nose, the strongly marked lines on the forehead, the bold eyes and arrogant bearing of the head reveal to us a man of genius and of force, a man born to rule, impatient of restraint, and of inflexible resolution. We have but to look at the portrait of Fust to see that he, also, was accustomed to having his own way, and that he and Gutenberg were not at all adapted to each other as partners.

But Fust would not have broken with Gutenberg if he had not been prepared to put a competent successor in his place. In Peter Scheffer, a young

John Gutenberg .... From an Old Print in the National Library at Paris.

[From Lacroix.]

GEORGE BRUCE'S SON & CO., TYPE-FOUNDERS, No. 13 CHAMBERS-STREET, NEW-YORK.

FIG. 5. The text of *The Invention of Printing* used by George Bruce's Son & Co. to display various type faces and sizes, distributed with the company's type specimens of 1878 and 1882.

De Vinne would become honorary vice president of the 1900 Gutenberg Festival in Mainz, an occasion that inspired him to publish two further articles.[43] In 1901 he would review a book published in London by George Washington Moon titled *The Oldest Type-Printed Book in Existence*, demonstrating that he was still ardently interested in the subject, was keeping up with the literature, and had a mind open to new scholarship.[44] Indeed, in private correspondence he expressed the hope that he would live to revise *The Invention of Printing* and rewrite parts for a new edition.[45]

In 1988 Paul Needham observed that "a generation from now, our picture of the early years of printing will have changed again."[46] More recently Needham has called that picture in for scrutiny himself. Working with Blaise Aguera y Arcas and digital scans of the earliest European printed works, he has suggested that the punch-and-matrix method of type casting – the type mold that has come down to us through the centuries – may not have been the technique Gutenberg was using.[47] Whatever the outcome of this trajectory of analysis, De Vinne's book still merits a place in the historiography of printing as a solid effort to raise the standard of scholarship.

It is important to remember that during the same time De Vinne was indulging his passion for history he was the principal spokesman for New York City printers on a range of trade issues and the principal proprietor of an ever-expanding and demanding business.

Two months before he died on 22 April 1877, Francis Hart wrote a will, providing the means by which De Vinne could acquire the remaining two-thirds of the business.[48] Aside from a $4,000 life insurance policy, his house, and six lots of land, Hart's assets consisted of his interest in the printing firm and its earning potential. The will called for $26,150 in legacies, the creation of a $40,000 fund for Hart's widow, and $2,500 paid annually to the widow until such fund had been created. These legacies together with legal fees, executors' commissions, and other estate expenses totaled about $80,000 to $90,000[49] in De Vinne's estimation. Once the fund of $40,000 had been created, Hart's interest in the firm was bequeathed to De Vinne on the condition that he pay the remaining legacies and debts. To satisfy these conditions, De Vinne had to continue in business as Francis Hart & Co. in partnership with the Hart estate for another six years before the business would be free of these obligations.

The relationship between De Vinne and Hart merits some reflection. The secondary accounts offer little insight. A trade journal indicated that they had different personalities: "Mr. Hart was enthusiastic, impatient, averse to drudgery, seeking great results too often by impossibly quick methods. Mr. De Vinne was sedate, studious, patient, thoroughly convinced that success could be had only by thorough attention to details." Nevertheless, the article depicts ultimate unanimity and harmony – just the image wise business partners would try to project to their employees, customers, and the public: "Disagreeing often about proposed policy, the partners always agreed when the time for action came. During business relations that lasted more than twenty-five years, there was never, on either side, any abatement of mutual esteem and confidence."[50]

It is, in fact, only through the earnest letter leading up to partnership and the anguished letters De Vinne wrote over the breakdown in partnership arrangements that his discontent is revealed. (The fact that De Vinne preserved these drafts along with legal documents that have been handed down through the family indicates the depth of his feeling on the matter.) In the 1850s De Vinne addressed Hart as a "personal friend" for whom he had a strong feeling of loyalty and whose "unlimited confidence" he valued highly. He patiently built up Hart's business without any financial recognition of his managerial services partly because he wanted to avoid the indelicacy of broaching the subject and partly because he trusted time. "I knew," he wrote to his employer, "that you were attached to me, and that it would eventually come out all right." Having pressured Hart to sell him a junior partnership, De Vinne no doubt returned to his duties with his old confidence and enthusiasm. He felt so sanguine – or was so naïve – that he did not call upon Hart to settle their partnership account periodically, trusting that delay would not harm his position. When, fourteen years into the partnership, Hart discovered that by various means of figuring interest he could claim seven-eighths of the business for himself rather than the original two-thirds, and silently entered this accounting into the books, De Vinne felt betrayed. Under the new partnership agreement that resulted, De Vinne could only wait out the remaining five years of Hart's life, a bit wiser, one suspects. Who expected Hart to live nearly three decades after he had tried to sell his business because of poor health!

That De Vinne did not leave Hart during that time in the face of other opportunities was partly due to his sense of loyalty and commitment. His father had certainly set a precedent for attending to the task at hand despite supervisors with whom one does not agree. More than that, except for brief setbacks, it seemed the most promising route. Early on, there was no other heir apparent except De Vinne. Hart's success was admittedly due to De Vinne's skill and efforts, and De Vinne simply trusted Providence to reward those efforts.

Proprietorship (1878–1886)

The prosperity of the house largely depends upon its reputation for good workmanship; and this good workmanship can be had only by attention to details and to little things.

TLD, 1883

D E VINNE naturally sought to pay the sums required by Hart's will as soon as possible. Despite such reverses as the loss in 1879 of $26,000 upon the failure of one of his long-time customers, McKillop & Sprague Co., he was able on 9 April 1880 – slightly less than three years after Hart's death – to complete the $40,000 widow's fund and sign with the executors a document that turned the ownership of Francis Hart & Co. over to him. It would be three more years before he paid off a bond of $6,000 for which he had mortgaged to the executors two lots in Jersey City. It also apparently took him that long to pay off all the legacies; the final accounting of Hart's will was dated 30 October 1883. Nevertheless, the firm was now his; and thus began De Vinne's two most productive and felicitous decades as a master printer, leavened in large measure by opportunities to write. He was also becoming a well-known historian of printing, thanks to *The Invention of Printing* and numerous articles addressed not only to fellow printers but also to book lovers and the general public.

Much of De Vinne's attention at this time was devoted to the Scribner Company's periodicals. As *Scribner's Monthly* increased in circulation, De Vinne's shop expanded to handle the demand. From the outset *Scribner's* had a British edition. It was identical to the New York edition except that it had British advertisements in the end matter, and the cover bore the name of the publisher, Frederick

Warne & Co., Bedford Street, Strand, London. No evidence regarding the size of the London edition has come to light.

Given the importance of this customer to De Vinne's career, the relationship merits exploration in some depth. Scribner and Company (to be renamed Century Company) began as the brainchild of Roswell Smith and Josiah Gilbert Holland. Smith had gained some experience in a New York publishing house while studying law. He practiced law in Indiana but harbored an ambition to return to New York and use his savings to publish a magazine or newspaper. Holland, a self-taught country doctor with an inclination toward letters, had written some moralizing essays and verse and was a popular lecturer on the lyceum circuits. He had been offered the editorship of Charles Scribner's literary and religious monthly *Hours at Home* but sought a wider, more general readership. Book publisher Charles Scribner agreed to participate, supplying his well-known name and 40 percent of the capital to the enterprise to be known as Scribner and Company. With Smith as business manager and Holland as editor in chief, *Scribner's Monthly: An Illustrated Magazine for the People* began publication in November 1870.

The promoters developed a formula that made the monthly an immediate success. Josiah Holland's evangelical Christian convictions were sufficiently in tune with the prevailing morality that through the pages of *Scribner's* he was quickly able to fulfill his ambition of securing "a pure place in the popular heart."[1]

When Holland died in 1881, his understudy and successor, Richard Watson Gilder, eased the magazine toward a more secular but no less earnest morality, making it a prime vehicle for what George Santayana dubbed the "genteel tradition." Gilder made his home a salon where artists and poets gathered, and he busied himself with many civic causes. Through multitudinous contacts he was able to keep the magazine in tune with scholarship, current events, belles-lettres, and the arts. He was careful, as Holland had been, to adhere to the "virginibus maxim" (printing nothing to offend a virgin).[2] Frank Tooker of the editorial staff summed up the magazine's essence:

It was the genial autumn of the Victorian age of literature, and we basked pleasantly in the golden glow of its rich fruitage. . . . Being comfortably assured in our own minds that we had arrived at the perfection of literary form, we were thoroughly resolved to keep our heritage unsoiled.[3]

The periodical had a decided visual emphasis from the start. Art director Alexander W. Drake was a trained artist and had been a professional wood engraver.[4] Since that medium was the preferred method of incorporating illustrations with printed text, his expertise was crucial to the new magazine; Smith and Holland wanted not only to feed the public hunger for graphic representations of events but also to educate their readers in the world's art.

The school of wood engraving ascribed to Englishman Thomas Bewick (1753-1828) was carried forward eagerly on both sides of the Atlantic and became the mainstay of illustrated magazines, which relied on wood engravings for their appeal to masses of readers. The technique involved cutting the design into the ends (perpendicular to the grain) of pieces of boxwood using engravers' tools rather than woodcut chisels. Because the designs were in relief, the blocks (or stereotypes or electrotypes of them) could be made type high and printed simultaneously with type – a great efficiency over metal-plate engravings or lithographs, which could not. The close-grained boxwood allowed exquisitely fine detail in these wood engravings (sometimes referred to as woodcuts or just "cuts").

Soon the process of engraving wood blocks received a fillip with the discovery that images could be photographed onto a light-sensitized block. The engraver, then, could keep the original design before him for reference rather than cut away an image that had been drawn on the block. *Scribner's* claimed to be the first magazine to adopt this method. It allowed the nuances of color and tone to be suggested by the minute shadings of tiny lines in this black-and-white medium. It was with this technique that Timothy Cole spent twenty-seven years in the museums of Europe transferring the great masterpieces of western art onto wood blocks and sending them back to Alexander Drake for the edification of the American public

---

FIG. 6.
Timothy Cole wood
engraving, *Century
Magazine*, November
1895, p. 2.

FIGURE FROM TITIAN'S "SACRED AND PROFANE LOVE."

(fig. 6). This "new school" of wood engraving, called "the American facsimile style – all tone and texture executed in microscopic detail,"[5] drew criticism from the likes of English engraver W. J. Linton, who expressed very spirited disapproval of the delicacy of the Cole style.[6] Nevertheless, it opened up a new avenue for such vehicles as *Scribner's* (to be renamed *Century*) to bring culture to the populace. It was as much through its widely acclaimed illustrations as through its content that *Scribner's/Century* achieved pre-eminence among popular monthly periodicals.

Eric de Maré, writing about England (in words that apply to America as well), said,

Proprietorship

Fig. 7.
Timothy Cole wood engraving, *St. Nicholas*, November 1901, p. 2.

FROM THE ORIGINAL PAINTING IN WINDSOR CASTLE, ENGRAVED BY PERMISSION OF QUEEN VICTORIA.

A LITTLE ENGLISH PRINCESS OF ONE HUNDRED YEARS AGO. PAINTED BY JOHN HOPPNER.

Indeed, the whole nineteenth century might be called the Boxwood Age because the wood-block illustration lived for just about a hundred years; it was born with Bewick and it died in the 1890s [when the halftone replaced wood engravings]. Thus the wood-block served with increasing and tireless application right through Victoria's reign, and by its means were recorded and immortalised every physical detail and every emotion of that long epoch when the tempo of life was changing at unprecedented speed.[7]

Another technique harnessed photography with light-sensitized gelatin to create, from about 1870, relief plates that did not involve the manual intervention of an artist or engraver. These "line blocks" were useful for reproducing ink drawings, maps, and facsimiles of

59

typography or calligraphy where no gray tones were involved. (In his 1876 *Invention of Printing* De Vinne delighted in being able to include photo-engraved facsimiles of early pages of type.) But it was wood engraving, which achieved the appearance of tone, that proved such a popular and satisfactory illustration medium for so many decades.

Wood engravings gave satisfactory results, that is, only when a satisfactory makeready was completed. It is here that De Vinne's printing of wood engravings for Century Company merits consideration. As in so many other instances, his contribution was not a particular invention but an improvement of existing techniques.

The key to making wood engravings ready for printing lay in a system of "overlays." This term (potentially confusing to the uninitiated) referred to layers of tissue *under* the paper (and, hence, laid *over* the surface against which the back of the paper rested before printing). These layers were meticulously cut out in varying shapes to give more pressure to darker areas and less to lighter. De Vinne was not the originator of the process by any means. In fact, he noted that "the graduation of impression by means of carefully cut overlays was brought in fashion by many printers, of whom Charles Whittingham [the elder, of the Chiswick Press in England] was most successful."[8] In America, overlays were first used extensively by Joseph A. Adams in the Harper's Bible published before De Vinne completed his apprenticeship. De Vinne said that Adams "developed the system of overlaying that is now adopted in all printing-houses of this country."[9] (De Vinne did not mention "underlays" by which paper is placed under certain parts of the wood block, to increase pressure selectively; apparently he did not use this technique.) While he took his cue from others, De Vinne experimented with paper overlays until he perfected the technique. He also used a "peeled overlay" technique in which a three- or four-ply cardboard was scraped and cut to give less pressure to "gray" areas and even less to white ones.

Even after his reputation as a printer of wood engravings was made, however, De Vinne continued to feel that this work was a good deal of trouble. He claimed that in general printers "do not covet the work; most of them say it is vexatious and unprofitable; some say they never want to see a wood-cut in their pressrooms." De Vinne admitted in private correspondence that he had to do a great deal of this sort of delicate work in *Scribner's/Century Magazine* and elsewhere but that he regarded it as "a perversion of the true function of printing." In 1878 in a two-part article for a London trade periodical he discussed how nearly impossible it was to achieve as good a reproduction in a regular press run as one typically achieved in a careful proof. The next year the same periodical published his three-part piece on the various pitfalls of printing wood engravings. Notwithstanding these feelings, in 1880 he described the state of the art in generous detail – both historical and practical – for *Scribner's Monthly*. Still considered an authority in 1911 (although it may have been a decade or more since he had personally supervised their actual printing), De Vinne would contribute "The Printing of Wood-Engravings" to the *Print-Collectors' Quarterly*.[10]

When *Scribner's* entered the field there were two well-established monthlies appealing to the educated middle class. *Harper's*, founded in 1850 by the book-publishing house of Harper and Brothers, relied heavily on serialized novels from famous British authors. *Atlantic Monthly*, founded in 1857, remained a New England periodical with respect to both contributors and readers. *Scribner's* proposed to go beyond both these monthlies in encouraging American literary talent from all regions. Moreover, it intended to be more meticulously illustrated and produced than either competitor. Pursuing these ambitious aims, it was able to build its circulation to 125,000 in its first decade.

Shortly after launching *Scribner's*, Roswell Smith recognized the potential of the juvenile periodical field. At his suggestion the company began publishing *St. Nicholas: Scribner's Illustrated Magazine for Girls and Boys*, its first issue appearing in 1873. As noted above, De Vinne was its first and only printer for forty-four years. In the financial panic of 1873, several other children's magazines foundered, and Smith was able to absorb *Our Young Folks* of Boston, *Little Corporal* of Chicago, and *School-Day Magazine* and *Children's Hour* of Philadelphia. Editor Mary Mapes Dodge (author of the 1865 classic *Hans Brinker, or The Silver Skates*) convinced many celebrated authors to write children's pieces. Authors represented in the periodical included Louisa May Alcott, Mark Twain, Rudyard Kipling, Robert Louis Stevenson, and Theodore Roosevelt. *St. Nicholas* quickly became the prime children's journal, reaching and maintaining a circulation of about sixty thousand for many years.[11] It had access to the same financial backing, illustrators, and production facilities as *Scribner's*. A contemporary evaluation of the art work noted that "nearly every illustrator of talent and note has got his handiwork between the covers of *St. Nicholas*."[12] As in the case of the senior periodical, its printer did not stint on excellent presswork. Less expensive line blocks were more prevalent in *St. Nicholas* than in *Scribner's*, but the children's periodical contained many fine wood engravings as well (fig. 7). Its cheerful trade binding, each holding six monthly issues, became familiar to many children and adults alike (plate 3).

For De Vinne, *Scribner's/Century* was not only a vehicle for polishing his manual skills. It also provided an audience for his articles, a wider one than was offered by the trade journals that customarily published his works. Over a period of twenty years he would contribute nine pieces of varying length, most of them historical. They had begun in 1876 with "John Gutenberg," an outgrowth of his investigation of historical sources that culminated in his *The Invention of Printing*, published the same year. His enthusiasm for his printing forebears also found expression in a piece about Aldus Manutius, "The First Editor," and in one about the Plantin-Moretus Museum in Antwerp, "A Printer's Paradise." His contributions to *Scribner's/Century* also included a letter and two articles on the actual printing of the magazine and, as mentioned above, articles on the printing of wood engravings.[13]

With great care devoted to its physical appearance and to its contents, *Scribner's Monthly* was a model of success both in critical approval and in circulation. Most notable in the mid-1870s was *Scribner's* series, "The Great South," a travelogue by Edward King. This was followed in the 1880s by the even more popular "Battles and Leaders of the Civil War," in which over a period of three years opposing military commanders gave their versions of battles and campaigns. Through these two series and the courting of southern writers, the publishers claimed to have helped heal sectional wounds.

It was not long before Smith and Holland yearned for independence from the loose association the magazine maintained with the book publisher, now known as Charles Scribner's Sons. They wanted the freedom to publish books and began doing so with the 1876 *Talks with Girls.* In 1877 Scribner & Co. published Edward King's *The Great South,* from the successful serialization in the magazine. There followed a series of hymnals and tune books (four between 1878 and 1880). As book publishing gained momentum, young Charles Scribner, son of the founder, took exception to this encroachment upon his territory. Not only would it confuse the public to have two book publishers with such similar names, but this energetic new source of competition – under any name – posed a potential threat to the established firm. It is also apparent that Smith and Holland chafed at the feeling that the magazine was somehow a stepchild of the book publisher. Roswell Smith brought matters to a head by purchasing enough of Josiah Holland's shares to gain a majority interest in Scribner & Co. Thus armed, he was able to convince Charles Scribner's Sons to sell him their 40 percent, severing business ties. The magazine publishers would continue business under another name, taking both the senior periodical and *St. Nicholas* with them.

The November 1881 issue of Smith's magazine appeared as *The Century Illustrated Monthly Magazine* with no alteration of format, business management, or editorial policy. The name change did not halt its growth in circulation. Charles Scribner's Sons waited five years, as agreed, before entering the periodical field. By the time their *Scribner's Magazine* began to appear in 1887, *Century Magazine*'s identity was secure, and there was no confusion. (The

Century Club was the inspiration for the new name, but club and company had no connection.)

The Century Company celebrated its separation from Charles Scribner's Sons by moving from its offices on Broadway near Astor Place to handsome quarters on Union Square, graced by rich carpets, polished woodwork, and stained-glass doors, and by framed originals of the magazine's finest art work on the walls. Smith was now free to build his own book list, which he did on a very gradual basis, the periodical business being preeminent for at least a decade. Two years after the name change, a Century Company entry appeared in *Publishers' Trade List Annual*: a half-column advertisement that listed *Century Magazine, St. Nicholas*, the *Imperial Dictionary of the English Language* (which would be named *Century Dictionary* when it actually began to appear in 1889), a botanical and zoological atlas, *Sport with Rod and Gun* (a subscription book), and ten hymn and tune books. During the balance of that decade Century added two dozen titles in fiction, poetry, sport, juveniles, and a biography. De Vinne was the happy recipient of most of this book-printing business.

Meanwhile, having at last satisfied all the terms of Hart's will, De Vinne conveyed one-twenty-fifth of the profits (but no ownership) of Francis Hart & Co., to his thirty-year-old son, Theodore Brockbank De Vinne, who was already on salary at the firm. The elder De Vinne then created a new firm in which the son owned one-twentieth of the capital. The partnership document of 1 January 1883, naming the firm Theodore L. De Vinne & Co., placed the power of management squarely in the father's hands. Nearly fifteen years later De Vinne would increase his son's share to one-tenth and would make him vice president when the firm eventually incorporated.[14] Nowhere is there much evidence that Theodore B. De Vinne inherited his father's devotion to the mechanics of printing, to its art, or to the study of its history. In fact, the younger Theodore remains something of an enigma. It seems that De Vinne always intended for his son to join the firm. He wrote the fifteen-year-old boy from Bath, Maine:

I think much of you now that I am away. To-morrow is to be your first day of school [this year] and I hope you will go resolved to make good use of your time. It may be your last year at school; or it may be the beginning of many years of a new school life. It shall be just as you please. If you wish to be a scholar I shall not oppose it. But I wish you would pay special attention to writing, drawing, and French. Oblige me by working hard to do all well. You will find all of great service as you grow up. When you come in the office to help me I want you to take a good position at once, and be qualified to do work. All you need is patience. Try to do your best.[15]

It appears that Theodore B. De Vinne's principal contribution to the firm was in its financial management. One of his few extant letters indicates that he continued his father's early cost accounting efforts.[16] According to his own grandson's recollection, Theodore Brockbank De Vinne preferred investment in railroads and bonds to the world of printing.[17] He had three children, one of whom (Theodore Low De Vinne II) died in infancy. He sent his surviving son, Charles DeWitt De Vinne, to Princeton, where he graduated in 1906 before joining the firm. Theodore Brockbank assembled a sizable library strong in early Americana, which would be sold at auction in 1919. He also took a rather limited part in the New York Typothetae, representing the De Vinne Press there after his father became less active. The De Vinne Press staff referred to the two men with the charming sobriquets "Our Senior" and "Our Junior." It must not have been easy to be the namesake and heir of such a remarkable patriarch. At any rate, T. B. De Vinne seems to have made his contribution – whatever it was – rather quietly. As we shall see, his name appears on a patent, suggesting that he perhaps did take an interest in some technical matters after all.

One of the first things De Vinne did under the firm name of Theodore L. De Vinne & Co. was to publish for in-house use a *Manual of Printing Office Practice* (1883). Its pocket size made it convenient for ready reference (fig. 8). It codified the procedures he had developed over the years. About 80 percent of the text dealt with the particulars of composition, proofreading, and presswork. Any

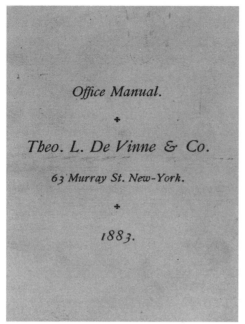

Office Manual.

✤

Theo. L. De Vinne & Co.

63 Murray St. New-York.

✤

1883.

FIG. 8. Cover, *Manual of Printing Office Practice*, 1883 (5¼" x 3⅜").

well-trained journeyman could have produced work up to the house standard by following this manual carefully.

The remainder of the manual dealt with more general policies of the firm. It gave the employees – said to be seldom fewer than one hundred fifty at this time – a strict description of the hours of work (fifty-nine and one-half per week) and other conditions of employment.

Apparently, the care De Vinne had taken to minimize union influence in his establishment had paid off for a number of years. His house was untouched by the several compositors' strikes that occurred in New York City in the 1860s and 1870s. In 1883 a trade journal reported that there had never been a strike in the house of Francis Hart.[18] Certainly the *Manual* made it clear to employees that De Vinne wanted to do no business with unions:

> All established rules and usages of the trade will be maintained, but no regard can be paid to the rules or orders of persons outside of the office. It is the desire of this office to be as liberal as any other in the same line of business; but it can deal only with the workmen employed in this house. As it is not bound, directly nor indirectly, to any association that undertakes to regulate wages or prices, it will prefer to deal with workmen who are equally free, who do not take orders from any society as to what wages they may receive, or where and how they may work.[19]

Also apparent in the *Manual* is De Vinne's stance about loyalty.

Proprietorship

It was not proper, he said, for workmen to reveal to outsiders the names of authors or customers or to talk about such details as sizes of editions, prices, or other matters the office "does not choose to advertise." The manual entreated employees to attend to details, to accept constructive criticism from each other, and to place a high premium on the quality of work:

> The prosperity of the house largely depends upon its reputation for good workmanship; and this good workmanship can be had only by attention to details and to little things. The office intends to provide perfect materials; the workmen must see that they are not made imperfect by the carelessness or neglect of their fellows.

To assist those responsible for determining which press (and consequently which size and format) to use, the manual listed the firm's forty presses, the sizes of their printing surfaces, and their speeds. The equipment included one proof press, two other hand presses, six power platen jobbers of various makes, two Adams platen power presses, and twenty-nine cylinder presses, some of which were capable of printing two thousand sheets per hour. One has only to compare this with Hart's inventory thirty-four years earlier to realize how the shop's business had grown.

In about 1883 there passed through the lives of the Century Company and Theodore L. De Vinne & Co. a young man whose name would later haunt them. Young Samuel S. McClure arrived at the office of Roswell Smith asking for an editorial position. Impressed with his ardor but having nothing to offer him, Smith persuaded De Vinne to give him a proofreading situation at twenty-five dollars a week (eighteen on the books – the prevailing rate for the position – and seven from De Vinne's pocket). McClure's wife was taken on the *Century Dictionary* staff at fifteen dollars a week to read "the best authors" and find examples of word usage. When they moved their belongings to the city De Vinne had them to dinner, took them to an art exhibit, and found them lodgings. McClure hated printing from the outset; the work was demeaning, the hours too long. In less than four months De Vinne turned him over to the Century Company. There he chafed at the dull routines of a junior editorial assistant. Instead of patiently working his way up through the system, he bombarded the management with grandiose plans to make big money for the company – "schemes to bring in the ducats," he called them. His style was so dissonant in the genteel offices at Century that Roswell Smith had to dismiss him, suggesting that he "go out and try to found a little business" of his own. In not too many years *McClure's* would be one of the cheap new popular periodicals that first challenged and later hastened the demise of *Century Magazine.*[20]

Almost exactly a year after De Vinne's vocation led to a company bearing his name, his avocation led to a very promising alliance. He was one of nine men out of whose 1884 meeting the Grolier Club arose. His note to Arthur Turnure dated 14 January reads, "My Dear Sir: I accept with pleasure, your invitation to meet some book lovers at Mr. Robert Hoe Jr's, on January 23d at half-past eight, evening. Yours very truly, Theo. L. De Vinne"[21] (fig. 9). He was, at the age of fifty-five, the oldest of the group. He already had an intimate association with some of the other founders. There was Alexander W. Drake, art director of *Century* and *St. Nicholas*, with whom De Vinne was in almost daily contact. Fellow-printer Arthur B. Turnure was a member of the Typothetae and had just launched *Art Age*, a monthly for those who "appreciate the importance of the art idea rightly applied in all forms of book-making." In the first number (April

FIG. 9. De Vinne's letter of acceptance to the founding meeting of the Grolier Club.

1883) Turnure had praised the quality of De Vinne's printing of wood engravings in *Century Magazine*. William Loring Andrews, another founder, had retired at the age of forty from the family leather business to become director or trustee of various institutions, including the Metropolitan Museum of Art and New York University. Andrews collected books avidly and published several dozen volumes, mostly on art subjects, twenty-six of them written by himself. He participated in every detail of their production, having De Vinne print many of them. Other founders were two men involved in publishing and bookselling (Samuel W. Marvin of Scribner's and Edward S. Mead of Dodd, Mead & Co.), an attorney (Albert Gallup), and a banker (Brayton Ives). Then there was Robert Hoe III (often referred to as Robert Jr. after the death of his grandfather, the first Robert Hoe), usually considered the prime mover of the club. He was a member of the press-manufacturing family with which De Vinne had done business for at least two decades and on whose web press he would soon be printing *Century Magazine*. In truth, De Vinne actually had more in common with Robert's uncle, the down-to-earth "Colonel" Richard M. Hoe, for whom he would serve as pallbearer in 1886, than the Grolier Club founder.[22]

Before long the Grolier Club rolls included numerous others with whom De Vinne had business and social dealings, such as Walter Gilliss and Richard Watson Gilder. New members in 1885 included his son, Theodore Brockbank De Vinne. The club soon achieved the prestige it would maintain through the years. It was a sufficiently potent symbol of New York high culture that in her 1920 *Age of Innocence* Edith Wharton made her protagonist, Newland Archer, a founder of the Grolier Club.

The club, like the Typothetae, engaged De Vinne's abiding interest. He participated fully, being a member of the council throughout his life. Before the first year was out De Vinne suggested that the club publish that famous statute that sought to regulate printing in England, the 1637 *Decree of Star Chamber Concerning Printing* (plate 4). He took responsibility for designing and printing it and also wrote an introduction that has often been quoted:

The people of England were boiling with discontent. Instead of trying to remove the causes that made the discontent, the ministers of Charles I preferred to destroy its manifestations. Annoyed by a little hissing of steam, they closed all the valves and outlets, but did not draw or deaden the fires which made the steam. They sat down in peace, gratified with their work, just before the explosion which destroyed them and their privileges.

This club, founded for the "literary study and promotion of the arts pertaining to the production of books," would be an ideal outlet for De Vinne's historic proclivities. From the earliest days he was happy to address club members on topics that interested him. A year after its founding he delivered a lecture to the club on "Historic Printing Types." With some additions and new illustrations, it became the sixth official Grolier Club publication. To some extent a precursor of his *Plain Printing Types*, this was meant to be a popular treatise on book types. Not all Grolier Club members, after all, were typographic experts. Yet he did not hesitate to document this excursion (from the Gothic types of the forty-two-line Bible through the revival of old-style roman and on to the variety of types available from American typefounders) with plentiful bibliographical references.

He chaired the Grolier's first house committee. In 1885 he was appointed a member of the Committee on Publications and its chairman the following year. He would later serve as vice president and president, but nothing engaged him as much as the Committee on Publications, which proved to be a deep and lasting interest through the years. In fact, the committee's minutes show that he continued to chair its meetings even during his presidency although he wasn't officially a member of it. De Vinne would print more than 80 percent of the fifty-seven books the club published during his lifetime, and his firm would print six of the next nine, ending its work for the club in 1917.

It was fortunate for De Vinne that the club was launched early in 1884 so he could be involved from the outset. For in May he left for three months in Europe, the first of five times he would cross the Atlantic. He was accompanied on the wharf by a sizable and apparently enthusiastic delegation of the Typothetae, including all the leaders of the New York City printing industry: Martin B. Brown, William C. Martin, Douglas Taylor, John Polhemus, Joseph J. Little, Howard Lockwood, and the like. *Art Age* reported that "the finest floral ornament of the day was in the form of a large ship, having on the side in purple violets 'Typothetae' and on the other 'Theodore L. De Vinne.'"[23] He could absent himself from the office for a trans-Atlantic voyage because he had trained his staff well and made explicit in the 1883 *Manual* what was expected of them. Loyalty to the printing house seemed to have been at a high level. De Vinne would soon establish for his employees (or at least endorse) the De Vinne Press Mutual Aid Association which provided medical and funeral benefits to those who chose to join. This was a very common type of insurance of the period. Founded on 13 April 1888, it thrived for years, perhaps until the sale of the company in 1923. In 1893–94 it had 112 members, including the De Vinnes, *père* and *fils*. Records show that it was still operating in 1918.

De Vinne's company continued to attract new business. His visibility as printer of *Century* and *St. Nicholas* magazines, as well as of Century Company's burgeoning book publishing trade, probably helped more than anything else to increase the quantity of customers. His careful printing, and in some cases editing, of Grolier Club publications further enhanced his reputation as a printer of high quality. By the middle of the 1880s De Vinne was clearly sought out by publishers and private individuals who wanted a printer for deluxe editions. Meanwhile the circulation of *Century Magazine*, which had been about 125,000 when the name change occurred, rose to nearly 250,000.[24]

The success of the Century Company's publications brought the need for increased printing capacity. Thus began the construction in May 1885 of the De Vinne Press Building, every detail of which was designed to suit the proprietor's needs.[25] He must have looked back bemused at the cramped and unsuitable spaces the printing house had occupied through the years. When he took up his position with Francis Hart in 1850, the shop had "occupied one-half of a deserted school-house in a narrow lane known as Thames Street" in lower Manhattan.[26] Hart had previously been at 1 Pine Street (or 106 Broadway, the same corner building referred to in two ways), which was a stone's throw from the Thames location. The four subsequent moves had not been too far from the business center of the city, for printing was the lifeblood of commercial communication. Whether the moves were to bigger and better quarters each time or sometimes merely an effort to avoid the "heavy rent and grasping landlords" referred to in an 1855 letter to Hart, one cannot say. The locations can be traced on a map (fig. 10); but, even when the footprint of a building can be determined, it is impossible to know how much of a given building the shop occupied. We do know that printers, with their heavy, noisy presses and their flammable materials, were not coveted tenants.

From 2 and 4 Thames Street Hart & Co. had moved two blocks north to 117 Liberty Street in 1851. Two years later they moved two blocks northwest to the corner of Washington and Courtlandt Streets (also spelled "Cortlandt" then and now), where they remained for nearly twenty years. This must have been convenient for De Vinne, because the ferry from Jersey City, where he lived at that time, landed one block from the office. In 1872 the shop moved about twelve blocks northeast to College Place, just beyond Park Row, famous as the home of many newspapers. The next move three or four years later was eight blocks west to Murray Street, where the firm remained for a decade.

In 1885 Century Company president Roswell Smith and Theodore De Vinne built a massive, made-to-order building some twenty blocks uptown from the Murray Street location on the northeast corner of Lafayette Place and Fourth Street. (In 1905, Lafayette Place would be extended, renamed, and renumbered; De Vinne's letterhead used "12 Lafayette Place" through September 1906, then "395 Lafayette Street: Old No. 12 Lafayette Place" through June 1911, and "393-399 Lafayette St." thereafter.) Numerous bookish concerns had located in the area earlier in the century, including Scribner and Co. until 1881. Nearby were the American Bible Society, the Astor Library, the New York Mercantile

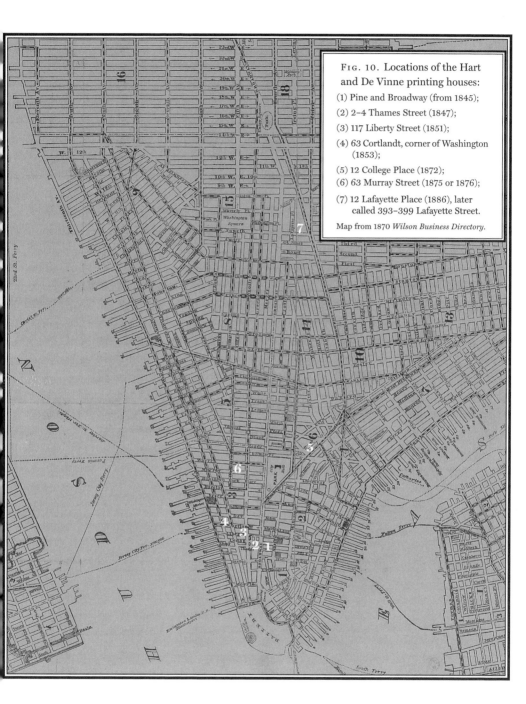

Fɪɢ. 10. Locations of the Hart and De Vinne printing houses:

(1) Pine and Broadway (from 1845);
(2) 2–4 Thames Street (1847);
(3) 117 Liberty Street (1851);
(4) 63 Cortlandt, corner of Washington (1853);
(5) 12 College Place (1872);
(6) 63 Murray Street (1875 or 1876);
(7) 12 Lafayette Place (1886), later called 393–399 Lafayette Street.

Map from 1870 *Wilson Business Directory*.

Library, and publishers including Crowell, Wiley, Funk, and Wagnall. Earlier yet, Lafayette Place had been the site of elegant town houses of the Astors, Vanderbilts, and Delanos.

For architects, Smith and De Vinne chose the firm of Babb, Cook, and Willard, whose other works of distinction included Andrew Carnegie's Fifth Avenue mansion at Ninety-first Street. The "De Vinne Press," as the building proclaimed itself under the eave of its gable end, was one of the finest examples of commercial architecture in the period between the introduction of elevators and the first use of structural steel. The building expressed its neo-Romanesque design in rough brickwork trimmed in terra cotta, suggesting the utilitarian purpose for which it was intended. Its mass and solidity hinted at the heavy machinery within. With thick load-bearing masonry walls accented by massive archways that extend two and three stories, it has been called a "monument to honesty and restraint in architectural expression and in the art of printing." Architectural historian Talbot Hamlin found it "an exquisitely and originally detailed building . . . a typical example of that flurry of real originality that eddies through much of the best building of the 1880s and 1890s." Lewis Mumford said it was one of those fine survivors of another day that "attracts the knowing eye" and has "a special bouquet to those who know the vintage years."

Such acclaim was sufficient to have the building designated a New York City landmark in 1966. Encomiums have not abated. Says Paul Goldberger, "This is truly New York's equivalent of the great nineteenth-century brick mill structures of New England. And it is far and away the finest work of the architects. . . ." "The best thing here is the brick quoining, by itself enough to make this one of my favorite buildings in Manhattan," says Francis Morrone. Sarah Landau declares it "New York's handsomest surviving commercial structure of the 1880s, and one of the nation's outstanding architectural monuments." Andrew Dolkart praises the "sophisticated fenestration pattern and subtle terra-cotta detail." "Roman brickwork worthy of the Roman Forum's Basilica of Constantine," declares the *AIA Guide to New York City*. Christopher Gray says it is "among the most sophisticated works

FIG. 11. De Vinne Press Building at the time of its completion. *Sanitary Engineer*, 13 May 1886, between pp. 560 and 561.

of masonry in New York, a tour de force of honestly simple bricklaying."[27] In 1977 the building was placed on the National Register of Historic Places and in 1980 on the New York State Register (fig. 11).

The De Vinne Press Building, with the sense of solidity and success it suggested, was noted by viewers across the Atlantic as well as in America. One London trade journal reprinted the description of the De Vinne Press, its proprietors, and its new building with this introduction:

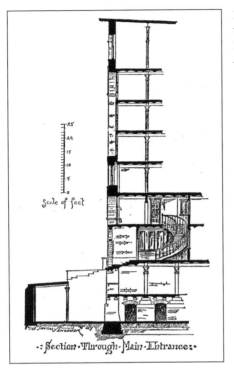

FIG. 12.

Vertical section of the De Vinne Press Building, looking north. *Sanitary Engineer*, 13 May 1886, p. 561.

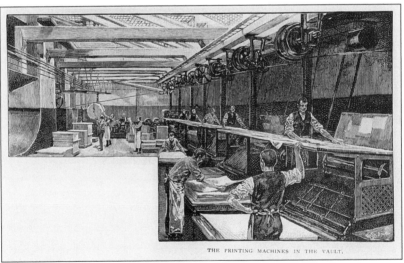

THE PRINTING MACHINES IN THE VAULT.

FIG. 13. Presses in the vault of the De Vinne Press Building. *Century Magazine*, November 1890, p. 95.

Proprietorship

In these days of cut and slash, and of reckless competition in the American Printing Trade, it is refreshing and comforting to read of a Printer able to maintain an establishment on a large scale and do his Printing in beauty and a high degree of art. Such an establishment is known to the United States, and, indeed, to the whole reading world – it is that of Theodore L. De Vinne and Company, of New York."[28]

Unfortunately but inevitably, the interior of the building has been changed considerably to accommodate later uses. In its heyday, the visitor entering through the front door on Lafayette beheld a vestibule containing a decorative spiral staircase that led to the second floor and Theodore De Vinne's office. Aside from these details, the design of the interior was strictly utilitarian.

The building was designed especially for a printing house without any attempt to anticipate subsequent use. Construction throughout was sturdy enough to permit heavy presses and other equipment to be used on any floor. The floors themselves were covered with a layer of asphalt to absorb vibrations of the machinery. Interior structure consisted of iron beams and brick arches supported on iron columns topped with angular capitals that upheld classical notions even though the mood was utilitarian. Wood appeared mainly in the window frames. In a business whose product was paper and in which such substances as benzene were in daily use, it was important that most construction materials not be highly flammable.

Covering a lot that was one hundred by seventy-three feet, the building had a total of nine stories, the use of each one carefully planned for minimum movement of bulky and heavy materials (fig. 12). The lowest level, called the vault, stored stereotype plates and paper and housed boilers, the coal pit, and a machine repair workshop. It was "the only place in the building in which gas burn[ed] all day."[29] The vault was also the home of a web press (i.e., it used a continuous roll of paper rather than sheets) which produced unillustrated pages of the *Century Magazine*. To accommodate the web as well as six two-revolution Hoe cylinder presses, a thirty-foot-wide strip was excavated under the sidewalk on the Lafayette Street side of the building. Lighting of this three-thousand-square-foot underground extension was enhanced by bulkheads of "patent lights" consisting of squares, circles, and hexagons of translucent glass set in iron which allowed natural light to fall from Lafayette, a much wider street than Fourth, into this pressroom. "This is prob-

FIG. 14. Vestibule of the De Vinne Press Building. *Century Magazine*, November 1890, p. 90, from a drawing by Harry Fenn.

ably the best-lighted vault in the city," said *The Sanitary Engineer*[30] (fig. 13). Panels of patent lights closest to the exterior walls swung open to ventilate the vault. (By 1911 New York City would deem these bulkheads to be sidewalk obstructions, whereupon they were removed and replaced by cellar windows flush with the building line. The stairway leading to the main door was moved closer to the building and the huge iron gates lengthened to accommodate the modified stairway.)

On the next level up, which could be entered from the sidewalk on the Fourth Street side, were the large drum cylinder and Adams presses as well as the 130-horse-power Corliss steam engine that provided power for the building.

The next story, the "first floor," was entered by stairs and the main door on the Lafayette Street side. Beyond the vestibule (fig. 14), the stop-cylinder and other small presses printed the illustrated forms of the *Century* and sundry deluxe editions for a variety of customers. Most color work was also produced on these machines (fig. 15).

The second floor held the office and "counting room." As noted above, De Vinne's office was a slight departure from the otherwise functional décor. It was, in effect, a modestly furnished and appointed library lined with bookshelves that held a working collection of treatises on printing, specimens of other presses, and office copies of De Vinne's own imprints. Also on the second floor were proofreaders' desks, paper-cutting and pressing facilities, and the packing department.

The third floor was the job composing room, the arrangement of which was planned to take maximum advantage of natural light, with racks for storing type cases in the center and composing stands near the windows. The foreman of this room had access to management offices directly below by means of speaking tubes and copy boxes. The book composing room occupied the fourth floor, its arrangement being similar to the third. On the fifth floor were the electrotype foundry, the roller-making department, and the carpentry shop. The sixth floor was a bindery where sheets for Century Company's periodicals were folded, cut, gathered, collated, and wire-

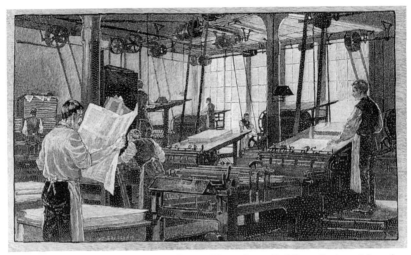

FIG. 15. Stop-cylinder presses at the De Vinne Press Building. *Century Magazine*, November 1890, p. 95.

FIG. 16. Women gathering sheets in the De Vinne Press bindery. *Century Magazine*, November 1890, p. 97.

stitched, and then covered with paper wrappers (fig. 16). It was presumably also where conventional trade binding of books was carried out. For, as later copyright records show, the De Vinne Press did that too. Finally, the seventh floor was used by Century Company as a storage room for surplus stock and for valuable cuts (wood engravings and electrotypes of illustrations) and manuscripts.

Construction began in May of 1885, and at least some printing was taking place as early as April 1886 even though the building was not officially completed until July. By all accounts, Babb Cook and Willard served their clients' needs well. The building, which cost a relatively modest $200,000,[31] was praised for its architectural distinction and hailed as a model design for efficient operation of a large printing business. It also suited the proprietor's own personal style of management.

De Vinne's approach was to make clear the specific standards of his house (instilled in his workers by many years of close personal supervision and codified in his 1883 *Manual of Printing Office Practice*), to take advantage of each technical innovation and adapt it to his own production, and to delegate authority to longtime, trusted employees. The new building, with its separate departments on different floors, suited this delegation scheme particularly well.

Each of the five major departments of Theodore L. De Vinne & Co. had its foreman who hired workers as needed. Pressmen and compositors reported on printed tickets the work they did each day. The foremen reviewed and registered the tickets, making daily written reports to the manager, Robert W. Brown, who could thus keep a better running account of each worker's performance than he could have done through direct personal supervision.

Management could also keep track of the status of each job as it passed from department to department. On all long orders each foreman received specific written instructions together with a projected date for completion of his portion of the job. To the extent that this system was used and worked as intended, it saved time in following up on orders.

It became apparent that the growth of De Vinne's operations would necessitate some systematic approach to management. A number of efficiency procedures were inherent in his pioneering cost-accounting work of the late 1860s and early 1870s; others were developed prior to publication of his 1883 office manual; still others, from 1886 on, were facilitated by his design of the De Vinne Press Building. Together they comprised an approach very much in keeping with the systematic management movement: a running account of the capacity and performance of each press, announcement of the precise hours of work and a steam whistle to signal them, location of functions within the building to minimize movement of materials, speaking tubes and copy boxes to facilitate communication between floors, coordination of work flow by means of a ticket that accompanied each job, delegation of hiring and operational responsibility to foremen, and an accountability system based on daily written reports.

While other businessmen and manufacturers were experimenting at this same time to find the means of rationalizing their expanding operations, it is fair to say that De Vinne did not wait around for techniques to be proven and expounded in management literature. Indeed, he tried most of these methods before the proliferation of systematic-management articles at the end of the century and the books published early in the twentieth by such leaders of the management revolution as Frederick W. Taylor, Alexander Hamilton Church, J. Slater Lewis, and Henry Metcalfe.

As some of the reformers took the next step from "systematic" to the more mechanistic "scientific" management with its time-and-motion studies, they moved out of De Vinne's realm of applicability. Printing, with its custom nature, simply did not lend itself readily to such mass-production efficiencies. It was not possible to find the "one best way" for many nineteenth-century printing office tasks. De Vinne always held that his men were *not* interchangeable parts; it took special inclinations and talents to produce the work on which the firm's reputation rested.

The efficient running of the De Vinne establishment was further enhanced by the longevity of its managerial and supervisory staff. General manager and "confidential clerk" Robert W. Brown had been with the firm since the days of Francis Hart – in fact, he had been one of the executors of the Hart estate. He was described by Frank Hopkins, an employee during the 1890s, as a workhorse who oversaw everything personally and never took a vacation. Hopkins indicated that it was Brown, above all, who concerned himself with profitability. Other key employees dated from Francis Hart & Co.: Theodore's brother Daniel S. De Vinne, foreman of the composing room; pressroom foreman Hazeldine Hamilton; and a compositor named James W. Bothwell, who would become the most critical employee of all in years to come. In addition, there was the younger partner, Theodore B. De Vinne, his father's faithful management surrogate.

The business card of the firm at the new location featured modern type with just a touch of gothic (plate 1B). Its clean lines contrasted considerably with the Hart & Co. card of a few decades earlier.

De Vinne's ability to produce *Century* at its peak circulation of a quarter of a million, as well as *St. Nicholas* and the many other works issued from his press, rested not only on perfecting various technical details but also on equipping his now-commodious establishment with appropriate and modern printing machinery. For instance, to speed up the printing of the *Century* in the mid-1880s, he asked the Hoe Company to design one of their rotary web presses especially for the unillustrated pages.[32] This was a "perfecting" version, which required only one pass through the press to print both sides of the page. Although common for newspapers for some four decades, rotary presses had not previously been used for book or magazine work. One of the unique features of this web press – De Vinne's own modification, not part of the Hoe design – was a device that caused a jet of steam to dampen and hence soften the paper from the roll ever so slightly as it unwound. This particular web press was designed for *Century Magazine*. It would soon be printing, cutting, and folding the text and advertising pages of regular editions of the magazine and would be kept fully employed doing only this. All reprint editions, pages containing illustrations, and other Century

Company publications (as well as work for other customers) were done on other presses where the type and plates lay on a flat bed.

The illustrated pages of *Century* and the whole of *St. Nicholas* were printed on stop-cylinder presses that printed sixteen pages on one side at the rate of about 750 impressions per hour. Needless to say, it took a number of these machines to deliver the many illustrated pages on time each month. "To get the superior quality of presswork demanded this delay in performance," said De Vinne, "and this multiplication of machines has been submitted to for many years."[33] However, encouraged by the success of the rotary web press, De Vinne asked Hoe to develop a new press based on the rotary principle for the printing of illustrated forms. In 1890 the "rotary art" press was set up at the De Vinne Press (fig. 17). It was still sheet fed and still printed on one side of the page (as De Vinne explained, because woodcuts needed time to dry before printing the other side so the ink would not offset); but it did the work of four stop-cylinders. "The gain in performance," De Vinne noted, "is not as great as the gain in quality of presswork, but quality was considered more than speed." The De

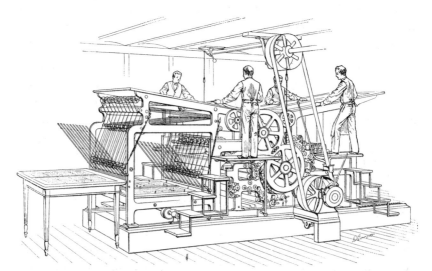

FIG. 17. Rotary art press at the De Vinne Press. *Century Magazine*, November 1890, p. 94.

Proprietorship

Vinne-inspired rotary art press in some measure superseded the Adams power platen press, which had been favored for fine work for so long.

With the relocation of his business further uptown, De Vinne moved his family from Jersey City to 150 West Fifty-ninth Street in Manhattan where they would live for three years until their residence on Seventy-sixth Street was completed.

In full control of his printing establishment for less than a decade, De Vinne was in an enviable position. He had just settled into a commodious new building built to his specifications where he could experiment with new equipment and techniques. He had one large established customer and many lesser ones. The security of his business position allowed him to indulge his passion for printing history.

Fig. 18. The terra cotta cartouche at the left of the De Vinne Press Building's main entrance was the basis for the press's device. *Century Magazine*, November 1890, p. 89, from a drawing by Harry Fenn.

[6]

Top Form (1886–1900)

I bind myself to do your work fairly. The Century Co. is not bound to any thing. It can take much or little of its work away at any time it pleases without assigning any reason. I make this concession because I believe that I shall make it your interest, as well as your pleasure, to have us your printers. I don't care about keeping the work on any other terms.

TLD, 1886

FIG. 19. The De Vinne Press device.

AT THIS TIME De Vinne began to use a printer's device based on architect George Babb's terra cotta cartouche that graced the left side of the main entrance of the De Vinne Press Building. The cartouche depicted a tablet that bore a saying of Prometheus in Greek. (It can be translated, "and further I discovered for them [i.e., mankind] numeration, most striking of inventions, and composition, nurse of the arts, producer of the record of all things.") To the tablet's right was a ribbon that said "IMPRIMATUR" (fig. 18). For the press's device, a new ribbon bearing the words "THE DE VINNE PRESS" (in common use long before the firm was incorporated under that name in 1908) appeared to the left and below the tablet, which had become spiral bound (fig. 19). There seems to be no record of whether Theodore requested this device or influenced its design.[1] But he was clearly fond of it and used it beginning in 1886 on letterhead and as a colophon on his more ambitious imprints in lieu of the tiny all-caps "THE DE VINNE PRESS" that modestly identified the printer on the typical title-page verso.

87

It was not very well known that the $200,000 De Vinne Press Building and the land on which it stood were owned jointly by Smith and De Vinne, the publisher contributing three-fourths of the capital and the printer only one-fourth. De Vinne complained privately more than two decades later, "That big building has its disadvantages as well as its compensations. My pecuniary interest in that building is small; yet it has the demerit of giving me a rating in financial circles that is misleading."[2]

Even more interesting than the financial arrangements were the obligations and duties each party agreed to perform. Notably, De Vinne agreed to maintain a printing house of sufficient capacity to manufacture *Century Magazine* and *St. Nicholas* and all other publications of Century Company and to "give a preference in attention and dispatch" to Century work. Century, on the other hand, could withdraw its publications if it pleased, and a partial withdrawal would not constitute forfeiture of its rights to preference for the remainder of its work. An earlier draft of the contract had Century notifying De Vinne two years in advance of any complete withdrawal of its business, but this safeguard was stricken. Outfitting the press was to continue to be the sole responsibility of De Vinne. There seems to have been some consideration of Century's participating financially in the printing firm itself, but this notion was discarded. Century retained the right of access to the premises to examine and supervise its work. In fact, Century's editorial department took temporary space in the De Vinne Press Building while its own building was being repaired after a fire in 1888.

The contract said Theodore L. De Vinne and Co. would pay an annual rent of 5 percent of the cost of land and building. Presumably, this meant that the firm paid rent to the two individuals who owned the premises; extant records do not confirm how this worked. The contract specified a ten-year lease with option for two five-year extensions (rental fee to be agreed upon). Such a second five-year term would expire 30 April 1906. In fact, the lease would be extended another twenty years after that.

The De Vinne-Century relationship rested for many years on the mutual respect and personal integrity of the two principals. Nowhere is this clearer than in the note, in Smith's hand, written on the last page of the contract signed by both men:

> The parties of the first, and second parts, in the foregoing Contract, gratefully record the fact – after thirteen years of intimate business relations without any formal Contract whatever existing between them and their respective houses – that no "root of bitterness" has ever sprung up to bear fruit . . . and that no differences have ever arisen which required resort to arbitration.
>
> In executing this their first formal written Contract, which has become necessary, by reason of the uncertainties of life, and the magnitude of the interests involved, they counsel that all differences be adjusted in the future, as in the past, by agreement.

Both men seemed vaguely embarrassed by this attempt to codify their gentlemen's agreement. Smith attached a note to De Vinne's copy: "P.S. Your notes about the contracts [*sic*] show just what I had concluded – that we have both been on the wrong track and must simplify things and trust each other . . . rather than attempt to provide for the future by stringent contracts."[3]

The contract can be read in more than one way. On one hand, the power and privileges it outlined seem to be skewed in favor of the Century Company. On the other, some clauses sound as though they might have been contributed by a self-assured printer, quite in control of his business and fully aware of the asset he represented to the Century Company. There was, for example, a provision that the De Vinne firm endeavor to reach even higher degrees of excellence, to be alert to and if necessary test new inventions, as it had previously done, and give Century Company the benefit of such advances in their printing. Smith might have asked for that clause, but it seems rather gratuitous and could have been instead a bit of printerly pride and self-confidence. Such an interpretation is supported by the tone of a letter De Vinne wrote to Richard Watson Gilder, *Century Magazine* editor:

> I bind myself to do your work fairly. The Century Co. [is] not bound to any thing. It can take much or little of its work away at any time it pleases . . . without assigning any reason. I make this

concession because I believe that I shall make it your interest, as well as your pleasure, to have us your printers. I don't care about keeping the work on any other terms. I don't like to feel, or make others feel the "you've got to" constraint.[4]

This display of bravura was not inappropriate at the time. Printer and magazine were at their peaks; Century's book list was growing; the printer-publisher relationship had worked out handsomely for both. It was hard to imagine the pact going sour.

Judging by extant correspondence, things continued to go smoothly for several years. De Vinne's tone was always respectful – at times obsequious. The very next year, for example, he wrote to Century Company secretary W. W. Ellsworth following the citywide compositors' strike, thanking Century for its moral support and promising, "I shall try to see that that faith and patience and generous appreciation of my services shall have a better requital [than] this note of thanks." In November 1890 De Vinne returned a check Century had sent him for a thirteen-page article written for the magazine, saying, "It is pay enough and honor enough to get your approval of my methods in the pages of the magazine. I am more than content with that."[5]

The relationship was at its apex during one of their major projects – the heroic publication of a major reference work. In 1882 Roswell Smith had purchased from Blackie and Son the American rights to John Ogilvie's 1850 *Imperial Dictionary*, which was based on Noah Webster's *Dictionary* and at the time was being revised and enlarged by Charles Annandale. Although he first intended merely to Americanize the text, Smith soon determined that it should be a new work. Ultimately, the *Imperial* was used for little more than a word list. *The Century Dictionary*, created by a team of leading philologists and scientific authorities, was much more encyclopedic and included quotations illustrating the use of words, much like the *Oxford English Dictionary* that was so long in preparation and whose first fascicle had yet to appear. When the *Century Dictionary* appeared, it was truly the most ambitious and authoritative work of its kind in the English-speaking world (plate 5).

The dictionary was published in 1889–91 in twenty-four parts, intended for binding in six volumes. The impact of this project on the De Vinne Press can hardly be overstated. Each page had to be read by various specialists before it could be electrotyped and the type redistributed for further use, necessitating the purchase of a great deal of type and the assigning of space to hold all the composed forms, which included some six thousand delicate wood-engraved illustrations.

The composition demanded access to many typefaces and special sorts for each page of composition. De Vinne designed an elaborate stand capable of holding a dozen cases of type within ready reach of the compositor. A trade journal reported in 1887 on these "new stands and cases which have been arranged by Mr. De Vinne for the easier composition of complex book work like dictionaries [by which the compositor] can reach more than seven hundred boxes without moving from his stand"[6] (fig. 20). He also devised an improved storage system for leads, wooden "furniture," and other spacing materials – all arranged efficiently to avoid unnecessary movement for compositors and those making up pages on the composing stone. He presented these ideas to the trade at the 1890 convention of the United Typothetae of America.

This great dictionary project, happily, would be concluded before Roswell Smith died in 1892. Reportedly, he was able to take the $1 million[7] he invested in the first edition directly from *Century Magazine* profits.[8] *The Century Cyclopedia of Names* was added in 1894 and *The Century Atlas of the World* in 1897. A supplement in two volumes was published in 1909, and other editions of the dictionary followed.

The dictionary was financially successful and has held up well in subsequent critical evaluations. It was cited in a 1971 court case as an authority on nineteenth-century usage.[9] A 1984 history of lexicography says,

> [*The Century Dictionary*] includes much encyclopedic material even in its alphabetical section, many thousands of illustrative quotations, and numerous fine pictorial illustrations. Beautifully

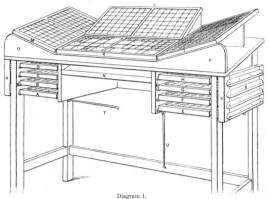

Diagram 1.
The De Vinne stand, with its under cases in rack and out of use.

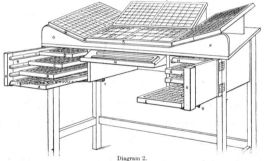

Diagram 2.
The De Vinne case, with swinging side-frames drawn out and locked, and with the galley exposed.

DIAGRAMS 1 AND 2. A and B, cases for extra and irregular sorts; C, nonpareil accents; D, nonpareil antique; E, brevier antique; F, nonpareil roman upper; G, nonpareil roman lower; H, nonpareil italic; I, brevier italic; K and L, brevier roman, upper and lower; M, brevier accents; N, drawer, containing galley; O and P, angled support for cases; R and S, swinging frame with racks; T and U, iron rods that hold the swinging side-frame.

FIG. 20.
Composing stand designed by De Vinne to make many typefaces available simultaneously to the compositor. *The Practice of Typography: Modern Methods of Book Composition,* pp. 24, 25.

printed and bound, it is surely one of the handsomest dictionaries ever made. In spite of the competition of other large but less expensive dictionaries . . . it was highly successful. . . . [I]n many instances the Century's treatment has not been surpassed.[10]

As if to ratify that 1984 assessment, *The Century Dictionary* – a wealth of information about late-nineteenth-century American culture – is now available in graphic form on the Internet.[11]

While the *Dictionary* and other substantial projects kept De Vinne's printing plant humming, he became busy once again with the revived employers' organization, The Typothetae of the City of

New York. De Vinne had been one of the thirty-one printers who signed the call for a meeting in 1883 "to improve the trade and cultivate a just and friendly spirit among the craft" by establishing a permanent organization. At this resurrection of the Typothetae, he was elected vice president, a post he held until 1892 when he was elected president upon the death of the much-revered William C. Martin, who was, at the time of his death, the oldest employing printer in New York City. In 1887 similar societies were founded in Chicago and St. Louis, and before long there were more than fifty around the country. De Vinne was on the board of trustees much of the time after the New York Typothetae incorporated in 1892, and a valued adviser always. When the national organization (the United Typothetae of America) took shape in 1887, he was elected its first president. Through the mid-1890s De Vinne would remain active in the national organization, speaking at its annual conventions (held in a different city each year) and chairing such important committees as those on standards for the measurement of type and on international copyright issues.

De Vinne was long considered the spokesman for the New York employing printers on labor questions. He chaired the "committee of employers" that met with journeymen representatives to determine standard prices for labor during the two decades before the Typothetae began to speak for its members on labor matters in the 1880s. As indicated above, he had always advocated proprietor independence and a free-market economy, making his views known publicly as early as the 1860s. By 1886 De Vinne was speaking with authority on all matters pertaining to the printing trade. The theme of self-reliance appeared again and again in his public statements, such as in an article he wrote for *Century Magazine* in 1886. "The thoughtful workman," he said, "must see that there are rewards for labor which no society can get for him – rewards to be earned by the discharge of duties which he must do himself; that it is better for him to be expert and active at his trade, trying to do more rather than less than is required of him, . . . than it is to lean on any association. . . ."[12]

In his presidential address to the United Typothetae of America later that year, De Vinne continued to maintain that employer and employee were not fundamentally different. He advocated informal clubs in which both, without compromising principles, could meet informally to exchange views. As naïve as this sounds now, he persisted with this approach for decades.

At every opportunity he seemed to return to one refrain – that trade unions were assuming and promoting an unnatural and unnecessary antagonism between capital and labor:

> The trade union spirit teaches a boy that he must look more to the trade union for fair wages and decent treatment than to his own exertions, or to his employer; the consequence is there is a marked degree of stiffness between employer and employee which never ought to exist.[13]

Notwithstanding the efforts of De Vinne, his managers, and foremen, however, unions did creep into his household. In late 1886, Theodore L. De Vinne & Co. experienced its first strike – a strike, said one report, "fomented from without." Forty press feeders, assuming the firm could not produce *Century Magazine* on schedule without them, walked out. The web press, which did not require feeders, had been installed but not fully tested at the time. "Egregiously underrated by the trade union which ordered the strike," the web press completed the work handily, and the strikers surrendered.[14] From that time on, however, it would be a struggle for De Vinne to keep his shop free of union control.

In September and October of 1887 the New York City printing proprietors negotiated with the Typographical Union an increase in wages but did not agree to a reduction of hours to nine a day with no reduction in pay, much less a clause that would have forbidden proprietors to employ anyone without a union card. With both sides clearly intransigent, a strike ensued that crippled some shops for nearly three months. Pressmen, feeders, stereotypers, and electrotypers briefly joined in a sympathy strike, bringing the total to a peak of about twelve hundred employees throughout the city.[15]

Theodore De Vinne, who was chairman of the Typothetae emergency committee during the crisis, was again wounded personally and professionally by this strike. His presses were idle for fifteen days. Writing to W. W. Ellsworth at the Century Company, De Vinne spoke of protecting his nonunion men and seeing "that the power of the mischief-making men who plotted the strike be broken." He felt confident that his men would not go out on another strike because this one had cost them too much:

> They have found and will find that our house is a better friend and paymaster than the Union. For the last week I have been excessively busy in bringing employing printers together, in considering plans for the getting of our men out of the Union, which plans I think will be successful.[16]

De Vinne and four other employers immediately set about to establish a "Printer's Guild," the objectives of which would be to promote better employer-employee relations, encourage skill and efficiency, and acknowledge the "just claims" of workers. "Trade disputes come largely from the infrequency of social intercourse between employer and employed," they maintained. Members would include proprietors and employees ("good workmen" only) of every branch of the trade. The Typothetae approved the concept and made plans to meet with employee representatives.[17] (What became of the idea is not clear; the Printer's Guild is not mentioned further in Typothetae minutes.) This proposed organization may have been the "plans" De Vinne mentioned to Ellsworth. It was clearly designed to subvert the unions' growing power, yet it was couched in De Vinne's refrains that employers and employees needed to emphasize their common interests.

One can readily understand why proprietors would want to attempt to make common cause with their employees in this period. The 1886 Haymarket labor riot in Chicago must have shaken even the most sanguine employer. With the formation in that same year of the American Federation of Labor, "pure and simple" trade unionism gathered momentum. The 1887 compositors' strike fell near the beginning of more than a decade of labor agitation and violence. The eight-hour day would be a major focus of this struggle until that goal was attained.

No Art Without Craft

By the end of 1887, with the strike ended, De Vinne was able to take his leave and make a four- or five-month tour of Europe. His companions on the trip included William Fayal Clarke, editor of *St. Nicholas*, and Charles F. Chichester, one of the business managers of *Century Magazine*. They reported that De Vinne's temper was never ruffled – that, although older than his companions, he took on the journey with wholehearted zest. Predictably, De Vinne turned the trip into a printer's pilgrimage with stops at the National Printing Office in Paris and, most notably, the Plantin-Moretus Museum at Antwerp. It is from this latter visit that we have his reverent biographical sketch of Christophe Plantin and description of Plantin's shop as it then existed in the museum that had been opened a decade before his visit. His companions noted De Vinne's boyish enthusiasm for the museum and his pride that a master printer of the sixteenth century was also a well-to-do burgher with a magnificent home.[18]

It was De Vinne's good fortune to live in a time when there were organized groups through which he could socialize with kindred spirits. Toward the end of the nineteenth century there flourished in America many clubs built around literary or bookish interests. In 1889, the writer and soon-to-be Columbia University professor Brander Matthews enumerated the New York City associations "made up of little knots of men interested in one or another manifestation of literature or art": The Grolier, Authors, Nineteenth Century, Century, University, Tile, Salmagundi, Kit-Cat, Greek, Library, Fellowcraft, Aldine, and Players Clubs, and the Architectural League.[19] His list could be expanded by moving slightly backward or forward in time or by relaxing one's definition of literary interests; for there was a plethora of men's clubs with more or less serious intentions in that period.

In 1882 seven men with literary inclinations had met at the home of *Century Magazine* editor Richard Watson Gilder to form the Authors Club. Membership was confined to men who had written "a published book proper to literature" or who had "a recognized position in other kinds of distinctively literary work." De Vinne had been elected to membership in 1887 on the strength of his *Invention of Printing* (1876) and *Historic Printing Types* (1886). When the club decided to publish a book made up of contributions from each member (and signed by each author in each copy), De Vinne offered to print this *Liber Scriptorum* at cost.[20] The edition of 251 copies netted the club over $10,500, allowing it to furnish the rooms donated by Andrew Carnegie in the Carnegie Building and to begin a library. De Vinne's contribution to the text was his argument against eccentric types called "Do You Know the Letters?" He also did some printing of the association's annual "Reports, Constitution, By-Laws and List of Members."[21]

De Vinne was one of the forty-four charter members of the Aldine Club, established in 1889 on Lafayette Place near the De Vinne Press. Founded for "the encouragement of literature and art, and social intercourse and enjoyment," the club originally limited its membership to publishers, authors, artists, and printers. It functioned chiefly as a luncheon place for "men who make books" in the printing and publishing district then located around Lafayette Place. In 1894 it followed the uptown movement and had quarters at Fifth Avenue and Fifteenth Street. In 1898 it was amalgamated with the Uptown Association, modifying its original emphasis.[22]

The Century Association (also called the Century Club) was the oldest of the literary clubs, dating its origin to 1847, when it grew out of a small group of artists known as the Sketch Club. The object was to be "the cultivation of a taste for letters and the fine arts, and social enjoyment." The forty-two original members included artists, merchants, physicians, bankers, clergymen, and lawyers, as well as authors. The constitution limited membership to professional and amateur authors and artists. While the club was always composed of more amateurs and appreciators of the arts than actual practitioners, it retained its artistic and literary emphasis. De Vinne would join in 1893 when the membership had grown beyond the original goal of one hundred to about one thousand. Like the Authors Club, the Century Association also used De Vinne's printing services at times.

No Art Without Craft

De Vinne presumably partook freely of the benefits of membership of the Century, Aldine, and Authors Clubs, the result of which
would have been to extend his sphere of acquaintances beyond his
Century Company, Typothetae, and other printing and publishing
contacts. Aside from serving on the Aldine committee of admis-
sions, and possibly other minor posts, he held no offices in these
organizations. At his death De Vinne would also belong to the
Hispanic Society and the American Numismatic Society, having
printed for both. Since there is no other evidence of any interest in
these specialized subjects, he may have been made a member as a
result of his printing for them; or he could have joined them for
business promise or to study the rare books in their libraries. All
these societies notwithstanding, however, De Vinne was involved
more intensely with the Grolier Club than with all the others combined. For the Grolier was – at least in its early years – focused precisely on De Vinne's interests: the arts involved in book production.

De Vinne was also able at this time to build for his household
(which included his wife, son, daughter-in-law, and grandchildren)
a handsome residence in Manhattan. He looked at property along
the western edge of Manhattan as far north as Ninetieth Street. But
in July 1886 he purchased a lot on the southwest corner of West
Seventy-sixth Street and West End Avenue, known as Eleventh
Avenue until the mid-1880s. De Vinne must have been aware of the
predictions that this was to be Manhattan's next fashionable residential area. The area now called the Upper West Side developed
slowly and was still open land with occasional shanty villages, farm-
houses, and taverns until the opening of the Ninth Avenue elevated
train in 1880. As utilities and other services were put in place, it
began to attract investors who constructed luxury housing, both
private residences and apartment buildings. Housing clustered at
first around the elevated railroad or "el" stations at Seventy-second,
Eighty-first, and Ninety-third Streets. By the time De Vinne built
his home, the Upper West Side was in the midst of a housing boom.
Writing of the blocks in the Seventies and Eighties between West
End Avenue and Riverside Drive, Moses King in his 1911 edition of

King's Views would call it the finest residential district in the city.[23]

De Vinne's was one of the earliest houses on his block. In 1885, Eleventh Avenue residences were still all below Sixtieth, and West Seventy-sixth Street was still inhabited no farther west than Tenth Avenue. Only in 1887 did building along Seventy-sixth Street reach beyond Tenth Avenue and then only six dwellings and a stable. When construction began on De Vinne's corner house in October of 1888, the only houses in the immediate vicinity were across West End Avenue to the south. The house of the neighbor to his immediate west was under construction and was finished three months before De Vinne's July 1889 completion date. Within five years most lots one block in any direction from De Vinne filled up. Of the fifty-seven residences built within one block of De Vinne between 1886 and 1896, the 100-foot lots averaged 21.5 feet in width. Their estimated cost averaged $23,000. They were largely four stories high with a few of three or five. Most were brick and stone like De Vinne's until 1891 when limestone and brownstone fronts led the field.[24]

To design his four-story house De Vinne chose the same architectural firm that had handled the De Vinne Press Building four years earlier. The corner lot gave them some flexibility, and they used it well. They put the entrance, reached by a stairway of nine steps, on the long 84-foot side of the building that ran along Seventy-sixth Street. The West End Avenue side (26 feet, 7½ inches) was rounded on the first three stories; a bow bay at the other end of the house unified the design. The mansard roof was topped by a decorative iron rail that repeated the fence and stair rail below. An 1889 photograph in the *American Architect and Building News* shows much of the first floor facade covered by ivy (fig. 21). De Vinne took a hand in the interior design, experimenting with the stairway from parlor level to second story before settling on an easy slope of not more than thirty degrees for the benefit of Mrs. De Vinne in light of her frail health. This $40,000 residence was larger and quite a bit more expensive than its typical neighbor.[25] Although not ostentatious and not as grand as the residences along Riverside Drive, it was one of the finest of its type.

FIG. 21. De Vinne's residence, 300 West Seventy-sixth Street at West End Avenue, New York City. *American Architect and Building News*, 24 June 1899, 64: 1226, following p. 104.

Top Form

In 1890, De Vinne and Roswell Smith undertook another building project: an addition to the De Vinne Press Building, extending the edifice along the Fourth Street side, continuing the design of the original structure (fig. 22). This extension, officially "21–23 East Fourth Street," was no doubt necessitated by the production of the massive *Century Dictionary* and its supplements, the composition and presswork of which called for the hiring of additional hands as well as more space for storage and production. In addition, the Century Company was at work on two ambitious subscription books, both of which had been serialized in their magazine (*Battles and Leaders of the Civil War* and *Abraham Lincoln: A History*). The company had some thirty other titles in print at this time.

By now, De Vinne had a well-developed patronage among publishers, private clubs, and individuals. During the 1890s, in fact, his reputation was fully developed and his clientele numerous and varied. In that decade, De Vinne's declining stamina for physical work, together with the financial security he had attained, inspired a considerable amount of travel, including trips to Europe in 1892 and 1894 and an extended Mediterranean trip with his wife and niece in 1897.

This freedom from daily supervision at his printing house was a circumstance made possible only because of the trusted, competent employees at Theodore L. De Vinne & Co. and the company's clearly established house policies. One such employee at this time was Frank Hopkins, who had started in 1887 as a proofreader on *Century Magazine* and had risen to assistant manager and official representative to major customers. By 1891 Hopkins was taking major responsibility for negotiating, planning, and seeing through the press most of the house's finer printing. The elder De Vinne came to the plant less and less, even when he was in town; and then he typically arrived after lunch (fig. 23).

Yet despite this seeming leisure, De Vinne could not shrink from his position as leader of the proprietors who resisted union control. In the 1890s, as the Typographical Union members grew bolder and more numerous, De Vinne became even more outspoken against the closed-shop principle and the union's tactics against strikebreakers. "The prevention of a free man from getting work," he said, "is a grosser violence of the Constitution than any other possible act. It strikes at the very foundation of civil liberty."[26] Nevertheless, he did not abandon hope of returning to the practice of a joint committee of workers and proprietors sitting down together to discuss proposed changes in rates and rules. It was, in fact, a matter of great ambivalence for De Vinne. By the end of that decade he could declare, "The time is coming . . . when we shall have to imitate the tactics of our opponents . . . to resist some of the unreasonable demands made by the socialistic and anarchistic elements of society." Yet, virtually in the same breath, he predicted a return to the joint-committee tradition, saying cheerfully, "There is surely fairness and justice enough in each party. . . ."[27]

Within his own shop he tried to maintain loyalty in part by force of his personality and reputation for fairness. On the occasion of the De Vinnes' fiftieth wedding anniversary, 25 December 1900, the employees presented to him and his wife a specially designed, framed shield of "gold and iron repoussé" depicting scenes from Bunyan's *Pilgrim's Progress*. In accepting the "Pilgrim shield," De Vinne expressed gratification that he still retained the "good will and love" of his employees:

> I dare not say that I have always lived up to my ideal of what an employer should be. I have made mistakes which I regret. Yet I do say that I have always tried to be just, and I accept this testimonial, to which men have contributed who have been in the employ of our house for periods ranging from ten to fifty years, as evidence of their belief that I have always meant to be fair to all.[28]

At times there were specific incentives for loyalty. In April 1892 the Messrs. De Vinne had divided a portion – reportedly 5 percent – of their profits for the past year with their employees. One year earlier, in an obvious effort to retain his workers' steadfastness and to reward the faithful, De Vinne had announced his intention "to give, in cash, a share of the receipts . . . to every man and boy, woman and girl, union or non-union, . . . who has fairly done his or her duty" during the intervening twelve months.[29]

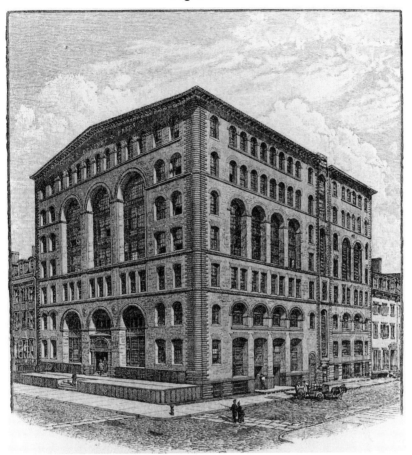

FIG. 22. The De Vinne Press Building with its addition on Fourth Street. This wood engraving was used in numerous publications; it was the frontispiece of the 1907 *Types of the De Vinne Press*. (See plate 8.)

"Profit-sharing" enjoyed a vogue in the late nineteenth century, inspired in part by a book of that title written in 1884 by an Englishman, Sedley Taylor. A number of American firms adopted the technique in the hope that it would provide incentive for better production and mollify trade unrest by giving employees a stake in company profitability. De Vinne's interest in the plan can be seen by articles he collected and labeled "Labor Unions/Profit Sharing."[30] The Typothetae discussed it as early as May 1888. The principal

FIG. 23. Theodore De Vinne in his office at the De Vinne Press, mid-1890s.

FIG. 24. The likenesses of Theodore L. and Theodore B. De Vinne on a brochure produced for the 1892 De Vinne Press banquet to celebrate its profit-sharing program.

American proponent of the idea, Nicholas P. Gilman, even published a journal devoted to the subject until 1896 when enthusiasm for the idea waned after the depression of the 1890s. It is not clear how far beyond one year the De Vinne Press plan was in effect. It reportedly ceased "after several years" under union pressure.[31]

At the banquet organized on 30 April 1892 by the De Vinne Press employees to celebrate the distribution (fig. 24), superintendent Robert W. Brown read a testimonial that said, in part,

> We, the employees of Theodore L. De Vinne & Co., in meeting assembled, unanimously feel that we cannot allow the present occasion to pass without expressing our deep sense of the generous consideration displayed toward us by our employers. . . . To Mr. Theodore L. De Vinne, the founder of the firm, we offer the assurance of our enduring esteem. In him we recognize a man who has advanced the art of printing to its highest development in the nineteenth century; a man who by his genius and indomitable energy has established a printing-house whose work is famous both in America and in Europe; above all, a man filled with kindly solicitude for the welfare of his Employees, ever ready with wise counsel and generous contribution in all undertakings for their social advancement. Appreciating as we do the enormous responsibilities involved in the conduct of such a vast establishment as The De Vinne Press, we cannot refrain from expressing our admiration for his uniformly kind manner toward us, by which we are encouraged in the performance of our respective duties, while he has endeared himself to all.

Afterwards, Brown "uncovered the beautifully engrossed testimonial, which in its splendid Florentine frame, thirty by forty inches, rested on an easel, covered with the national colors."

In De Vinne's response, he mentioned by name and praised the major employees, referring to them as his "own household." He used the occasion to touch on three of his favorite themes. This "festival," he said, was "one of many evidences that capital and labor are not enemies." No one served him "grudgingly or fearfully." There was, he noted, "a mutual feeling of kindliness" between the owners (himself and his son) and the employees. De Vinne started to say something against the nine-hour day but confined himself to these remarks on the "time is money" theme: "The less you work, the less the production; the less the production, the less the profit. Neither Henry George, nor Edward Bellamy nor all the trade-unions, nor all the legislatures can ever juggle these premises to any other conclusion." Finally, he touched upon the notion of individualism, by which he meant, in part, not relying on trade unions for advancement. "In your business life you make your own fortune or misfortune. No employer can make it for you, nor can any trade-union or any legislature – each and all may help you a little or hinder you a little – in the long run you will have to depend on yourself." De Vinne closed with the hope that years to come would knit his household closer together and further consolidate their mutual interests.[32]

Apparently the business aspects of his firm were not all-consuming, because he found time for typographic design, both historical and practical. One project was making *Century Magazine* more readable by designing a new typeface for its two-column format. In 1895 the magazine quietly switched from the gray, modified old-style type it had used since its inception as *Scribner's* in November 1870 to this new face. In an editorial in the November 1895 issue, *Century* congratulated itself on twenty-five years of literary and moral leadership, citing its pioneering work in the revival of wood engraving and its "attempts to improve the newer and more autographic methods" of illustration, but not mentioning the typeface new to that issue. In the December issue, the editor did refer to it briefly:

> We therefore trust that our readers were pleasantly affected by the appearance of the November pages of THE CENTURY, when the new type was put in use for the first time. The story of the designing of this type . . . perhaps Mr. Theodore L. De Vinne ought to record, if not here, at least for the benefit of a technical audience. Meantime we hope our readers like the change; we hope they find the new type clearer and more elegant.

Three months later De Vinne obliged with a two-page "open letter" to *Century* readers, acquainting them, as he could never resist, with a bit of history. He told of Caslon's type of the early eighteenth century, later dominance by the modern styles of Didot and Bodoni, the revival of Caslon types by Pickering and Whittingham,[33] the continued prevalence of the delicate moderns, the changes wrought in type appearance by new printing techniques, and what he described as a current demand for bolder types – demand on his part, certainly. This demand, he said, had been answered to some extent by types like Jenson, Monotone, and De Vinne (about which more later). The *Century* publishers, he continued, decided to "swim with the tide" (as though their printer had nothing to do with it).

The Century face was indeed bolder and blacker than the magazine's earlier type. It accomplished this boldness by greater contrast between thick and thin strokes of the letters (without allowing thin strokes to become too delicate) and by more prominent brackets.[34] These characteristics were more pronounced on *Century Magazine's* paper printed at high speeds than they were on the softer paper of type specimen books (fig. 25). To provide more white space within the letters, one of De Vinne's criteria for legibility, the letters were elongated a trifle and the x-height increased. (De Vinne called it Century Roman or Century Expanded, meaning "expanded upward.") This gave it a slightly narrower or compressed look, even though the lower case in the old and new types were almost exactly the same a-to-z width. The result was that the same amount of text could be fitted into the crowded two-column format as before, but it was more vivid and readable. It was, in fact, precisely for the narrow measure that the face was developed.

Linn Boyd Benton of the Inland Type Foundry, inventor of the pantographic punch cutting machine in 1884, modeled and cut the face on De Vinne's instructions. They began with ten-inch drawings, using "minute geometrical accuracy," which had to be modified on some letters "for the humoring of optical illusions in the reader." Each character, said De Vinne in this *Century* piece, "was scrutinized by editor and publisher, printer and engraver, and often repeatedly altered before it was put in the form of a working model."[35]

As a part of this new face, De Vinne offered the quotation marks in use in France since the time of the Didots, which looked like

CENTURY EXPANDED

THIS face of type was first made on 10-point body, for use on THE CENTURY MAGAZINE, and it has been used for many books of The Century Co. The expansion of the letter is upward, enabling one to get much matter in small space.

Capitals 28   Lower-case 20

18-point.   A. T. F. Co.

Legibility first, Decoration last

PRINTING, in its early days, was a masculine art. The value of the printed book was in its readability. The types used might be large or small, thick or thin, but they were always distinct. There were thin and thick strokes in the many forms of letter then in use, but the thicker stroke was always protracted, and the thin stroke always of a perceptible width. Knowing well they could not compete with skilled copyists in refinements of decoration, the old printers wisely gave their best efforts toward making print plain. The change that came with the new method of engraving on wood, in its imitation of copperplate delicacy, was damaging to typography.

FIG. 25. Century type from *Types of the De Vinne Press*, 1907, p. 229.

boomerangs turned on the side and printed in the middle of the type line («, », ‹, and ›). They may have been more rational than apostrophes and inverted commas, but they did not last beyond the April 1898 issue of *Century*.

Judging from colleagues' remarks quoted by De Vinne in his article, the typeface itself was well received. Carl Rollins testified years later, "I can well remember the elegant appearance of the rejuvenated magazine as it came in each month. Nothing so fine and refined had hitherto appeared in America."[36]

The periodical switched again to a rounder, slightly larger face with the November 1902 issue. Publicly the magazine merely said the new type was "more readable than ever." It was Bruce's Modernized Old-style No. 20 that had appeared in the De Vinne specimen books as early as 1877. The 1907 De Vinne Press type specimen would explain that No. 20 was used as the text type of *Century Magazine* and *St. Nicholas* because "its light lines, that will not take or impart a strong black to print, commend it to all who desire a greater prominence to be given to engravings."[37] Significantly, De Vinne did not say that *he* was among those who desired type to be subservient to illustration.

De Vinne had only intended Century Expanded for matter set in columns and for poetry where a compressed type avoided frequent running over of lines. Benton also cut Century Broad-Face for the De Vinne Press "for service on books to be set in a broad measure which do not require a compression of letters for the saving of space." Other than its horizontal expansion, it had the same characteristics as Century Expanded. In *Plain Printing Types*, De Vinne said his aim on Century Broad-Face was "to give to each letter a larger face than is usual in text-types of this body, with as much boldness of line as would be consistent with the greatest legibility," noting that there is a limit beyond which further thickness of line actually makes types less legible when printed in mass.

Although De Vinne apparently had nothing to do with Century faces beyond these two, a whole "family" was created for the American Type Founders Company (ATF)[38] by L. B. Benton's prolific son, Morris Fuller Benton, who designed eighteen different variations from 1900 to 1928. (Confusingly, one of those variations is also known as Century Expanded, De Vinne's name for the original prototype.) Later, British typographer Stanley Morison judged this to be "probably the finest type family of related weights and series" in what had become a large field indeed of type families.[39] While De Vinne's original Century Expanded type inspired these variations, credit for their creation goes to Morris Fuller Benton or perhaps to the ATF's Henry Lewis Bullen, who may have had the idea.[40]

The Century family of types has fared quite well in legibility studies, news that would have pleased De Vinne immensely.[41] Beginning as foundry type, Century proved to be a favorite with typographers even as it was being transformed into versions for typesetting machinery, film, and digital use.[42] Century and its familial descendants have survived through the years in a way the "artistic" types De Vinne decried have not. As Paul Shaw has summed it up, despite all the redesigning of Century, "De Vinne's original conception has survived virtually intact. Like an accordion, Century has had the vitality and strength to undergo repeated stretchings and squeezings without loss of identity."[43] Indeed, Century is one of the faces generally embedded in today's word processing software.[44]

Attention to *Century Magazine*'s typeface was appreciated by some, but illustrations were an even more important ingredient in its success and that of its chief rivals such as *Harper's*. Needless to say, wood engravings, while exquisite in their charming detail, were time consuming to create, difficult to print, and therefore expensive. Producers of illustrated material were naturally intrigued by new techniques that would cut costs and speed up production. A relief plate that could suggest tone but could be produced mechanically was of considerable interest. Experiments from the 1860s sought to photograph an image onto a photosensitive block through some kind of screen that broke it up into lines or dots on the printing plate. (This would create the impression of lighter and darker tones, even though any specific point on the illustration was either black or white.) The first "halftone" (as these images were dubbed) to appear in a newspaper, where speed was truly of the essence, is thought to be "Shantytown" in the New York *Daily Graphic* on 4 March 1880. Further experimentation led, in time, to smoother results through use of a crossline screen, and finding the optimum screen distance and lens aperture. The result was the optical-dot halftone still widely used today.

In late 1884 and 1885, illustrated magazines were experimenting with these various methods of creating plates mechanically. Tracing this development must be done with great care, since some wood engravers were able to reproduce a variety of tonal effects that simulated processes such as charcoal drawings and even photographs with uncanny faithfulness.

The first halftone in *Century Magazine* appeared in May 1885 (p. 138). It was labeled "process reproduction from a photograph" and had been touched up with a graver to give better definition to the overall gray appearance of this scene of an Army of the Potomac encampment. Halftones in the November 1885 issue depicted two sculptures, and then no more appeared until the fall of 1886, when they began to be used very sparingly and typically for scientific subjects. *Harper's* had run its first halftone in December 1884 amid its many exquisite wood engravings. In *Scribner's Magazine* (the monthly launched by Charles Scribner's heirs after the required interval from the formation of the Century Company as an independent publishing concern), halftones dominated from its first issue in January 1887.[45]

It is worth noting that even the most fastidious wood engravings were still subjective, whereas the photographic halftone allowed objective depiction of physical phenomena. As Ellic Howe put it, "The hand of the wood engraver could not do the impossible, to dehumanize itself and make purely objective statements."[46]

As always, De Vinne was keen on new techniques. In a moment when candor overcame modesty, De Vinne said that "Francis Hart & Co. were probably the first printers in New York to experiment with the Meisenbach process of printing from relief plates produced by photographing through fine meshes on gelatin films."[47]

(Meisenbach, says Bamber Gascoigne, was an early technique whose widespread use caused the name to be used for any relief halftone block that used a crossline screen.[48]) Alexander Drake said that De Vinne "was among the first to embrace [the halftone] and bring it to the highest state of perfection."[49] We know that De Vinne's shop contained an electrotype foundry, but there is no evidence that he had the in-house capacity to produce the many photo-mechanical and photo-chemical blocks from which he printed. There were companies that specialized in this sort of thing. In his printer's note in the 1896 reprint of Moxon's *Mechanick Exercises*, he credits the line-block plates to the Hagopian Photo-Engraving Company. The three portraits (of Gutenberg, Coster, and Moxon himself) were "reproduced by the artotype process of Bierstadt," artotype being another term for the planographic collotype process.[50] For the historic Moxon reprint he felt it was worth including three pages of this more sophisticated illustration process even though they had to be printed separately from the typography.

Although *Century* editors were reluctant to relinquish wood engravings where they, along with *Harper's*, led the field, they eventually surrendered to the halftone, which was about one-tenth as expensive to produce. John Tebbel reported that by 1893 the halftone accounted for approximately one-third of the *Century's* illustrations, as compared with half of *Harper's*, two-thirds of *Scribner's Magazine*, and nearly all of *Cosmopolitan's*.[51] By actual count in Volume 51 (November 1895 through April 1896) of the 398 illustrations on its 960 pages, 31 percent are line blocks, 19 percent wood engravings, and 50 percent halftones. Interestingly, though, on fully 56 percent of those halftones, the plate had been further enhanced by an engraving tool to get the crisper definition and contrast to which wood engravings had accustomed the eye. Grayness was a problem with early halftones partly because the plates were in such shallow relief. Some way around the tedious handmade tissue cutouts was more desirable than ever. De Vinne spoke for the whole industry when he said, "Every printer will be thankful when the days of overlays and making-ready come to an end."[52] In the narrative accompanying the

1900 census of manufactures, four such new processes were mentioned. One of them received a detailed description:

> The De Vinne-Bierstadt process utilizes the action of light upon gelatin in combination with other substances. A print taken on a thin sheet of transparent celluloid is dusted with plumbago to thicken the lines, and exposed in a photographer's printing frame over a film of gelatin. This film is afterwards swelled in those parts not made insoluble by the action of light, and from it a plaster of paris mold is made. From the latter a flexible reverse in gutta-percha is formed, and the gutta-percha, backed, becomes the overlay, being thickest in the darkest parts of the illustration.[53]

Products of this process can be seen at the St. Bride Library in London, which has a 1904 portfolio consisting of four halftones on coated paper. Each one is labeled with the photographer and the photoengraver and says, "Printed with the De Vinne-Bierstadt Mechanical Overlay, 5 New-Street, London, E.C." The portfolio indicates that the process was patented in the United States, Great Britain, France, Germany, Austria, Russia, Switzerland, and Belgium. Curiously, the patent for the De Vinne-Bierstadt process was registered in the names of Edward Bierstadt and De Vinne's son, Theodore Brockbank De Vinne.[54] T. B. De Vinne's role at the press, by all accounts, was a managerial one, but this patent suggests that he actually did play a role beyond his quiet front-office presence. It has not been confirmed, but Bierstadt was probably the same Edward (1854–1906) who promoted the "artotype" process of printing images and was the brother of Albert and Charles, painters and photographers.[55]

Interestingly, another approach to avoiding the onerous handmade overlay was gestating among De Vinne Press employees. Walter J. Wickers, head of the engraving department, and Patrick M. Furlong, electrotyping foreman, began to experiment in 1897 with an idea to make electrotype plates thicker in the dark areas, thus obviating the need for overlays altogether. In conversation with Furlong, Theodore L. De Vinne had suggested shaving the back edges of vignette cuts so those edges would print more faintly. Furlong thought this idea of variable thickness of the plate could be taken a step further so that the makeready of overlays was built into the plate. He and Wickers tried several methods of making the plates slightly thicker in the darker parts of the illustration, and by the time they had a marginally workable model a decade later, someone else had patented a very similar process.[56] Wickers and Furlong indicated that De Vinne had taken little interest in their idea, since he "was absorbed in other experimental work." Perhaps that included what became the De Vinne-Bierstadt mechanical overlay.

The elder De Vinne did make another contribution to the printing of illustrations: the development of coated, "calendered" paper. One source gives Alexander Drake partial credit for this collaboration with the S. D. Warren paper manufacturers of Boston.[57] However, Drake himself said, "It was [De Vinne's] demand for and use of glazed paper [coated with fine white clay and machine-smoothed] that had much to do with the introduction of this kind of surface that has meant so much to reproductive processes."[58] Moreover, Charles M. Gage, the actual inventor, made it clear that he had developed paper coated on both sides in Massachusetts in late 1874 or early 1875 at the specific request of De Vinne (through New York paper dealer William P. Dane) who needed it for a catalogue with colored wood-engraved illustrations. At that time paper coated on only one side was in use for "box covering, lithographing and other purposes" but no coated paper had been used previously for book work. A year or so later, when *Scribner's* required this kind of paper for its illustrations, Gage was employed by S. D. Warren & Co., who would supply the paper.[59] Other printers soon followed suit. As one historian saw it, "De Vinne won the thanks of an entire industry."[60] This coated paper was particularly critical for the printing of shallowly engraved halftones as they proceeded to replace wood engravings. Later De Vinne would admit that he did not like the glossy paper at all but used it because he couldn't get the necessary smoothness without the coating.[61] And, although he had been a pioneer in the use of dry paper to meet the exigencies of speed, he admitted to a "returning kindliness for damp paper."[62]

The energy required to build a successful business venture and keep it at the forefront of the industry's technological developments must have been exhausting. But De Vinne never lost sight of a further goal – to educate fellow printers in the history of the craft. This side of his career continued to gain momentum. He proposed that the Typothetae of the City of New York publish a reprint of the most important English-language printing manual, Joseph Moxon's 1683 *Mechanick Exercises on the Whole Art of Printing*. De Vinne, aware of only three copies in America, one at the Library Company of Philadelphia, one in the Typothetae library in New York, and his own, considered it such a seminal document that he convinced the Typothetae to undertake a reprint.[63]

The original had so many broken letters, wrong font characters, and presswork blemishes, De Vinne said, that a photographic facsimile was not advisable. Instead, he chose type that had been cast from matrices struck with punches (ca. 1740) of the first Caslon type. This was as close as he could come to the flavor of the original. This "line-for-line and page-for-page" reprint repeated the irregular spelling and punctuation, use of capitals and italic, etc. to convey the mannerisms of seventeenth-century grammar and typography.

De Vinne supplied a nine-page historical preface and thirty-two pages of notes to explain various terminology and techniques, comparing them with current practices. He printed 450 copies from type on handmade Holland paper and certified that the type had been distributed. The book was offered in 1896 by the Typothetae, bound in half calf in two volumes at $12 a copy. The cachet of a limited edition did not work any wonders with sales. When anticipated subscribers did not come forth in sufficient numbers, the Typothetae authorized De Vinne to sell the remaining copies on whatever terms he could, in order to recover part of his expenses.

The New York Typothetae and its principles continued to be important to De Vinne, although he gradually became less centrally involved. The organization honored him, even as his actual participation decreased. While poor health prevented his attending the annual Benjamin Franklin birthday celebration in January 1896, his portrait hung across from Franklin's at the traditional fête. In October 1897 – his first Typothetae attendance in a year – he tried to resign the presidency, but Douglas Taylor announced from the chair that his resignation would not be permitted; the sense of the meeting was that De Vinne "should not be allowed to withdraw." The following year the organization bowed to his wishes, electing him vice president instead. At the March 1898 meeting De Vinne said, "I wish that I could be more active amongst you, but am glad to know that our typothetae is prosperous, that we are working on a sound basis, and that my son and grandson may share in its benefits."[64] (By this time it was common for typothetae to be used as a generic, singular term without capitalization.)

While less involved now in business issues, De Vinne found his interest in typography itself growing ever deeper. He was very much in touch with the work of contemporary creators of books, taking full and early notice of William Morris and his work. By 12 July 1891 he had a copy of the first Kelmscott Press book, *The Story of the Glittering Plain*, issued only two months earlier. And on 4 January 1892 he said he had obtained *Poems by the Way* "some months ago," which would have been shortly after its publication as well.[65] De Vinne wrote about Morris's printing in some two dozen of his pieces.

Sometime in late 1892, De Vinne visited Morris in his "workroom" at Hammersmith. Correspondence ensued. In the preface to his *Plain Printing Types* (1899), De Vinne acknowledged assistance from, among others, "the late William Morris of London," and on page 207 is a passage written by Morris, composed in Golden type at the Kelmscott Press in 1894 and "kindly sent as a contribution to this book,"[66] a gesture one would not expect from Morris, considering the disdain he felt for Americans and American printing.[67] De Vinne's earliest remarks (1892) merely praised Morris's typefaces as "practical protests against the effeminacy of modern types."[68] Here De Vinne was referring to the Basle face, which he later learned Morris had not cut but had obtained from the Chiswick Press, and the Jenson, by which he meant Morris's Golden type that was used first in 1891 in *The Story of the Glittering Plain*.

When Morris's Troy type and the smaller Chaucer appeared, De Vinne could not disguise his distaste for these modified black-letter types. Gothic types, he argued, had been rejected by readers three centuries earlier. Nevertheless, he conceded, they were bold and simple; what's more, they were easier to print and more durable than modern-style romans.

A look at the final editing of his *Plain Printing Types* is instructive. De Vinne printed each volume of the *Practice of Typography* in a "proof" edition, giving himself an opportunity to circulate the text to colleagues and refine it further. The 1894 proof copy of *Plain Printing Types* at the Grolier Club shows some editorial changes he considered making regarding Morris. These comments are written in the margin in his hand near the example of Golden type:

> Mr. Morris is certainly more of a poet than of a printer. He speaks of the ugliness of Bodoni, but are for inst. his hyphens correct in *roman* types? And what is the use of the strokes crossing the ascending letters? Of his capitals "ugliness" might be a well merited denomination. Look at the N, the C, the E, the H, the M, quite out of proportion with the forms of the lower case types.
>
> I should think the Morris types are hardly anything better than a curiosity, one of the peculiarity artists and poets are often given to when they are trying to apply their fancies to matter foreign to their knowing.[69]

But the final version, copyrighted in 1899 and published in 1900 (after Morris died in 1896), included none of this. In the section where these marginal notes were made De Vinne had regained his sense of balance:

> When William Morris determined to make a new style of roman type, he selected for his model the roman type on great-primer body of Nicholas Jenson. Morris put his adaptation on english or 14-point body, but he made it very much bolder and blacker. The Golden type, for so Morris named it, approximates the thickened face known in America as antique, and in England as egyptian, more closely than it does any style now known by the name of roman. It first appeared in 1891, in "The Story of the Glittering Plain." Bibliophiles welcomed the new style as a pleasing return to the simplicity of the early printers, as a vindication of the superior merit of old-fashioned masculine printing. . . .

The merit of the Golden type is not in its sturdy medievalism, but in its simplicity and legibility.[70]

Between the 1894 proof and 1899 final versions of *Plain Printing Types*, De Vinne added one chapter entitled "Quaint Styles of Plain Type." This gave him a place to discuss Morris's Troy type:

> It is held by some artists that roman types as now made are too uniform and too monotonous, too "typy," and altogether inartistic. William Morris is reported as saying in 1890 that no good book printing had been done since the middle of the sixteenth century, and that the degradation of the art is largely due to mean types.[71]

It was this feeling that had led Morris to design the Golden type, but he had an "aversion" to the classic and preferred the Teutonic, hence his decision to devise a black-letter type. Morris's Troy type, based on the broad-faced round gothic of early German printers, De Vinne thought, had "unexceptionable" lower-case letters and unsuccessful capitals. He included a page of "Satanick" type (The American Type Founders' version of Troy) and concluded: "Morris went too far in the exposition of his theories, but the reading world is indebted to him for his demonstration of the merit of a really masculine style. He has shown as no one ever did before that typography need not imitate photography, lithography, or copperplate."[72]

As time went on, De Vinne's critique became more elaborate. Predictably, he took issue with Ruskin's and Morris's view that a return to handwork would be a panacea for laborers' discontent, for he believed that machinery, in fact, liberated both worker and capitalist. His fundamental disagreement with Morris's antimodernist stance elicited an acerbic tone that belied his customary restraint:

> Then came William Morris, practically crying out, "There is but one good school or style of printing, and that is the Gothic or Mediaeval, and I am its prophet." He did his best, and did it with signal ability, to turn back all the wheels of improvement and to cause the reading world to accept the style of book made in the fourteenth and fifteenth centuries. He set the fashion for many of the peculiarities of the Vale, the Roycroft, and other presses that try to startle the reader with the roughness of their composition and their contempt for the usages of the craft.[73]

In a more generous mood, De Vinne praised Morris for "his attempts to put typography back in its proper field" by countering the trend toward delicate typography that imitated engraving. He said that, given Morris's preference for medieval themes and for "the literature of the North over that of old Rome," it was natural that the Englishman's work would have Gothic mannerisms.[74] "The Kelmscott books deserve high praise for faithfulness to the best features of fifteenth-century printing," said De Vinne, "but not every feature calls for praise." One such feature was the surface of paper. He claimed the early printers regarded smooth paper as having great merit, using it when they could obtain it. Strangely, though,

> The books of William Morris and of Cobden Sanderson, and of Ricketts, and their numerous American imitators have a roughness rarely found in any book of the fifteenth or sixteenth centuries. . . . A paper that . . . makes your fingertips sore as you pass them over the leaves, is accepted as the culmination of high art in paper making. Why smoothness is a merit in vellum and roughness is a merit in hand-made paper I fail to discern.[75]

Another feature of which De Vinne disapproved had to do with spacing. He disliked title pages with text so huddled together that it required deciphering. This practice, he suggested, was "apparently devised by an illuminator who wanted nearly all the page for his own handiwork." Similarly, he objected to the lack of space between words and of adequate leading between lines. In the fifteenth century, "thin leads and graduated spaces were almost unknown," but one should not repeat practices that have "no excuse but that of unavoidability." Morris's close spacing led naturally to unsightly bits of white at the ends of paragraphs that he then felt obliged to fill in with "unmeaning and unpleasing bits of ornamentation." To support his own views, De Vinne quoted Morris's mentor, Ruskin: "The eye is not saddened by quantity of white, but it is saddened, and should be greatly offended, by quantity of black."[76]

On the other hand, De Vinne found much to be admired in Morris's work. One was the unity his books displayed:

In every feature of his books, from the selection of the paper to that of the tapes that tied the covers, Morris was the only controlling force. . . . The result of his energy was a book that showed completeness, with a unity not to be had when the book has been the joint work of many men, even when all are able or expert. [77]

And Morris's craftsmanship also received De Vinne's endorsement. Despite Morris's amateur status in the difficult trade of book production, "no one can examine a book made by Morris without the conviction that it shows the hand of a master." De Vinne particularly appreciated Kelmscott presswork. "No printer of the fifteenth century did better;" he said, "few did as well." [78]

It was distasteful, De Vinne admitted, "to note blemishes in the work of a man who has done so much for virile typography." However, he was disturbed by inappropriate imitation of Morris's style by others. Although it was suitable for medieval subjects, enthusiasts would do well to avoid putting modern texts in monastic dress. And, when shortcuts were taken in Morris's painstaking methods, the results were deplorable. [79]

Taken at random or even chronologically, De Vinne's notions about Morris might seem ambivalent. But thematically they form a consistent pattern. He appreciated the virile boldness of Morris's Golden type and the conceptual unity of his products. He gave somewhat grudging praise to the Hammersmith "poet's" technical accomplishments. He did not approve of turning the printed page into a tapestry of design rather than a transmitter of information, and he was totally out of sympathy with Morris's medievalism and with the Arts and Crafts preference for handwork over machinery.

In addition to the Kelmscott Press, De Vinne was well aware of the work being done in England by other private presses. He had enthusiastic praise for the work of Cicely and C. H. St. John Hornby of the Ashendene Press, especially their revival of the type used in Subiaco in 1465. (He meant no disrespect when he wrote that they "deserve recognition as amateurs of superior merit.")[80] He felt that the quality of their 1902 edition of Dante's *Inferno* stood out in a field of the many recent books that had come "dressed in some new style of type, or in a revived style of old type" that were "too often so mediocre in merit" that he paid them little attention.[81]

De Vinne underestimated Morris's long-term impact in both England and America. He predicted that the appeal of Morris's books would be "to the limited number of English-born readers of similar education and tastes, for whom the mediaeval style of book-making has an indefinable charm," noting, as have others, the irony that this socialist's products could be purchased only by the wealthy.[82] In 1907 he said that "the taste for the style of artistic printing developed by William Morris is nearly over. . . . The simpler taste will win in the long run, and the monastic styles will soon disappear."[83] He was right, of course. But in focusing on Morris's medievalism he failed to see the Englishman's more lasting contribution – the possibility of the book as a means of artistic expression. As Lawrence C. Wroth put it, after Morris the book was, to printers and booklovers, "a thing to be noticed for its own sake, not a pale, negative vehicle for the conveyance of words."[84] In De Vinne's vision, the book was a conduit for an author's ideas – little more, nothing less.

Suffice it to say, De Vinne did not stand idly by while the Morris-inspired typographic revolution affected customers' tastes. Whereas the Century typeface had been a utilitarian response to a practical problem, Renner was De Vinne's bid to participate in the revival of incunabular types. Cut in 1898 and 1899 at the Bruce Type Foundry, Renner was "a fair copy but not a servile imitation" of the type Franz Renner used in his 1479 *Quadragesimale* in Venice (fig. 26).

De Vinne carried on extensive correspondence about the new face in 1898 with J. W. Phinney, a Boston typefounder with whom he shared an intense interest in historic type design. Selected paragraphs from six letters of that year to Phinney reveal the laboriousness of the process:

> Before you begin on your new roman [Jenson], I should like to show you a specimen of an entirely new roman letter, cut by Francis Renner of Venice, in 1472. It was undoubtedly made in rivalry of the faces of Jenson and De Spira. In design I like it better than either. Unfortunately for him it was badly cut, badly

founded and badly printed. . . . I have serious thoughts of having a font of it cut for my own exclusive use, and am only prevented from doing so by the extraordinary high rates asked by Mr. Benton.

I enclose a proof of the Colophon of one of the books of Francis Renner of Hailbrun (printed at Venice, 1472), the type of which I admire. . . . The general effect of a large page is quite pleasing. I propose to have each character re-drawn on an enlarged scale (not so big, however, as that adopted by Mr. Benton, for that enlargement seems to mislead) – say for a four-line size. . . . No italic.

My experiments with the Franz Renner type are moving very slow.

I have had cut and rejected, several punches; possibly I may have to reject some more. For many reasons I should have preferred you to do this work, as you are the only master founder I know of that takes any interest in the revival of old styles, but I find, as I suppose you do, that it is necessary to supervise the punch-cutter continually, and this I could not do if he were in Boston.

I thank you for your comments on the Renner face. Some of them have been anticipated and corrected. My study of the early Venetian types leads me to the conclusion that to make a very distinct and readable letter, the small letters should be put in the middle of the body, and that ascenders and descenders should be of nearly equal length. These are my proportions: Dividing the body into 100 points, give ascenders 31, round letters 30, descenders 30. This gives the leaded appearance that Morris objects to; but I think the experience of the reading public is a safer guide. It likes leading. My objective point is readability, and I let nothing stand in its way.

My first experiment in making a 10-point of the Renner face was not a success. I am trying again, and hope to show it to you in a month. I am not entirely content with the 14-point. I have some changes to make that may startle you, but not in the way of eccentric forms of letters. The Grolier Club folk are well pleased with it, but I do not want to publish it until it is right. All this takes time.[85]

De Vinne wrote Robert Hoe that Renner had "some archaisms that are not unpleasing" and that its "great mint" was its readability.

FRANZ RENNER of Hailbrun, Germany, was the sixth printer of Venice, in which city he practised his art with success between the years 1470 and 1494. He found there the brothers de Speyer and Nicolas Jenson, rivals of great ability, who were trying to please Italian readers with new roman types. Renner was moved to emulation, and gave to his readers a roman letter of much lighter face than those of his competitors. It had some crudities but much merit.

The type of this page was remodelled on that of Renner's "Quadragesimale" of 1472. In 1899 it was recut for the service of the De Vinne Press, to meet the wishes of buyers who objected to the thinness of modernized old-style.

Measurement in 12-point ems

CAPITALS... $21\frac{1}{2}$
SMALL CAPS... $16\frac{2}{3}$
Lower-case.... $13\frac{1}{3}$
ITALIC CAPS $20\frac{3}{4}$
Italic lower-case. $12\frac{3}{4}$
1234 5678 *234 567 890*

The legibility of printing does not depend so much upon a type of thick lines as it does on the clearness and instant visibility of every line in every character. To this end the hair-lines of this style were made firmer and thin letters were widened. Old rules were observed. Short letters occupy but about one third of the body and ascenders and descenders are of equal length. This treatment gives the white space between lines that is needed for easy reading.

This modernized Renner type, first used in 1900 by the Grolier Club of the City of New York for the printing of a limited edition of Boccaccio's Life of Dante, has since been employed in many other books of importance. ¶ *Of this face we have five pairs of cases for roman and one pair for italic.*

FIG. 26. Renner type from *Types of the De Vinne Press*, 1907, p. 224.

Designed to give relief of white space between lines, it was "flatly opposed . . . to the rules for good type laid down by William Morris." [86]

This new face, first used in the Grolier Club translation of Boccaccio's *Life of Dante* in 1900, received critical praise. [87] But thirteen years later William Dana Orcutt would say of Renner "The oblique serif of the *e*, the fancy curve to the *h*, and the superfluous curl at the top of the *g* introduce features which are foreign to the model, and give to the modern type a 'jobbiness' which unquestionably detracts from the otherwise dignified appearance of the face." [88]

De Vinne used Renner again in his *Title-Pages As Seen by a Printer* (1901), also published by the club. When Doubleday, Page & Co. used Renner in 1903 for its Elizabethan Shakespere [*sic*] series, editor Mark H. Liddell exulted,

> We have secured the prime beauty of early printing without having to resort to mediaeval man's revisions, and in so far we *have beaten William Morris at his best* – no borders, no black illegible type, no crowding of matter, no sacrificing of sense to aesthetic demands – all clear, straight, legible printing – simple, direct and forceful . . [89] [Liddell's emphasis]

In his 1910 *Notable Printers of Italy During the Fifteenth Century* De Vinne would isolate the model for the Renner face for particular praise:

> [Franz Renner's] most characteristic type . . . is that of the Quadragesimale of 1472, which does not betray imitation of or indebtedness to any rival printer of his period. The extreme lightness of structural lines in all characters, the smallness and roundness of lower-case and grace of the capitals give to this type strongly marked individuality. It is plainly the outcome of an intent to produce in easily readable type some of the delicate features of fine Italian penmanship, but it did not prove popular as a type, for it was too frail and slender for the ordinary book, and four books of this type seem to have been enough for the book buyers of this time. [90]

Indeed, his version of Renner's type was not much more lasting. Even for *Notable Printers* De Vinne himself would revert to the modern Lindsay face that had found favor in earlier Grolier Club publications. Although the Monotype Corporation offered a version of Renner that extended its life a bit, it soon disappeared from use.[91]

There is another typeface with which De Vinne's name has been associated but which he did not design or even really endorse. The Central Type Foundry of St. Louis cut a face that they wanted to name "De Vinne." Frank Hopkins's account of De Vinne's response indicates the honoree's ambivalence: "Mr. De Vinne told me that he did not approve the design and feared that people would think he had designed it, but he felt he could not be ungracious and decline the honor, wherefore he gave his consent."[92] De Vinne actually had more to do with it than this isolated passage suggests. His 1907 type specimen book says that the face was the outcome of correspondence (1888–90) between himself and J. A. St. John of Central Type Foundry about the need for plainer display types. De Vinne had suggested a "return to the simplicity of true old-style but with some adjustments." St. John had insisted on "grotesques" on some capitals "to meet the general desire for more quaintness."[93] De Vinne objected, and correspondence reveals the typefounder attempting to make some accommodation: "Dear Mr. De Vinne, The farther we get into this new series the better we like it. We will cut duplicate letters for those you rather object to – C G R S M – and they will be [sent?] into fonts, giving the printer his choice"[94] (fig. 27).

Having allowed the use of his name, De Vinne could hardly denounce it. In the chapter of *Plain Printing Types* on fat-face display type, he noted that there had been attempts to graft old-style peculiarities onto fat-face (by definition a modern type), including one "made by Central Type Foundry and *by that house* named 'De Vinne.'"[95] Elsewhere he reiterated the face's unsuitability for books: "The De Vinne face, designed for job-work only, is another unacceptable type for the title-page of an ordinary book, for it is over-bold, and has some eccentricities of form that are not graces."[96] Numerous variations appeared, forming a type family that grew, as Mac McGrew put it, in helter-skelter fashion from several sources.[97] In 1898 Central Type Foundry asked Frederic W. Goudy to adapt its

De Vinne display type into a book face, which was called De Vinne Roman.[98] Linotype cut a De Vinne that, presumably, was the version included in the 1908 *Machine Faces in Use at the De Vinne Press.* The De Vinne face had a surprisingly long run. It is a pity there is no way to assess how much the name itself influenced the type's use and longevity, for "De Vinne" had and continues to have a certain resonance in the printing world, even among those who lack a grasp of the historic details. The Linotype version was still appearing on type specimens in the mid-twentieth century.

De Vinne has been credited with the naming – though not the designing – of one further typeface. J. W. Phinney of Boston's Dickinson Type Foundry designed a type that everyone, including De Vinne, acknowledged as the American adaptation of Morris's Golden type. According to Bullen, Phinney admired the Golden typeface and had asked Morris three times "for permission to pay for the privilege of reproducing the design, but Mr. Morris did not

DE VINNE

ESTEEMED
By Every Advertiser

Capitals 45   30-point   Lower-case 34$\frac{1}{2}$

BOLDNESS
With Simplicity

Capitals 51$\frac{3}{4}$ 36-point   Lower-case 43

FIG. 27. Type designed by J. A. St. John at the Central Type Foundry and named in De Vinne's honor. *Types of the De Vinne Press,* 1907, p. 275.

want to popularize it or make its reformatory influence available in general typography, but rather to keep it for the narrow purpose of enhancing the value of his limited edition publishing business."[99] Phinney therefore created his own version, supposedly going back to the original Jenson letters. (In his 1907 *Types of the De Vinne Press*, however, De Vinne would say, "Jenson is the American reproduction of the style made by William Morris of the Kelmscott Press, and by him called the Golden Type," with no mention of its being modeled on Jenson's original face.) De Vinne had been in correspondence with Phinney regarding old typefaces as models as early as 1883 and visited him in Boston several times in the 1890s to discuss mutual interests in earlier type designs. Several of De Vinne's letters dealt explicitly with the attributes of the face Phinney was developing. The Dickinson Foundry wanted to call it "Morris," but De Vinne persuaded Phinney to name it after Morris's model, Jenson, since the Golden was not an original face. [100] De Vinne's letter to Phinney (in which he had ordered some and was already calling it "Jenson" before the name was settled) says,

> I have been notified that the hundred-pound font of "Jenson" old-style has been received, and is now going in case. . . . We propose putting it in a thin book for the Grolier Club to be called "Incunabula," from a collection of Mr. David W. Bruce. We shall give facsimiles from every book that mentions the invention of typography. The translations of these passages will be in your new type. We think that we can make a book, not only pleasing to the eye, but really instructive to the student of typography.
>
> Pardon the freedom of my criticism when I say that I like "Kelmscott" no better than "Updike." Why not call your new type "Jenson"? It copies the Jenson type more faithfully than William Morris has done, and I am sure it would be preferred, not only by every printer, but by every bibliophile. If you do not like the term "Jenson" why not call it "Early Italian," or "Renaissance," or "Old Venetian"?[101]

"Jenson" it was, and it became a very successful face, keeping several foundries busy supplying the printers' demand. Apparently Daniel Berkeley Updike, proprietor of the Merrymount Press, considered the type his exclusive property but, when he discovered it was being distributed to the trade, abandoned it after using it in one circular.[102]

It was during this period (1891–94) that the Episcopal *Book of Common Prayer* of 1892 made its way through the De Vinne Press. Numerous interesting and amusing stories attend the history of its production.

Frank Hopkins was just coming into his own at the press and had significant responsibility for the project. As he remembered it in his memoirs, negotiations with the Episcopal hierarchy began in the winter of 1891–92 while De Vinne was in Florida. Hopkins's daughter and son-in-law, Amy and Thomas Larremore, subsequently corrected this by citing a letter dated 20 June 1891 to Messrs De Vinne & Co. from the Rev. William R. Huntington, rector of Grace Church.[103] The Larremores made it clear that the initial negotiations took place before De Vinne's trip but that Hopkins did, indeed, handle the finalization of the contract and propose the production details to De Vinne for approval. In early 1892 Hopkins wrote De Vinne,

> I have drawn up a form of contract which the Rev. W. R. Huntington and Mr. J. Pierpont Morgan have signed for the Committee [on Revision of the Prayer Book], and which you are requested to sign for the De Vinne Press. I assure you that the estimate and specifications have been made up with all possible care. Mr. Brown and Theodore have read and approved them.[104]

De Vinne's reply said,

> Try to make these books a faultless piece of work. Spare no time or expense. . . . Much of our work is trivial and ephemeral, but this will last. You seem to have a good price for it. It should be at least equal to any Prayer Book of the Oxford or Clarendon Press. We must make it better if we can. . . . Be very careful about the paper. We can't get it good unless we are very critical.[105]

The "form of contract" Hopkins mentioned was a one-page typescript entitled "Specifications for Printing the Standard Book of Common Prayer of the Protestant Episcopal Church" and was signed by Huntington and Morgan on 19 February and by De Vinne on 29 February.[106] It outlined the numbers of copies to be printed on each of four types of paper and stipulated the size of the type. It mentioned an additional allowance in the event that decorative borders were decided upon. The Larremores cited two further signed documents in their possession that modified the details of the original specifications.

As Hopkins continued the story, the Committee on Revision of the Prayer Book wished to have one printed proof copy available at the Triennial Convention in Baltimore (October 5–25) and then, after they approved the revisions, several hundred final copies printed, bound, and delivered to the delegates before adjournment. To be sure, the revisions had been studied before the Convention opened; they had been championed for some years by their tireless architect, William Huntington.[107] However, accomplishing this printing of approved text in "about two weeks' time," said Hopkins, was infeasible: "With the magazines, the dictionary, and many important books in hand, any suggestion of haste with the Prayer Book might have disorganized the entire establishment." It was agreed by all parties that one complete copy, with approved revisions, would be presented to the convention before adjournment.

Hopkins ordered a new font of modern-face type from James Conner's Sons of New York in the size specified by the committee: great-primer, that is, 18-point. (The 1907 *Types of the De Vinne Press* indicates that it was Conner's "Great-Primer No. 4.") The composition was entrusted to James Bothwell, "who personally set a large amount of the type and kept strict watch over his assistants." They composed and electrotyped the pages, distributed the type in its cases, and repeated the process to the end. Each sheet was printed on a proofing press and sent to the convention in Baltimore, approved, and returned to the De Vinne shop to be finished. Ultimately, to meet the deadline, the "one complete copy" was made up of as many printed sheets as possible and the missing pages filled in with nice proofs.

The press also managed to get the 650 large octavo copies (11" x 7½"), with a title page bearing the date 1892, ready for distribution

---

by December.[108] As modified by the two subsequent addenda, the agreement between committee and printing house called for seventy-six bound folio copies without borders, one of which was the standard on vellum, and 436 bound folio copies with borders on all pages. Of this latter group, eleven were to be printed on vellum as a gift from Morgan to the members of the committee. (Hopkins reported that the best skins at that time were found in Germany and the best dressing done in London. The De Vinne Press placed an order for the twelve vellum copies, which "called for the sacrificial slaying of about 700 young animals.")

Borders were indeed ordered for some of the folio copies, and the first designs, apparently provided by a relative of a committee member, were unsatisfactory. Huntington then asked fellow Episcopalian D. B. Updike to rescue the project by planning a scheme of decoration and selecting a designer. Updike declined, the financial offer was doubled, and he consented reluctantly, enlisting the talents of Bertram Grosvenor Goodhue. Updike composed an essay for distribution with the large-paper edition of the prayer book, detailing the symbolism employed and making it clear that the decorations were added to "a book practically *already printed*" (Updike's emphasis) rather than being integral to the design at the outset.[109] He later wrote that Goodhue's line was very far from De Vinne's typography and it must have been painful to De Vinne to have his press produce the "uninspired but dignified book" with these appliqués on every page. We have no comment from De Vinne on what he felt, but it would not be like him to criticize a customer's choice, particularly after the fact. "Sad to relate," said Updike, "the edition had an immediate and astounding success! We [he and Goodhue] were congratulated, and we blushed. Our shame was taken for modesty and we were congratulated more!"[110] Updike retained his embarrassment about the stylistic incongruity of the resulting bordered copies. He wrote to Hopkins's daughter in 1936 that, given her father's central role, the prayer book should be included in a bibliography of Hopkins's work – that is, the edition "before those wretched borders were put on it. Such copies do exist and the [unadorned] book is a much more impressive piece of work than it became later" with the borders added.[111]

In 1934 Updike referred to the version without the borders as "handsomely printed by Theodore De Vinne in his chilly but workmanlike style."[112] We can say with certainty that Theodore De Vinne did not "print" or even design it but, rather, that it was in the style he had taught his staff to emulate. He would have been very pleased at both "handsomely" and "workmanlike." As for "chilly," that term probably would not have offended him, for it was not De Vinne's goal to infuse typography with personality or "warmth." Nor did Updike mean to disparage De Vinne's accomplishments. He respected the older man's scholarship, quoting De Vinne's work in his own *Printing Types*. Updike also sought advice from De Vinne on various technical matters once he had his own printing establishment.[113] And he particularly respected De Vinne presswork, sending the 1896 *Altar Book* there for printing before Updike had the facilities for printing such a project. Updike wrote that De Vinne "turned out a magnificent piece of work, although he [De Vinne] was frankly out of sympathy with the style of the volume."[114] Indeed, after Updike developed his own confident style he fell out of sympathy himself with his early Morrissian work and looked upon the *Altar Book* as a period piece in his own development as a designer. In 1940 he wrote the Larremores, "I can scarcely congratulate you on securing the worn-out Altar Book which, in its best estate, I am not, now-a-days very fond of – it is too reminiscent of a particular period. So I don't think I want to autograph it."[115]

Although De Vinne delegated production of the *Book of Common Prayer* to his staff, he was still personally involved in the work the press did for the Grolier Club. All during his prime he continued eagerly chairing its publications committee. This enthusiasm is hardly surprising, since he was the author of four Grolier Club titles and the printer of most club books published during his lifetime. We do not know how much profit, if any, De Vinne allowed himself on Grolier Club printing, but much of the preparation must have been a labor of love. Reportedly, his customary pricing, even toward philanthropic customers, included a 10 percent margin.[116]

At the outset the club established the practice of printing two or three copies on vellum (a printing surface De Vinne said all printers at all times have disliked) to be auctioned and the remainder of the edition on handmade paper to be sold to members (and occasionally others) to cover the cost of production. At first De Vinne gave considerable attention to these titles, but eventually he came to trust Frank Hopkins with many of the details. Hopkins said he was *"even* allowed to assist Mr. De Vinne" in carrying Grolier works through the press (emphasis added); he had a large part, for instance, in overseeing the club's 1889 publication of Richard De Bury's *Philobiblon*. For the 1894 version of William Bradford's *Facsimile of the Laws and Acts of the . . . Province of New-York*, De Vinne could not even correspond with the person writing the introduction because Hopkins, who had the address, was out of town.[117] De Vinne apparently never relinquished Grolier Club printing entirely to Hopkins, but by 1895 he was clearly proud to prove to his Grolier Club associates that the press's best work could be done in his absence.

In fact, it is during one such absence that we glimpse the personality of the relaxed De Vinne. While on a cruise up the Nile he wrote *Century* editor Richard Watson Gilder about the pleasures of the trip and how restorative it was for him and his wife. The seventy-one-year-old Mrs. De Vinne "felt so chipper that she thought she would try a donkey at Memphis. It was a mistake, but she bore up bravely," thereafter resorting to a sedan chair to get about. He was amused by the donkey boys, who were both a "delight and a terror," called him "Father," and adopted him as a kinsman. Mrs. De Vinne's grandniece, Belle, who accompanied them, was "as enthusiastic as a kitten over all she sees. . . . To me it is a great delight to see one rejoice in her youth."[118]

It is appropriate here to say a word about Frank Hopkins and follow his career at De Vinne's to the end. Soon after he came to the De Vinne shop Hopkins was taking on ever-increasing responsibility, estimating and seeing works through the press, stepping in for ailing general manager Robert W. Brown. During his decade there Hopkins became the designer (in all but name) of some of the press's most ambitious works. The Larremores, although far from dispassionate observers, provide convincing evidence of his central role. He was clearly a very significant asset to De Vinne. Indeed, Hopkins also benefited both professionally and personally from his association with the press. In the course of his duties he enjoyed frequent and cordial contact with Century Company worthies, bibliophiles, and other significant patrons of the press. De Vinne sponsored Hopkins for Grolier Club membership. In the spring of 1890 Hopkins proposed marriage to De Vinne's stenographer while the patriarch dozed in the afternoon sun, seated next to them in his Plantin-Moretus armchair.

In 1892 Hopkins built a house for his family in Jamaica, Long Island, and within a few years had thoughts of setting up a press in his attic for his own amusement, a desire no doubt stimulated by his brief publishing association with fellow bibliophiles Paul Lemperly and Francis Adon Hilliard for whom, in 1895 and 1896, Hopkins had designed and supervised production of four limited editions on behalf of their "Société de Trois." De Vinne took a dim view of Hopkins's setting up printing equipment at home, saying that he and Mr. Hart always felt this sort of thing took a man's mind off his regular duties. However, De Vinne withdrew his objections upon Hopkins's reassurances. Thus began the Marion Press. When several modest but well-executed Marion imprints began to receive critical praise, Hopkins found himself in trouble with the boss. Shortly after the *New York Times Review of Books* said, "Aside from the beauty of its typography, some collectors claim that the presswork of the Marion Press is among the best in America," De Vinne had a word with him. The aging proprietor said he was beginning to plan for the continuation of his firm after he was gone. It seems unlikely that he actually felt a commercial threat from the little private press, but, fully cognizant of Hopkins's importance to the firm, he feared that the De Vinne Press would lose the battle for Hopkins's heart. He asked

Hopkins to choose. After thinking about it for a month, Hopkins resigned his "beloved position" in February 1898, relinquishing his salary of twenty-four dollars a week (hardly an adequate recognition of his contribution). For the next three decades he had all the work his little hand shop could manage, always taking care not to solicit current De Vinne customers. After Hopkins's departure, De Vinne took a larger part once again in the production of Grolier Club books and seems to have attended personally to their 1899 edition of *The Life of Charles Henry Count Hoym*. And it was at this time that De Vinne began to pin his hopes on another young employee, James Bothwell. One can speculate about the long-term effects on the De Vinne Press had Hopkins accepted the mantle of heir apparent rather than leave it to the faithful but less aesthetically attuned Bothwell; but we will never know.

Although De Vinne was truly in top form during this period, there were naturally challenges: difficult decisions regarding his administrative personnel, coping with union demands, finding his place in the Grolier Club leadership, properly equipping his plant, maintaining an appropriate flow of business, striking the aesthetic balance he believed in. There was, however, one constant: the enduring esteem of his peers in the printing industry. As evidence of this high regard, for his seventy-first birthday on Christmas Day in 1899, the New York Typothetae presented him with a loving cup, accompanied by speeches from five of his fellow printers.[119] Yet he never let admiration from others go to his head. Throughout his prime and, indeed, up to his death, De Vinne valued "substance" over "show." He would later express this to Bullen:

> If I have fairly prospered in the business world it has been by fol-
> lowing Carlyle's advice "to do the duty that lies next to you and do
> it as well as you can." I have no sympathy with the too common
> feeling that prefers show to substance. This love of show has been
> the degradation of typography in more ways than one. I recollect
> Horace Greeley and his associate editors sitting down at pine
> tables on an uncarpeted floor in company with many associates of
> high merit. I recollect Gordon Bennett, senior, and many promi-
> nent editors of that time, dwelling, as you rightly say, in garrets

and attics, under very unpleasant conditions. Not one of them cared for show. They did their work thoroughly, and prospered by contemning show. During a long business life time I have seen the rise like a rocket and the fall like its stick of some men who began a book and job printing business with black walnut furniture, plate-glass, and other accessories, intended to entrap the unsophisticated.[120]

Honor and Foreboding
(1901–1904)

Many thanks for kind words about the degree of M.A.
Yet it makes me feel somewhat apprehensive. When
much is given much is required. More than ever we
must be careful of our printing. I must beg you and all
of us to "live up to our reputation."

TLD to Bothwell, 16 June 1901

B Y THE TURN OF THE CENTURY De Vinne was the undis-
puted dean of American printers. His Typothetae participation
would have been cause enough for him to rise to a position of
leadership within the industry. But his prodigious writings cemented
his stature and gave him visibility far beyond the trade. In recognition of his accomplishments, Columbia University awarded him the
honorary degree of Master of Arts on 12 June 1901; Yale had done
the same on 6 May. In presenting him for the degree at Columbia,
Dean J. Howard Van Amringe said, "As author and typographer,
in the broadest sense, his name will be associated in the coming
time with those of Gutenberg, Aldus, Caxton, Plantin, the Elzevirs,
Baskerville, the Didots, the Whittinghams, and our own Franklin.[1]
The Pittsburgh Typothetae took up this theme of "printing luminaries" and struck a medal for the annual meeting of the United
Typothetae of America, held in that city the following year, that
depicted Gutenberg in heaven viewing a roster of names: Coster,
Caxton, Aldus, Plantin, Elzevir, Franklin, Didot, Blades, De Vinne
(plate 1C).

Many members of the printing fraternity expressed pride in De
Vinne's honorary degrees, and not only in America. The *British and
Colonial Printer and Stationer* commented,

Honor and Foreboding

Mr. De Vinne has been recognized for many years as the dean of American printers, loved and respected by competitors, employees, and unions [*sic*], and now honoured by a great university. Heretofore such degrees have been conferred mainly upon the men who have sprung from the colleges, or who have been conspicuous as inventors, statesmen, and the like. Now that the printer has been thus recognized, let us hope that during the century just beginning there may be developed a considerable number of other printers who shall elevate the craft and be deemed worthy of like honours.[2]

There was other evidence, as well, of De Vinne's stature. When Moses King had compiled his *Notable New Yorkers of 1896–1899,* he included only two letterpress printers among the 2,337 men: one was ex-Congressman Joseph J. Little and the other was Theodore Low De Vinne. De Vinne had sufficient status to be interviewed at his home in August 1901 by the New York *Herald* on the upcoming mayoral race. (In one of his very few nonprinting utterances to be recorded, he said he favored Seth Low, former Brooklyn mayor and current Columbia University president, as someone everybody could depend upon to clean up existing police scandals and improve the city.)[3] As further evidence that he was considered more than a tradesman, De Vinne was one of the 105 "captains of industry" (the only printer) invited by the likes of J. P. Morgan, William K. Vanderbilt, and William Rockefeller to have breakfast with the visiting Prince Henry of Prussia in February 1902. Moreover, his was one of the eighty-odd portraits the *Herald* chose to print when covering the various events attending the prince's visit.[4]

De Vinne was also well known by the general reading public through his numerous articles in general periodicals. An excellent example was the 1901 "Printing in the Nineteenth Century" in the New York *Evening Post,* excerpted in *Current Literature* and reprinted in *Scientific American* and in a volume covering various nineteenth-century achievements. Here he was at his lucid best. There is not one superfluous word in this recitation of technological changes that printing had witnessed in the preceding century.[5]

Nearly all of De Vinne's writings were to some extent didactic. As

Stanley Morison said, De Vinne was "not so much an inspirer as a teacher and guide."[6] Nowhere are his instructional talents in higher gear than in his four-volume *Practice of Typography* (1900–1904). Because these treatises, taken together, filled a void in practical printing literature, they were received eagerly and gratefully. Originally published by Century Company, they merit a detailed discussion.

Volume 1, *Plain Printing Types* (1900), was the culmination of three decades of note taking. The *appearance* of type on a page was truly a lifelong preoccupation for De Vinne. The first half of the book concerns practical considerations such as how type is made, traditional names of type sizes (in the United States and six other countries) matched against their numerical values in the new point system, how composed type is measured for paying compositors and charging customers, and how many of which characters make up a font. There follow thirty-seven pages demonstrating different sizes of type from 72-point down to 4-point. It does not surprise the reader to find that each of these pages gives a bit of printing history (a work within a work, an act of subliminal didacticism). The second half of the work covers the history of types. The introduction says that each chapter has been revised "by experts in different branches of printing." He also acknowledged the encouragement and cooperation of the late David Bruce Jr., Charles Jacobi of the Chiswick Press, the late William Morris, and various type founders in several countries.

Volume 2, *Correct Composition* (1901), was a much-appreciated style manual for compositors, proofreaders, and authors. It filled a need before the advent of such standards as the University of Chicago Press and Modern Language Association manuals.[7] As late as 1965 De Vinne's discussion of the effect of punctuation on meaning was cited by a United States Court of Appeals judge.[8] For this volume De Vinne acknowledged the assistance, among others, of *Century Dictionary* editor Benjamin E. Smith, Columbia University English literature professor Brander Matthews, and *Nation* editor Wendell Phillips Garrison. His preface sets forth his reason for addressing this book to printers:

Next to clearness of expression on the part of the author comes clearness in its reproduction by the printer. An incorrect expression may be overlooked in speech or in letter-writing, but a slovenly arrangement of words in type-setting is rated as a serious offence by the critical reader, who practically requires the printer to be more exact or at least more systematic than the author.

The importance the printer must place on getting it right, and the cost of doing so, are made very clear in his chapter on proofreading, but standards on proofing vary with the nature of the product:

Ordinary news work, for the most part, receives but one reading. Sometimes the errors marked on the first proof are revised on another proof, but this proof is not always re-read. Sometimes revising is done in the metal. In the cheapest forms of hurried auction-catalogue printing the composition is not even proved on paper: the copy-holder reads aloud from the copy while the corrector follows him, reading from the type on the galley and correcting, as he proceeds, the grossest errors only. . . .

Every book of reference or authority should be read on three or more proofs. . . . The cost of reading and revising with this care is large, usually about one half as much as that of the first type-setting.

The slighted catalogue reading which costs about one tenth that of type-setting, and the careful dictionary reading which costs more than first type-setting, are the extremes of book-work. The cost of the reading of the ordinary novel . . . is small when it is a strict reprint, large when it is in manuscript and not entirely in the full control of the printing house. . . .

Volume 3, *A Treatise on Title-Pages* (1902), originated as an illustrated lecture at the Grolier Club, which the club had published in 1901 as *Title-Pages As Seen by a Printer*. The 1902 expansion of the subject with its emphasis on practical considerations was aimed not at bibliophiles but at printers. There are 256 illustrations, mostly facsimiles of title pages, ten of them from the De Vinne Press (half of which were Grolier Club imprints).

A Treatise on Title-Pages has three parts. First is the origin and development of the title page, beginning with history, as always. Second is an instructional section: every title page needs a plan;

three bits of information must be readily apparent in any design (author, title, and imprint); white space is valuable; any decoration should not be blacker than the type; when choosing title page type, consider the text; avoid extremes; the title page is the architecture of words. De Vinne admits that there are no universal rules for designing title pages (any more than for garments, houses, or furniture). Nevertheless, he clearly prefers the typographic over the "artistic" solutions, centered lines with varying sizes of type to emphasize important words, but few different faces. The third part is a critique of title pages, culminating in ten different designs for one title provided by Charles T. Jacobi of London's Chiswick Press. Buried quietly in a discussion of "the modern title-page," identified only in a footnote, is the first title page he designed as an apprentice and on the facing page the way he would arrange the same words as a mature printer.

De Vinne was familiar with Alfred W. Pollard's 1891 *Last Words on the History of Title-Pages*. Indeed, he cited Pollard and reproduced the title page of that very work as a method of composing capital letters to be preferred over that used in William Morris's *Golden Legend*. Pollard's work, which originated as several articles in the 1880s, may have provided some inspiration, but De Vinne went far beyond what Pollard attempted in his strictly historical essay.

The most "printerly" of the *Practice of Typography* manuals was Volume 4, *Modern Methods of Book Composition* (1904). Whereas *Correct Composition* addresses the literary aspects of type setting, this covers its mechanical aspects. It gives a step-by-step outline of equipment, composition (including such tricky areas as mathematical symbols, music, and non-roman alphabets), making up pages, adjustments made on the imposing stone, and principles of imposition (arrangement of blocks of type so the pages on the two-sided printed and folded sheet will be in proper order). A final chapter on machine composition was written by Philip T. Dodge, president of Mergenthaler Linotype Co. The sections on music, Greek, and Hebrew were written or revised by experts in those fields.

Honor and Foreboding

Reviewers of *The Practice of Typography* volumes found very little fault. William Dana Orcutt felt De Vinne had shortchanged Aldus and the American presses in his *Treatise on Title-Pages*. But reviews were full of praise for De Vinne's conservative standards. "No student who takes Mr. De Vinne for a guide will pursue any of the false gods that have recently arisen to beguile the craftsmen," said George French in reference to *Modern Methods of Book Composition*. In a backhanded compliment, an unsigned piece in *The American Printer* marveled at the inclusion of such a wide range of title-page styles presented in Volume 3: "This tolerant spirit owes its existence, no doubt, to his long practical experience as a printer, which shatters ideals." *The Literary Collector* expressed the gratitude of "hundreds of young printers in this country" for De Vinne's work, which left nothing out on the assumption that everyone knows it.[9] French, who reviewed each volume as it appeared, did complain about the unnecessary length of the titles, and not without reason. Following are the full subtitles:

A Treatise on the Process of Type-Making, the Point System, the Names, Sizes, Styles and Prices of Plain Printing Types

Correct Composition, a Treatise on Spelling, Abbreviations, the Compounding and Division of Words, the Proper Use of Figures and Numerals, Italic and Capital Letters, Notes, etc. with Observations on Punctuation and Proof-Reading

A Treatise on Title-Pages, with Numerous Illustrations in Facsimile and Some Observations on the Early and Recent Printing of Books

Modern Methods of Book Composition, a Treatise on Type-Setting by Hand and by Machine, and on the Proper Arrangement and Imposition of Pages.

This wordiness gave the manuals an old-fashioned look De Vinne apparently thought appropriate. It is difficult to reconcile them with his statement that the more words in the title, the more ineffective the composition. The trade bindings were an unassuming, utilitarian brown cloth with printed cloth spine labels. The understated decorations confirm his advice to show restraint in books on serious themes. In the first volume he allowed himself, at the beginning of each chapter, a modest line-cut headpiece and a chaste five-line decorated initial; and at each chapter a small vignette appeared when room allowed. In the second volume the headpieces are slightly more elaborate and each contains a filled-in black portion, as do the initials. In the third the bold, bordered headpieces and initials have a stippled black background with white entwining branches and leaves – definitely a nod to the Kelmscott style – and the initials are nine type lines high. In the final volume the decorated initials have been reduced to seven type lines, and both they and the headpieces, while still floral in décor and retaining the rectilinear borders of Volume 3, have a lighter horizontal-rule background. Each headpiece displays a medallion portrait of a figure in American typography: publishers (James Harper, Henry O. Houghton, Horace Greeley), typefounders (George Bruce, David Bruce Jr., Samuel Nelson Dickinson, and Thomas MacKellar), writer-printers (Isaiah Thomas and Joel Munsell), German-born Linotype inventor Ottmar Mergenthaler, and American printing icon Benjamin Franklin (fig. 28).

With a more recent perspective, Carl Rollins noted that "if not as selective and discriminating as Updike's great work of a quarter of a century later, [*Plain Printing Types*] is a mine of information on nineteenth-century type-faces."[10] (Rollins neglected to mention their different purposes: De Vinne was discussing text types then in use, whereas Updike was covering the broad sweep of history.) In 1935 Lawrence C. Wroth reviewed a dozen printing manuals from Joseph Moxon's 1683 *Mechanick Exercises* down to De Vinne's turn-of-the-twentieth-century work. He claimed that after Moxon all of them were largely derivative until *The Practice of Typography*, which was

> an original, creative study of the printing craft, informed by knowledge of the past and enlightened by faith in modern mechanical methods and by the conviction that through their thoughtful use the great traditions of typography might still be carried on. Looking backward for his standards of excellence, he took the tools provided him by his age and taught himself and others their best and most dignified use.

FIG. 28.
Headpiece
depicting
Isaiah
Thomas. *The
Practice of
Typography:
Modern
Methods of
Book
Composition,*
1904, p. 39.

ISAIAH THOMAS

II

EQUIPMENT

Galleys and galley-racks . . . Compositors' tools . . . Brass
rules and cases for labor-saving rule . . . Dashes and braces
Leads . . . Furniture of wood and metal . . . Furniture-racks
Quotations . . . Electrotype guards

GALLEYS AND GALLEY-RACKS

HE galley is a tray of wood or
brass with a raised rim on two
or three sides, made to hold
composed type, for which service it is kept in an inclined
position. The galley of wood,
which has its rim at the head
and on one side only, is frail and seldom used.
The galley of brass, with a rim at the head and on
each side, is stronger and much more durable; it
holds the type securely, and allows it to be locked
up and proved on a press. Galleys are sometimes

39

Wroth said that De Vinne "reassembled the typographic lore of the
centuries and adapted it to the click-clack and whir of the electri-
cally controlled printing-office of the new industrial age."[11]

To *The Practice of Typography* must be added the many articles
in which De Vinne shared his expertise with neophyte printers. As

one unsigned review put it, De Vinne was not like some successful businessmen who consider the hill they have climbed "a monument whereon they may pose." Rather, he was one who looked back at those who were only part way up and helped them avoid some of the roughness of the road.[12]

Apparently De Vinne was not satisfied that he had done enough for those still climbing the hill. He wanted to add a volume on presswork to *The Practice of Typography*. And near the end of his life he asked Henry Lewis Bullen to consider several writing projects he lacked the energy to undertake, including a volume on "the planning of books, giving mechanical directions about all details from the writing of the copy to the binding of the book."[13] This is one of the very few times De Vinne mentioned binding although, as revealed by copyright records, his firm did execute cloth binding for trade books – occasionally even for books he had not printed. (Some of his type specimens also mention the binding services at his press.) De Vinne said he regretted that the need for speed in binding thick magazines of large circulation, such as the ones he printed, required quick side stitching rather than sewing through the center of each gathering. For side stitching through the whole issue rendered the gutter margins too narrow and prevented the magazine from opening flat. (To be sure, when binding together the six issues that constituted a volume, the owner had a later opportunity for conventional sewing.)

The Century Company continued to be a major De Vinne Press customer throughout this period. There were a few signs of strain in the Century-De Vinne relationship after Roswell Smith's death in 1892, but nothing of major proportions. Century was forever vigilant about the proofreading and promptness of each issue. Apparently in response to criticism, De Vinne composed a paper in 1894 titled "Concerning Composition Done for the Century Company." In generous detail he outlined the composing and eight proofreadings given to *Century Magazine* copy. He blamed delays in this process on poorly prepared copy and frequent alteration. He concluded, however, "These remarks are not made in a captious or fault-finding spirit. We speak about it only in self-defense; only in explanation of delays in time and increased expense which are unavoidable."[14]

A few years later De Vinne agonized over a problem encountered in the production of the eighth edition of *The Century Dictionary*, the binding of which was done by Tapley & Co. The De Vinne Press was doing the folding but could not meet the schedule Century desired so passed some unfolded sheets along to the binder who then shared this task. Tapley & Co. did their folding on fast but inferior machinery, causing much waste. Again, De Vinne elaborated on the history of the problem and argued that his firm should not bear the entire loss for the waste and the re-inspection that detected Tapley's mistakes. But he redrafted the letter twice, each time becoming both more succinct and more conciliatory. The third version ended thus: "It is not for us to say how much the other party should contribute. We leave the adjustment of the matter entirely to your sense of fairness, and shall not quarrel with your decision, for we shall accept it without another word of controversy and close the matter forever."[15]

As De Vinne gradually withdrew from active participation in the daily life of his firm, the tone of correspondence between the press and Century lost its gentility and became more and more matter-of-fact – occasionally even testy. In the ensuing years Robert W. Brown and James W. Bothwell spoke for the press, though they did not hesitate to invoke De Vinne's name when it seemed called for.

While this was a period in which De Vinne reaped the harvest from his years of effort and care, the seeds of his firm's undoing were beginning to be sown.

The number of men who spent their entire careers at the De Vinne Press was considerable. There were, however, some noteworthy departures around the turn of the century. The case of Frank Hopkins is a curious episode, leaving one wondering at De Vinne's inflexibility. One has to ask what benefits would have accrued to the De Vinne Press had Hopkins been given a significant promotion and further responsibility rather than an ultimatum to choose between his career there and his hobby press. It is not exactly clear who took over the manifold duties he had performed when he left De Vinne's in 1898. Perhaps Brown, the up-and-coming James W. Bothwell, De Vinne's son, and the proprietor himself all filled in. According to Hopkins, sometime in the 1890s, pressroom foreman "Major" Hazeldine Hamilton (who, like so many key employees, had worked there since the Francis Hart days) walked out of the building one day with presses running and was never seen again. In 1901 the supervisor of book composition was the subject of a terse note to the Century Company from Theodore L. De Vinne & Co.: "Mr. William Bigger's connection with this establishment ceases from this date. All Communications in the future should be directed to the firm." In 1904 James Morrow, one of the compositors mentioned by Hopkins in his survey of De Vinne personnel, wrote on De Vinne letterhead notifying the editors of *Century Magazine*, "It is with a feeling of regret that I inform you that I leave the De Vinne Press . . . after a clean record of thirty years." His departure sounds abrupt; he was apparently not retiring, for he asked the Century Company for job recommendations.

Also in 1904, Daniel S. De Vinne, Theodore's younger brother, retired. He had begun working at Francis Hart & Co. on 27 November 1850 as an office boy and rose to the foremanship of the composing room of his brother's business. In 1908 Robert W. Brown, for years the manager and, Hopkins claimed, the "real money-maker" of the firm, would leave under strained circumstances. Brown had been an employee of Hart's firm and may have even predated De Vinne there. He was one of Francis Hart's executors. Hart's will, probated in 1877, had said, "I expect [my executors] to repose great confidence in the integrity of Mr. De Vinne and in his advice and skill as a printer and it will be a great satisfaction to me to think that my friend Brown will become permanently attached to the business and will aid in its prosecution." When the De Vinne Press incorporated on 1 May 1908, Brown would be announced as vice president. On 17 June, however, De Vinne would write to his attorney, requesting the following amendment to his will: "As Robert W. Brown has voluntarily resigned the office of Vice-president of the corporation known as the De Vinne Press and has refused attendance at the printing-house and the duties connected therewith, I hereby revoke the bequest of $7500 as stated in article 13 of my last will."[16]

The record is silent on why so many top managers left the firm. Perhaps at its zenith the De Vinne Press depended too much for its sense of purpose upon the daily presence of the founder. His increasing absence to pursue outside typographic interests may have created room for discontent and jealousies to manifest themselves. Perhaps he paid them too little in money or praise for the superior work expected of them. One can only guess. Somehow the magic had been lost.

Loneliness and Frustration (1905–1907)

I will call on you soon. I intended to do so today, but I am too weary.

TLD to Ruth Granniss at the Grolier Club 3 April 1907

D<small>E</small> V<small>INNE</small> G<small>AVE</small> even more time and effort during the early years of the twentieth century to Grolier Club publications. As chairman of its Committee on Publications, he personally coordinated and supervised their design. Now in his late seventies, he worked out of his home because he was frequently not strong and because his wife was ill. In May 1905, De Vinne was "warned by the doctor that Mrs. De Vinne's death was possible at any hour." She was "still living but failing fast," and he could not leave the house. (Her obituary revealed her final illness to be typhoid fever.) After his wife of fifty-five years died, he went to Atlantic City to try to recover his own health. But, after losing seven pounds in one week, he was glad to get back to New York.[1]

By 1905 James Bothwell had risen within the De Vinne Press and was taking considerable responsibility for Grolier Club printing. Although he sent proof to club librarian Ruth Shepherd Granniss and talked over details with members of the publications committee, his role was something of an emissary; nearly every letter mentioned De Vinne: "This is Mr. De Vinne's preference;" "I want to talk over the matter with Mr. De Vinne before complying."

Some club publications engaged more of De Vinne's attention than others. Two of them, *Researches Concerning Grolier* (1907) and *The Scarlet Letter* (1908), were particularly engrossing, largely because of the problems with the Paris firm of Léopold Carteret, which was producing the illustrated plates.

Loneliness and Frustration

As early as 1904 De Vinne had felt forebodings about the *Jean Grolier* book:

> I foresee a din of disagreement in the making of this book – disagreements as to dates and spelling of proper names, as to size of leaf, method of printing color plates, quality of paper, etc. Let us try to get on as smoothly as we can and avoid discussions that are of no advantage. My patience, and yours too, will be strained on more important matters before this book is made perfect.[2]

Agreement within the committee on these details was only the beginning. There were delays in getting the paper; the sheets of illustrations from Carteret stuck together and were insufficient in number; the copy for the catalogue of Jean Grolier's library was "a tangle, interlined and written on side and back by two or more editors"; the translator made errors; and the expense went well beyond what the club had anticipated. De Vinne said the book had been "a hoodoo to every one connected with it."[3]

De Vinne took great care with *The Scarlet Letter*, saying it was "probably the last important book" he would see through the press. By a poll of members, Hawthorne's story had been selected as the American classic the club should undertake to publish. George Henry Boughton was engaged to create illustrations – a reasonable choice since he had addressed Puritan themes in his oils. There had been some sentiment in the Committee on Publications for putting it in seventeenth-century dress through the use of Dutch types common in England and its colonies at the time in which the story is set, or even in the eighteenth-century Caslon type. De Vinne, as chairman of the committee, had held out for a current look, saying, "All the imitations that I have seen of XVIIth century printing, even when from the best presses, are sorry counterfeits." He said he believed that "every good bit of typography should be the work of its own time." He secured the committee's agreement to use the modern Lindsay typeface. It had been designed originally on 14-point by John Lindsay at the Bruce Type Foundry. The next point size was customarily 18-point, but De Vinne had ordered it cut on a 16-point body as the exclusive property of the De Vinne Press. The result, although the face was compressed, was an openness even when no leading was used between the lines.[4] In this case, given the size of the page, 11" x 7½" and the generous margins, he did use slight leading to balance the white space on the page. Illustrations for *The Scarlet Letter* were being engraved and printed in Paris by Carteret from Boughton's watercolors. When the book first came up in committee meetings in October 1903, De Vinne proposed that the book be printed without ornament of any kind (apart from the illustrations). Seven months later, however, he had decided that some ornament would be desirable to create a transition between Boynton's full-page illustrations (each presented twice – in a warm black ink, and in color) and the open look of the type pages. For this purpose, De Vinne wanted a headpiece and a decorated initial to introduce each chapter – made from "open" designs harmonious with the typeface. His idea was that each headpiece would depict, in a center medallion, an aspect of colonial life, appropriate to the upcoming chapter. This was one of those few occasions where he approved of decoration. He wanted this edition to be special, he said, unlike the "bald," undecorated duodecimo editions of *The Scarlet Letter* that he could recall. In a lengthy letter to Boughton, De Vinne laid out his rationale, asking the artist himself to provide the decorations. Boughton agreed to provide sketches, and De Vinne told him that they would be printed from photoengraved plates of high relief on "the regular type-printing press." He assured Boughton, "Our house has done stipple work, tint and line work from relief plates that have been highly commended by lithographers who have fancied that their process was inimitable."[5] Boughton died in 1905 before completing the sketches, so the decoration was reduced to a tailpiece at the end of the introduction (a vignette in warm black ink of three Puritans in a gossiping pose) and a decorated initial in color in the stipple technique De Vinne mentioned, showing the "oaken" prison door with the wild rose growing to one side[6] (plate 6). Frustration over decoration, extra expenses, and delays notwithstanding, De Vinne seemed satisfied with the result: "Mr. Morton sends me word that he has subscriptions for more than 215 of the Scarlet Letter [out of 300]. If so we need have no fear about the threatened loss. I think it is a good book."[7]

In these years, a truly monumental project was finally drawing to a climax. In the works for some fourteen years, *The Bishop Collection: Investigations and Studies in Jade* was completed in 1906 in an edition of one hundred, primarily for presentation by Heber R. Bishop, the collector and compiler, to libraries and museums. Its lavish illustrations employed several techniques: watercolors, copperplate engravings, lithographs, and multicolor wood engravings. The type was the "Great-Primer No. 4" that had been purchased from the Conner type foundry for the 1892 Episcopal *Book of Common Prayer*. The two-volume elephant folio catalogue, when clothed in its red morocco binding, weighed 114 pounds. Writing much later, Carl P. Rollins pointed out that its size rendered it a librarian's nightmare: "Today it is but a curiosity, a great printer's aberration, so ungainly a production that in one large library it does not bear even a shelf number, but reposes in isolation in a little used corner, where even the staff is unaware of its existence." The variety of illustrations, he said, made it "a sort of enormous scrapbook." He noted that "the presswork is, of course, beyond reproach."[8]

By way of contrast, in the 1928 Grolier Club exhibition celebrating De Vinne's centenary, this gargantuan work was displayed next to De Vinne's smallest book, which stood all of six centimeters high in its binding: *Brilliants: A Setting of Humorous Poetry in Brilliant Type* (1888, reprinted in 1895 from the original plates). This tiny book was De Vinne's homage to the celebrated miniatures of Pickering and the Didots and included an essay in which he discussed small types of the past (plate 7).

De Vinne's health, resources, and peace of mind were put to a severe test when the International Typographical Union struck for the eight-hour day in 1906. His stance against the closed union shop had been successful for years. In earlier strikes he had prevailed, but this one was better organized, national in scope, and of greater consequence. It absorbed all De Vinne's energies.

The depression of the early 1890s had forestalled a showdown over the shorter workday for a time. With the return of prosperity, however, the unions became more adamant. The Typothetae, sensing the inevitability of this longtime cause, conceded the fifty-four-hour week in 1898. De Vinne, agreeing to the shorter workweek, continued to be conspicuous in his support for the open shop. That same year he wrote to Robert Hoe III, "Ours is the only large book house in New York not entirely controlled by the Union."[9]

The ITU waited only three years before pressing on toward the eight-hour day. In addition, it revived the union-foreman concept and demanded that – in closed union shops – business managers and even proprietors who performed any labor on their own machines would have to hold union cards, a notion that infuriated De Vinne and others. The union label was the last insult, as far as De Vinne was concerned. He called it "the badge of a minority, whose set purpose is to deprive the free men who are in the majority of a fair chance to earn a living."[10]

By the time the ITU's package of demands (the eight-hour day, the closed shop, union foremanship, and the union label) reached the point of strike on 2 January 1906, De Vinne and several other leading printing proprietors had made elaborate preparations for the fight.[11] *Publishers' Weekly* reported that "of 247 printing shops in New York City manned by members of the local union, 200 of the smaller ones gave up the struggle a day after the men went out."[12]

The Typothetae of the City of New York could claim only forty-four printing houses (of varying sizes) committed to its policy, and four of them capitulated within the first two weeks. De Vinne was one of the staunchest resisters, saying he considered eight hours and the closed shop to be business suicide and would not discuss the matter unless "bound hand and foot and laid helpless upon [his] back."[13]

One week into the strike, De Vinne told Ruth Granniss that the strike was "annoying." Three days later he said, "The affairs of the strike, which are much more serious now than it was [*sic*] last week, have kept me for two days from attending to Grolier business.

. . . Mr. Bothwell and our Junior are overworked. . . ." It was in connection with this strike that De Vinne's correspondence made two of its very few references to his son. The other came the following week: "The strike is wearing but our side is in and winning but it will be a month or more before we shall have peace, and I shall be free from care. My son is of great service to our house and the trade." The strike clearly put a strain on all the resources of the De Vinne establishment. With his son and staff carrying as much of the load as possible, De Vinne himself had to come out of semiretirement to give office matters daily attention. In February he even resigned as president of the Grolier Club. He had been vice president from 1888 to 1892 and president beginning in 1904. He wrote Miss Granniss in February 1906:

> Mr. Gilliss writes that my resignation as president of the Club was accepted in a kindly way. Mr. Holden takes my place with Mr. Lawrence as the vice president. Good selections. I do not know how Mr. Holden will constitute the committees. I shall give him no suggestions, but it is probable that I will be, (at least for some months), an active worker of the Committee on Publications.[14]

After two years of conflict, with heavy expenditures on both sides, the strike came to an end. While eventually giving their employees an eight-hour day, a handful of New York City printers – De Vinne among them – refused to accept union shop control. This claim is corroborated by a 1912 pamphlet, "Know Your Printer," produced by Big Six, the New York City chapter of the ITU; it lists the De Vinne Press as abiding by union conditions but not using the union label (not a closed shop).[15] For De Vinne it was less a question of the impact of shorter hours on the balance sheet than a conflict over prerogative. Since actual company records no longer exist, it is impossible to assess the economic impact on the De Vinne Press and how well it recovered. But it was clearly not salutary for a firm whose top management was beginning to fragment.

Needless to say, De Vinne had little time for writing in this period. Yet that did not stop trade journals from reprinting his articles from other sources or including bits of overgrown filler. An example of the latter is "To the Compositor," advice that a compositor should highlight the "who, what, when, and where" when designing a poster; *Printing Art* made this tip into a full-page piece dignified by a ruled border. Clearly, the 1906 strike deprived De Vinne of time and energy he would have preferred to devote to his avocations. He was already at work on his final monograph.

During this time De Vinne began to find the Grolier Club less and less satisfying. His presidential addresses in 1905 and 1906 provide a hint of his misgivings about the direction the club was taking. He said that members had become more interested in pictures than good typography. It was time to repeat the purpose of the club: the improvement of bookmaking arts. The preservation of literature, he argued, is more successfully accomplished by types than images, which are supplemental to text. "Our Grolier Club should try to lead the way in a return to the simple types and methods of early printers," he said. He proposed that membership be restricted to those who really love books and buy them – not those who join the club for its social features. In 1907 he confessed to Miss Granniss that he felt "not a little lonely" at the council meetings.[16] For the balance of his life he would struggle against a feeling of alienation from this organization that had originally seemed so compatible with his central interests.

Retirement (1908–1914)

I have always said, and here repeat, that I desire the De Vinne Press to be owned and managed by my heirs and those who have been helpful in securing its present position. It is no disgrace to lose in a fair and open fight for business; it would be a great disgrace to skulk out and to sell out for indefinite and unguaranteed promises of the better results that might come from a consolidation.

TLD, 1912

B Y T H E T I M E Theodore L. De Vinne & Co. incorporated as The De Vinne Press on 1 May 1908, its fortunes, as we have seen, were already on the decline. The strike had been a severe blow; the *Century Magazine* was losing circulation; and there had been attrition among his top personnel. De Vinne himself, less involved for more than a decade – except during the crisis of the 1906 strike – retired from active management. Theodore Brockbank De Vinne apparently never really tried to fill his father's shoes. From the time of incorporation on, James W. Bothwell was being groomed to manage the De Vinne Press. Thirty-seven years younger than his employer and mentor, Bothwell – like Brown, Hamilton, and Daniel De Vinne – had entered the shop as a boy. He was one of the superior compositors in the De Vinne shop, setting such important works as the Episcopal *Book of Common Prayer* mostly by himself. He participated actively in the councils of the trade; he was president of the New York Typothetae from 1913 through 1915. When De Vinne's son and grandson retired as officers of the press in 1919, Bothwell would carry on the firm. De Vinne's son proposed Bothwell for election to the Grolier Club in 1903, a membership he would maintain until 1921.

While the Grolier Club's *Scarlet Letter* was probably the last book
De Vinne actually saw through the press, he wrote one more for
club publication, relying heavily on Bothwell for production. By
1906 De Vinne had begun assembling facsimiles for a book he
wanted to write on early Italian printing. The proposed title changed
several times and finally came to rest on *Notable Printers of Italy
During the Fifteenth Century* ("printers of Italy," not "Italian printers," since most of them were German or French immigrants). As
indicated by his warm and frequent letters to Ruth Granniss, who
was not only librarian of the club but also secretary to the publications committee, now chaired by Beverly Chew, he wanted the text
to be accurate in every detail. She helped him check sources and fer-
ret out mistakes. At home he had at his fingertips at least twenty-
three of the twenty-five works in his bibliography of "authorities";
they would appear in the catalogue of his library auctioned by
Anderson Galleries in 1920. The remaining two were available in
the club library.

In selecting Italian incunabula for his subject, De Vinne focused
on the most fertile ground of early typography and one that had
long fascinated him. It also allowed him to avoid more than a passing reference to the black-letter or "Gothic" types used in northern
Europe, letterforms for which he had no admiration. A better title
for his study might have been *Notable Typography of Italy* since his
real focus was the types and their arrangement on the page; comments on the printers themselves were ancillary.

In his preface De Vinne revealed his objective. He noted that
"readers find the study of old types really difficult." Early types were
best seen in original works where ink, paper, and impression are
part of their character, but it was hard for most people to get access
to originals and harder yet to get them together to compare. Until
the advent of photoengraving, reproductions of typography had
been almost useless for study, consisting of a few lines traced from
an original and then manually engraved for reproduction.
Photoengraved facsimiles, though not as good as originals, were a
decided improvement. *Notable Printers* was illustrated by forty-one

numbered plates plus other smaller facsimiles integrated into the text, bringing the total to fifty-four. His list of facsimiles gives credit to Grolier Club friends for providing four of the originals. As for the remaining fifty facsimiles, his personal collection included at least forty-four of the original works.

In his text De Vinne warned against two common errors: judging the quality of all incunabula on the basis of the more sumptuous volumes popular with collectors and giving uncritical praise to all early books. Instead, with the eye of the experienced practical printer, he tried to make an unbiased appraisal of the typographical merits of each one. He said, "An old book may be highly esteemed for its age and rarity, for its quaint mannerisms or its association with a famous editor, printer, binder, or owner; but these peculiarities need not invest it with a sacredness that puts it beyond examination and comparison."

In cautioning against drawing conclusions based only on incunabula of larger size, he noted that even in the early days of printing there had also been a market for smaller, cheaper books, some of which were no longer available for comparison because they had been "thumbed to rags by persistent handling." That early books varied considerably in the quality of their production and in their legibility was a matter of great importance to De Vinne.

He discussed the books of twenty-three printers at work before 1500 in Italy, including the obvious Jenson, Ratdolt, Renner, and Aldus. But he also featured books by lesser-known printers in whose work he found merit or interest. He could not resist going beyond both his geographic and his chronological boundaries to cover the work of French sixteenth-century typefounder Claude Garamond. And then, as if he could not bear to bring his last monograph to a close, and giving in to the urge to instruct, he provided more context (type founding, printing ink, paper, composition, the handpress), occasionally drifting into comments on early twentieth-century practices.

It was an arduous task for an infirm, elderly man to write a text, collect the facsimiles, check references for accuracy, find someone to make an index, and incorporate the suggestions he gratefully received from Miss Granniss. Early in 1908 he noticed "constant reminders of increasing disability." Neuralgia was the only ailment mentioned in his correspondence. In November he confessed that he could work at his desk for only fifteen minutes at a time. In December he decided he could do no more toward perfecting the text of the work:

> For more than five weeks I have been poring over this last dummy of my Sketches of Italian Printers, hoping to clear it from the last error; but I have not been able to do anything to please myself. I should add something to it but I cannot. . . . I fear that I shall make faults that do not exist if I meddle with it more.[1]

The production details were also fraught with frustration. He originally projected a price to the club of $16 to $20 but pared it down to $12 at the behest of the committee, saying,

> I do not expect to make any money out of the book, but I do not want to lose more than I must. I have too much regard for the reputation of our Club and for the credit of our printing-house to put out a shabby book. The Printers of Italy is the last serious work I shall attempt, and it must not be inferior to its predecessors in mechanical construction.[2]

To keep the price to the club low, he used American-made Stratford paper, which he said was about half the cost of handmade Italian Fabriano. When he expressed misgivings about the surface of the paper in the dummy, Bothwell tried to reassure him:

> When we print the book this will be entirely done away with, as I intend to wet the paper after printing which will take off the finished appearance, and when we print the book proper we will give it a little more squeeze and color and that will give it the masculine appearance that you like.[3]

De Vinne guaranteed the club against loss by promising to take any copies unsold at the end of one year. Still, the price did not suit the publications committee, of which he was not a part for the first time since 1885. He made an impassioned plea to committee chairman Beverly Chew that shows poignantly how much he felt himself out of tune with the evolving emphasis of the club:

> I think the book would be taken up by Club members at $15 quite as readily as at $12. If we are warranted in printing four hundred copies of the Whistler Etchings, we ought to be warranted in printing the same number of a book that will cost the Club only one fifth as much. We have members who readily take prints with the elegant butterfly device of Whistler at $75, and facsimiles of the luxuriant colors and gilding of Grolier at $40; but I think we also have members who want substance as well as show. Would it not be discreditable for a club professedly devoted to books to care more for decoration than for information?
>
> There is a real need for a book on early Roman types. . . . I think it time that one who has practiced typography for fifty years and added to that knowledge a study and comparison of old books should be allowed in a literary club to express his notions.[4]

The publications committee approved his prospectus in February 1909; but the council must have been reluctant, for he made one last concession. In March he offered the club the edition of three hundred for $11 a copy ($50 additional for the three on Imperial Japan paper in folded sheets). He was granted permission to print one hundred copies (he actually printed ninety-seven) for his own use, provided he change the title page to omit the device and imprint of the Grolier Club (fig. 29).

Finally, in mid-1910, *Notable Printers* was published and sold to members for $15 a copy. De Vinne did take the unsold copies off the club's hands; fifty-nine of them would remain at the time of his death.[5] John Clyde Oswald would advertise *Notable Printers* in the July 1915 *American Printer* (along with his reprints of the four volumes of *The Practice of Typography*). Whether Oswald was disposing of extra stock of the De Vinne Press imprint or the Grolier Club imprint is not clear.

De Vinne's disaffection with the club continued. It was not merely because of the frustration caused by the last three publications with which he had been involved. He wrote Bullen, "Our Grolier Club was started to increase the love of good books, and they have done something of merit in that direction. But new members seem

NOTABLE
PRINTERS OF ITALY DURING THE
FIFTEENTH CENTURY

ILLUSTRATED WITH
FACSIMILES FROM EARLY EDITIONS

AND WITH
REMARKS ON EARLY AND RECENT PRINTING

BY
THEODORE LOW DE VINNE

NEW YORK
THE DE VINNE PRESS
1910

FIG. 29. Title page of *Notable Printers of Italy During the Fifteenth Century*, 1910, the last book De Vinne wrote (12½" x 9½"). One of ninety-seven he printed for his own use without the Grolier Club imprint.

to be more anxious to collect and to preserve copperplate prints than to keep up the standard of typography." He also complained that the occupation of printer was insufficiently respected: that (in Bullen's words) "among the dilettante[s] who so liberally support the club there was a disposition to rate a printer – even himself, he said – as a mere tradesman."[6]

Bullen later described this phenomenon to Beatrice Warde:

I want to improve printing and the condition of the workers in that vineyard; the G.C. is a dilettante affair with a right worthy reason for existence, but without scarce any mission other than to glorify itself. This was good old De Vinne's feeling. Not long before he died he told me that he could never overcome an inner (carefully hidden) feeling of "loneliness" (his word) when in the society of the Grolierites. He loved printing and printers (all grades of them, for he had lived with all grades), and he felt it in his bones that a large proportion of the membership looked down upon the printing fraternity, and therefore (to his sensitive soul) upon him; for such is the patronizing attitude of bond sellers, stock brokers, insurance agents, etc., who peddle other peoples' money. . . .[7]

Brander Matthews had called the club "a novel and fertile alliance of the dilettante and the professional."[8] In time, the balance shifted, and it pained De Vinne when the former gained the upper hand. Furthermore, special interest groups formed within the larger organization. There was the Society of Iconophiles, whose aim it was to preserve the visual record of old New York by collecting prints of the city and sponsoring new illustrations on that theme. There was the Club Bindery, which imported French artisans to do special binding for some members. There was the fad for extra-illustrating books (by inserting actual leaves from early printed books being discussed, for example). None of these sidelines interested De Vinne; typography and its history were everything to him.

The relationship between the club and the De Vinne Press also grew cool, as indicated by correspondence between Bothwell and the club in 1911 over the catalogue for an exhibition of first editions of the works of Alexander Pope. The Merrymount, the Riverside, and the Chiswick Presses began to appear on Grolier Club imprints, in addition to the Gilliss Press, which had already done occasional printing for the club.

De Vinne continued to produce articles even as his last book had finally gone to press. His mind was still agile and his desire to instruct strong. A good example is "The Printing of Wood-Engravings" for *The Print-Collectors' Quarterly*. A typescript with his editing in pen shows that his hand was less steady but he still had clear expression at his command.[9]

The fortunes of *Century Magazine*, meanwhile, had been declining for several years. As early as 1899 the finances of the magazine had alarmed Century Company staff, who recommended rational economies such as making corrections in manuscript since changes in proof were so costly. In 1909 the De Vinne Press was printing only one hundred thousand copies of each issue, as the decline continued. In 1911, calculating their circulation at 50 percent below a "normal" minimum, Century officers tried to think of a series that would raise circulation as their Great South series had done in the mid-1870s or as the series on battles of the Civil War had done in the mid-1880s, but no theme of sufficient promise presented itself.[10]

The main reason for *Century Magazine*'s continuing decline was the emergence of new, livelier, cheaper magazines. The development of economical halftone photographic illustrations paved the way for their success; a more popular style and contemporary content insured it. The tastes of the reading public no longer seemed to favor the long literary offerings of *Century* and the other old "quality" monthlies, which had also fallen on hard times. Some of *Century*'s readers were wooed away by *The Ladies' Home Journal*, which took a more practical and frank approach to women's issues. *McClure's* journalistic tone attracted male readers from the same pool as the *Century*, and it did so for fifteen cents at a time when *Century* cost thirty-five. There was a particular irony in *McClure's* success in that Samuel S. McClure, as noted before, had once worked for Century Company, where his innovative brashness did not fit in.

Retirement

The *Century* editors' response to this new competition (which in 1910 they considered to be forty or fifty magazines) was to hold fast to their standards: "graceful in style, accurate without being too heavily erudite, popular in the better sense." They continued "to bear aloft the flame of the ideal in an ever more raucous and changing world." They did bow – albeit reluctantly and slowly – to the new taste for realism in illustration as the halftone gained prominence; but "to manifest the eternal verities in print and picture was a duty that must be carried out, even if readership were reduced only to those capable of appreciating and sharing the editorial ideals."[11]

In 1913 Frank H. Scott, successor to the Century Company's founding president Roswell Smith, died. W. W. Ellsworth became Century president and decided on a new policy: the magazine would become "more journalistic and less aloof." Robert Underwood Johnson, more rigid than any of his conservative predecessors, resigned the editorship in disagreement, and newspaperman Robert Sterling Yard replaced him. Yard said, "It is time we looked this question of the present squarely in the eye."[12]

Not only editorial policy but also finances cried out for dispassionate examination. Century staff began scrutinizing De Vinne Press bills for printing and binding as never before. They even entertained estimates from other printers. The Carey Printing Company wrote to the Century Company on 14 January 1914 (one month before De Vinne died):

> In line with our conversation of a few days ago, regarding the printing of "St. Nicholas," I take pleasure in submitting our prices for this work as follows. . . . I understand fully what you mean, when you tell me of the long standing relation between The Century Company and your present printers. We have a number of customers just such as you on our books, and I am hoping that I may be able to show you good reason why you should be added to the number.[13]

Curiously, this letter was retyped on Century Company letterhead, presumably for circulation and serious consideration within the company. Nothing came of it immediately.

Overall, Century Company's business was not bad. The statement of capital distribution and earnings for the year ending 30 September 1913 had shown $134,700[14] in the profit column. The leading department was trade books at nearly $87,900. The dictionary was still showing a profit of about $52,300. Educational books made almost $15,900 and hymnbooks $5,900. *St. Nicholas,* counting circulation and advertising together, showed a profit of nearly $13,800. But *Century Magazine* spoiled the picture with a loss of $40,900. Were it not for its profitable advertising account ($51,900 or 73 percent of capital invested), matters would have been much worse; for *Century* circulation ran at a loss of $92,800, or 26 percent of capital invested.[15]

Although Century's book list continued to thrive, the De Vinne Press's role in printing their books decreased, a phenomenon that can be traced through the copyright records at the Library of Congress. Beginning in 1909, copyright applications were required to state the printer, typesetter, binder, and date printing was completed. Fortunately for today's scholar, those applications through 1937 are filed alphabetically by applicant. They give a partial picture of Century Company's printers and binders in this period – partial because much reprint and other work was being done aside from those newly copyrighted titles. From this source it is obvious that Century used quite a number of different typesetters, printers, and binders.

Trade books at this time were almost universally printed from electrotype plates, so one firm might have set the type while another did the printing from the plates, and binding could be jobbed out to yet another company. We see that the De Vinne Press by 1909 might be involved in one, two, or all three of these operations for Century Company books – or none at all. The De Vinne Press participated in the production of only 70 percent of the twenty newly copyrighted Century books in 1909. Judging from the copyright records alone, 1910 may have represented some sort of watershed in the relationship. For in that year the proportion of De Vinne Press participation dropped to 30 percent of the forty-two newly copyrighted Century books. Yet new editions of *The Century Dictionary* were in production at that time, and it is possible the De Vinne Press did not covet this mundane trade-book business. In the next five years the number of Century's new copyrights continued to climb to more than fifty per year, but De Vinne Press participation declined during the same period to a mere 5 percent in 1914. From 1917 onward, none of the Century copyright registrations would mention the De Vinne Press.

We must bear in mind that this officially registered documentation has to do only with copyright and lends no clue as to how many times books were reprinted to satisfy a continuing market. Consider the example of *Lady of the Decoration* by Frances Little, copyrighted and published by Century Company in February 1906 (before the printer-typesetter-binder detail was noted in copyright records). It says "The De Vinne Press" on the verso of the title page. Subsequent printings show that it was reprinted by the press in 1906 in September, October, November, and December (twice); in 1907 in January, February (twice), March, April, May, June (twice), July, August, September, October, November and December (four times); and in 1908 in January, February, March, May, July, and September. (Then it began to appear without the De Vinne imprint – the plates presumably handed over to another printer – in November of 1908 and several times in succeeding years.) The lively business represented by the numerous reprints of this and other popular books might be overlooked if one relied too heavily on the copyright records, useful though they are as a bibliographical resource.

On 1 October 1912, no doubt in an effort to reinvigorate its business, the De Vinne Press announced that it was

> prepared to Design and Execute all Printed matter of the better grade, its facilities being unusually well developed by many successful years of Printing de Luxe for Publishers.
>
> The exceptional skill heretofore devoted to Book Printing will be extended to commercial catalogue and Booklet work, and the opportunity is desired of presenting Designs and Estimates upon any work that may be under consideration.[16]

That same month the picture was so bleak that the younger men who actually ran the De Vinne Press had considered some drastic measure such as consolidation or other schemes to take in outside capital. De Vinne's reply "to the Directors of the De Vinne Press" bears quoting in full:

Dear friends and associates:

I see nothing in the plan of the London promoter that meets my approval. A proposition to secure a little present increased income cannot be entertained when it implies the extinction of the De Vinne Press, of a house that bears my name, with which I have been connected for more than sixty years. I have steadily refused propositions for partnership from applicants who wanted to buy and pay cash for an interest in the business. I have always said, and here repeat, that I desire the De Vinne Press to be owned and managed by my heirs and those who have been helpful in securing its present position.

It is true that we are in a season of adversity, and that the outlook is not satisfactory; but I firmly believe that the tide will turn and bring with it an increase of prosperity. It is no disgrace to lose or even to be beaten in a fair and open fight for business; it would be a great disgrace to skulk out and to sell out for indefinite and unguaranteed promises of the better results that *might* come from a consolidation with our brother master printers. For seventy-five years our printing-house has maintained an enviable reputation. To keep up that reputation means sacrifice and trouble; but it is better to face trouble than to sneak out by sale.

I am ready to be helpful in any feasible plan that promises improvement, and I will try to be more useful to the house; but I object to new partners and new schemes of consolidation.

Yours cordially,
Theodore L. De Vinne[17]

The magnitude of this "season of adversity" can be seen in the profit-and-loss account for the last three years of De Vinne's life. In 1911 the firm profits were about $27,000. In 1912 and 1913 the Press lost $23,500 and $18,000, respectively, making a net loss for the three years of $14,500.[18]

Retirement

Salaries paid to the four officers during those three years are also instructive. In 1911 and 1912, De Vinne and his son, as president and vice president, received $4,500 each. De Vinne's grandson, Charles DeWitt De Vinne, received $3,000 as secretary. James W. Bothwell, treasurer, received $4,500. However, in 1913 Theodore De Vinne drew no salary but instead transferred it to Bothwell, making the protégé's salary $9,000 and confirming that it was Bothwell who was "pulling the stroke oar," as De Vinne had said of himself in Francis Hart's shop nearly sixty years earlier.

De Vinne spent most of his waning post-retirement energies on such pursuits as his last book, discussed above, the 1910 *Notable Printers of Italy During the Fifteenth Century.* His eyesight was almost gone, but with help he was able to carry on correspondence. The *American Printer*, published at the time by John Clyde Oswald, was still eager to print De Vinne's writings, even those of his declining years that were rambling and dyspeptic in tone: "A Typographic Study in Retrospect" and "About Cheap Books." Writing in 1911 to J. W. Phinney, a typefounder in Boston with whom he had maintained a friendship for years, De Vinne said, "I am four miles north of our printing-house, and I do not go to that printing-house oftener than once a fortnight. My son and Mr. Bothwell are reconstructing it thoroughly. We have type-setting machines, . . . and a new cost system, a new method of bookkeeping, etc." No doubt part of the reconstructing was necessary for business survival. De Vinne continued, "Every time I visit the printing-house I am reminded that my day is over. And yet I retain most kindly remembrances of the many worthies with whom I had pleasing dealings years ago."[19]

De Vinne's currency among fellow printers and books arts professionals on both sides of the Atlantic remained as strong as ever, despite his troubles on so many fronts. He joined the advisory committee – or at least allowed his name to be placed on it – of *Imprint*, a periodical established by Gerard Meynell in early 1913. In response to De Vinne's honorary degrees from Columbia and Yale, the Typothetae had commissioned Victor D. Brenner to design a medal bearing the profiles of De Vinne and Benjamin

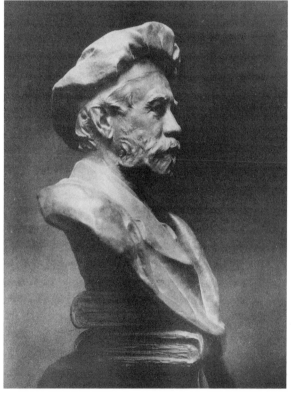

Franklin. It had been presented to De Vinne at the 1902 Franklin celebration where the two icons of American printing were jointly toasted[20] (fig. 30).

At its annual convention in 1910, the United Typothetae determined to have a bronze bust made of its first president and place it "in an appropriate institution of art and learning, in recognition of his services to the art and craft and as a permanent memorial of those distinguished services." The committee charged to carry out the plan selected sculptor Chester Beach and solicited subscriptions from throughout the printing industry to help finance it. In October 1912 the resulting bust was presented to Columbia University, where it currently resides in the south ground-floor corridor of Low Library. Two other copies were made at this time. One went to the Typographic Library and Museum of the American Type Founders Company in Jersey City, New Jersey; it is with the rest of the ATF Collection at the Rare Book and Manuscript Library at Columbia University. The other sat in the vestibule of the De Vinne Press Building; its subsequent whereabouts are still unknown at this writing. In 1918 Theodore Brockbank De Vinne would present the original plaster model to the Grolier Club; a copy in bronze for the club would be financed by subscription in 1926[21] (fig. 31).

When De Vinne died at age eighty-five in February 1914, the Boston Typothetae could say without a trace of hyperbole,

> In his death there has passed away the foremost printer of his time. The high quality of his printing, the ability he displayed in his contributions to the literature of our craft, and the time and energy he gave unselfishly to organized effort to improve printing trade conditions, earned for him a place in history and in the esteem of his fellow-printers that will not for a long time, if ever, be filled.[22]

Post Mortem (1914–1940)

His reputation does not, happily, depend on the later vicissitudes of the establishment the foundation of which he laid with such infinite pains. Nor is his influence in the world to be bounded by the term of his years.

D. B. Updike, 1923

W
HEN DE VINNE died on 16 February 1914, at least fourteen New York City and Brooklyn newspapers ran obituaries and tributes. More than one hundred out-of-town papers carried the story of his death, including those in such farflung cities as Fort Wayne, Dubuque, Detroit, Duluth, Kansas City, Omaha, Portland, Salt Lake City, San Antonio, and Charleston where printers, at the very least, knew his name. The Typothetae of the City of New York sponsored a memorial meeting on 10 March that was attended by scores of people associated with the printing and publishing trades.

De Vinne's will bequeathed $7,500 to each of his two grandchildren, Charles DeWitt De Vinne and Grace De Vinne. It gave $7,000 to his sole surviving brother, Daniel, $1,000 to each of six nieces, $250 to each of two nephews. To another niece he gave the income from $6,250, the principal to go to his son, the executor, upon her death. The sum of $15,000 was to be invested for the benefit of his two sisters, that principal also reverting to the executor when they died. Mrs. De Vinne's grandniece, who had been her companion and his secretary in later years, received $1,500. The remainder of the estate went to the son, Theodore Brockbank De Vinne.

The book value of the De Vinne Press at the proprietor's death was $365,818, of which De Vinne's interest was $287,895.[1]

Publishers' Weekly reported the entire De Vinne estate to be appraised at $1,455,677.[2]

Upon De Vinne's death, the Grolier Club Council met to compose a statement in appreciation of his zeal and contributions over the years. Subsequently the council decided to include a list of his writings in their Year Book of 1914. However, Grolier Club minutes hint that there was little residual sentimentality for De Vinne among council members. Two months after his death the De Vinne Press asked to borrow Volume 1 of the Jade catalogue (the two-volume elephant folio the press had completed in 1906) for a printing exposition at the Grand Central Palace; the council "regretted that they could not accede" to that request. The following month a letter was read from Bullen suggesting the publication of an address delivered by Robert Underwood Johnson at the Typothetae memorial meeting in De Vinne's honor, but "it was decided that such a publication would not be expedient."[3]

Nearly two years after his death the De Vinne Press issued a memorial volume for private distribution by his family (fig. 32). It contained a biographical sketch by Henry Lewis Bullen of the American Type Founders Library and Museum, a longtime De Vinne champion. There followed the speeches delivered at the memorial meeting of the New York Typothetae of 10 March 1914 (by John Clyde Oswald, editor of *American Printer*; Robert Underwood Johnson, former editor of *Century Magazine*; and Walter Gilliss, fellow printer and representative of the Grolier Club). Finally, there were thirteen official resolutions, thirty-six informal tributes, and the list of his writings from the 1914 Grolier Club yearbook.

Bothwell's brief introduction said that the collection of memorials had been selective rather than exhaustive, for "too pretentious a volume would have been distasteful to Mr. De Vinne." Fittingly, they dusted off De Vinne's Renner type and printed it on handmade, imported Fabriano paper watermarked "Umbria-Italia" (which is still made). Unlike the many garish "splendid" memorial volumes De Vinne had printed at the behest of customers, this one was bound modestly in light brown paper over boards, the pages trimmed only at the top, his favorite style for books in his own collection. The author's copy has a card tipped in: "Compliments of Mr. Theodore B. De Vinne." Yet various other bindings appeared on the volume. The copy listed in the Anderson Galleries auction catalogue upon the dispersal of the De Vinne collection in 1920 is described thus: "4to, old rose crushed levant morocco, gilt tooling, silk, doublures, silk-faced fly-leaves, uncut, in walrus case." This may have been a special binding for presentation to the family.[4]

By June 1914, Century made an effort to separate the magazines from the other affairs of the publishing firm. Negotiations for such a move broke off, and the company would struggle to keep the magazine afloat for another fifteen years before selling it.[5] In 1915, Century Company left its Union Square headquarters and joined the publishers' colony on Fourth Avenue, simultaneously removing its storage and shipping departments from the De Vinne Press Building, thus setting the stage for a divorce of the two firms. The Carey Printing Company won the contracts for both magazines. The October 1917 issues of *Century* and *St. Nicholas* were the last to bear attribution to the De Vinne Press.

Although the De Vinne Press continued under the management of James W. Bothwell, as it had in the past, it never again regained its financial strength of the late nineteenth century. In January of 1919 Theodore Brockbank De Vinne, president of the press, traded his common stock in for preferred.[6] In February he and his son, Charles DeWitt De Vinne, discontinued active participation in the firm.

If Theodore Brockbank had suffered in the shadow of a famous father, there was little to be done after the patriarch died; the son was already sixty-two years old. The founder had made arrangements for his son to reap the major financial reward from his life's work, but he clearly intended for the press to be operated and managed by practical printers whom he had trained and who had proved competent. (Theodore B. De Vinne's own 1926 obituary was perhaps typical of the way he was seen all his life: "Son of Late Founder of De Vinne Press" dies of pneumonia at the age of seventy-four.[7])

THEODORE LOW
DE VINNE

PRINTER

NEW YORK
PRIVATELY PRINTED
1915

F I G . 3 2 . Title page of the memorial volume published in De Vinne's honor in 1915 (10¼" x 7", untrimmed). The De Vinne Press device is in brown ink.

With the De Vinnes out of management roles in 1919, Bothwell's title was changed from "treasurer and manager" to "president and general manager," and the firm survived for three more years with new officers, including two of Bothwell's sons.

Meanwhile, the press continued to be one of the Grolier Club's printers. Reflecting hard times at the De Vinne Press, on an estimate in April 1917 Bothwell felt compelled to call the club's attention "to the several customs of the trade printed on the face of this estimate, each and all of which are made part of this proposal." Application to the Grolier Club of this very strict, businesslike list of provisions designed to protect the printer indicates how far the relationship had come from the days when Theodore De Vinne found the Grolier Club to be a vehicle for his love of printing. Except for a supplement to an earlier work, this item (*A Catalogue of Books in First Editions Selected to Illustrate the History of English Prose Fiction from 1845 to 1870*) was the last Grolier Club publication printed by the De Vinne Press.

There were several book collections with which Theodore Low De Vinne was associated. Most important was the one composed of 1,941 lots (plus four lots of furniture) auctioned on 12–16 January 1920 by Anderson Galleries (fig. 33). Like William Blades in England, De Vinne had assembled a very practical working library. It contained the standard bibliographical and typographical titles in numerous languages plus examples of printing in various periods. Fourteen lots (587 items) were "engravings, portraits, etc." One lot consisted of thirteen photographs of Rome, and one lot was four "plaster plaque portraits." Sixty-three lots (1,153 titles) were groups of twenty or so books; on those the catalogue did not give individual details. This leaves 1,862 titles, some containing multiple volumes, on which an analysis can be made.

The collection contained eighty-seven incunabula and ninety-three sixteenth-century titles. We can be sure they were well handled and studied, for that is why he owned them. Seventeenth- and eighteenth-century imprints numbered sixty-seven and 150, respectively. This dip in titles printed in the 1600s must reflect, in

FIG. 33.
Cover of Anderson
Galleries catalogue of the
De Vinne collection sold
at auction January 1920.

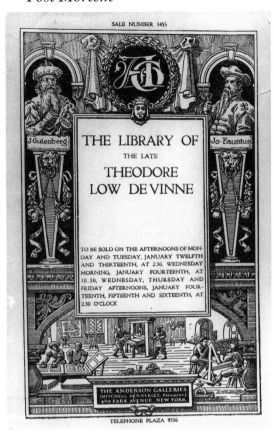

part, the relatively arid landscape of seventeenth-century printing. In the 1700s, on the other hand, not only did Bodoni, Didot, Baskerville, Caslon, and the Enschedés enter the printing scene to entice later students of the book, but typographic history blossomed in Europe, creating a body of work De Vinne needed for his research. He also owned works from the Kelmscott, Ashendene, and Doves Presses, an indication that he was abreast of the important private-press movement in England.

The 816 non-English titles give credence to reports that De Vinne studied several languages to aid his research. French works were the most numerous (356), the majority of them treatises on printing and typography, which he obviously collected for their content. The 257 books in Latin and eighteen in Greek reflect their role as the dominant languages of early printing. There were books in ten additional languages, German and Italian being the most numerous.

Apparently, De Vinne was less concerned with the coverings of his books than some of his Grolier Club cohorts. The Club Bindery was set up in 1895 by four Grolier members with Robert Hoe in the leadership. They found American binding inadequate and decided to import artisans who could turn out work equal to the best available in Europe. Bindings were executed only for subscribers, who were all Grolierites, but there was no official connection to the club. Although De Vinne was not one of the subscribers, thirteen volumes bound at the Club Bindery were in his collection, as described in the catalogue.[8] The binders of 129 other books are also identified. Most of them (ninety-five) were bound by Henry Stikeman, one of New York City's prominent binders. By and large, however, the bindings for De Vinne's collection were nondescript coverings – often cloth or paper over boards.

De Vinne began collecting in a time when books were purchased in sheets or folded into gatherings and perhaps covered with paper wrappers to keep them intact until bound to the purchaser's specifications. Often they were trimmed during this process at the top only (a dust-fighting feature) with the sheets left untouched, or "uncut," on the other three edges. For the serious bookman this continued to be the most unspoiled form of preserving a book, as it is for many collectors today. This must have been De Vinne's feeling, for a printer's finished product was sheets – not trimmed, bound pages. Even though his shop included a bindery where trade editions were enclosed in cloth case bindings with all three edges trimmed, this was not his preference for his own collection. Among the fourteen hundred titles (with individual entries in the catalogue) published during his career – and for most of which he was surely the first owner – a notable 56 percent were listed as "uncut." For books in formats smaller than quarto, where the sheet was folded more than twice, it was necessary to separate some edges with a paper knife to expose the full text. Two items were designated "uncut and unopened," meaning that the paper knife had not done its work.[9] Apparently Carl Purington Rollins was the successful bidder on one of these, because he returned to Yale University after the auction and composed this sonnet:

> O scholar-printer! Ripe with all the lore
> Which appertains to printing and to type,
> And, as becomes a man with learning ripe,
> A bookman with an ever growing store.
> From out their teeming pages you distilled
> The essence which you freely gave to us
> Who followed in your footsteps, envious
> To know it all, albeit far less skilled.
>
> Your learning oft my ignorance has vexed,
> But, Master, now you have me sore perplexed
> (although *nil nisi bonum* one believes):
> This book which so much pleases, also grieves,
> For when I open it to read the text
> *I find that you had never cut the leaves.*[10]

The Newberry Library of Chicago, whose income from the Wing Foundation had just become available, was the happy purchaser of 250 of the 300 titles it sought.[11]

This collection of De Vinne's, or parts of it, may have been at his office at one time, but it must have been at his home in later years, based on the substance of his correspondence from 300 West Seventy-sixth Street. The Columbia University Libraries' De Vinne Collection contains a typed list of some seventy-five titles headed "Books belonging to Mr. Theo. L. De Vinne in Office Library, October 1906." Three are incunabula; the books span the years through 1901. Most items on the list can be found readily in the Anderson catalogue. Perhaps, realizing that his time for contemplation and writing at the office had come to a close, he had asked his staff to round up the volumes that really belonged in his personal collection (as opposed to office copies of De Vinne Press books or other works needed for regular use in the shop). Or does this list represent duplicates that he allowed to remain at the office?

At least two annotated copies of the auction catalogue exist, both showing the amounts of the successful bids in their margins.[12] The item that brought the most money ($905) was the 1470 history of Rome by Titus Livius (two volumes, folio, containing numerous substantive marginal notes in a fifteenth-century hand), described as "of great rarity" and "probably the largest [copy] known." Second, ironically, was the 1910 Grolier Club book of the etchings of Whistler, which sold for $755. This was the very item De Vinne had cited – while pitching his *Notable Printers* to the Grolier Club Committee on Publication – as disturbing evidence of club members' growing preference of "decoration" over "information."[13] The third, at $450, was a two-volume morocco-bound collection (over a thousand pieces) of "Title-Pages, Dedications, Printers' Devices, etc., etc., cut from books published throughout Europe, from 1500 to 1800." These samples may have been assembled in the nineteenth-century enthusiasm for "extra illustrating" books, a practice with which De Vinne was not in sympathy, but he obviously found these printing samples of great historical and practical interest. (One assumes he acquired this collection after the cannibalization had been performed.)

The sale totaled some $25,000,[14] which for most sales of this era seems shockingly low even from a perspective of more than eight decades. As shown by auction-price results, De Vinne's library was clearly not in the same league as those of some of his Grolier contemporaries. The collection of Robert Hoe sold for nearly $2 million in 1911 and 1912, that of William Loring Andrews for $250,000 in 1919, Brayton Ives for more than $200,000 in 1891 and 1915, and Beverly Chew (his third library) for $160,000 in 1924.

The collection auctioned by Scott & O'Shaugnessy on 22 May 1919 has been mistaken by some writers as belonging to Theodore De Vinne, but it was the library of his son, Theodore B. De Vinne. In the 430 lots were printed books, broadsides, manuscripts, maps, newspapers, works of art, autographs, and objects such as powder horns. It included works about the discovery period, colonial times, native Americans, and railroads (1820–1872). It was strong in revolutionary tracts and rare early American imprints. The collection was offered for sale "with additions" from sources other than T. B. De Vinne. Without tracking down every item and examining it for evidence of ownership, one can't be sure exactly which had been T. B. De Vinne's or, for that matter, whether any had T. L. De Vinne's bookplate.

Stemming from his belief that printers needed to study their heritage, the elder De Vinne had also been a principal founder and benefactor of the New York Typothetae's library. Acting on his wish that fellow printers have access to the typographic reference works and printing exemplars he found so essential, he spearheaded the formation of a collection at the New York headquarters. Contributions of books and funds created an impressive collection that included type-specimen books, printing journals (French, German, English, and American), early printed books, and all manner of typographical treatises.[15] Wesley Washington Pasko (1840–1897), known for conceiving and editing the 1894 *American Dictionary of Printing and Bookmaking*, served as librarian for a time. After De Vinne's death, the collection fell into disuse and was later transferred to the American Type Founders library. Duplicates were auctioned by Anderson Galleries on 25 February 1924.

Apart from Theodore De Vinne's personal library, which was ultimately housed in his home, the De Vinne Press kept office copies of its imprints. Their bookplates were designed to keep their copies from straying from their proper locations (fig. 34). Accounts of the dispersal of this collection differ. Although a 1930 letter from Argosy Book Store certified to a customer, "On October (exact date unknown) 1928 we purchased the entire lot of proof copies of the De Vinne Press,"[16] the extent of their purchase is unknown. On 11 October 1928 Frederick Melcher wrote to Ruth Granniss at the Grolier Club while she was preparing the De Vinne exhibition that would open in December, "I have a De Vinne Press office copy of 'Jean Grolier' by William Loring Andrews, De Vinne Press, 1892. You may remember that the working library of the De Vinne Press was sold out by a bookseller on Fourth Avenue about two years ago,

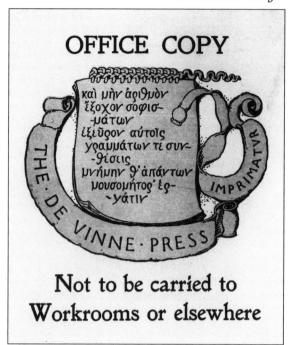

FIG. 34.

Office-copy bookplate for De Vinne Press imprints.

and this has that bookplate in it."[17] It may be that these are the same collection; perhaps Argosy's 1930 letter was incorrect about the year, and perhaps the bookseller mentioned in Melcher's letter was Argosy, which was indeed on Fourth Avenue in that period.

In a 1933 mimeographed account of the ATF Library, Henry Lewis Bullen gave this curious account:

> When the Library and Museum came to be recognized for its thoroughness its collections were strengthened from time to time by the acquisition of earlier similar collections. Theodore Low De Vinne was in his day the principal collector of books among American printers. He had two libraries – one of a general character in his home, another entirely related to typography in his printing office. His home library was, after his death, sold at auction, and contained only three items desirable for our Collection; the library relating to typography, containing many rare items, was acquired for our Collection in its entirety by private arrangement.

FIG. 35.

The De Vinne window of a set of twenty-four windows created in the late 1920s for the American Type Founders Library and Museum in Jersey City, N.J.

Theo. Low De Vinne, 1842‑1914

THE DE VINNE · PRESS

IMPRIMATUR

America's First Great Printer

These statements do not match known facts. Could the library of "general character" to which Bullen refers have been the 1919 T. B. De Vinne auction? It seems impossible that the 1920 home-library auction of such rich typographical content contained only three items "desirable" for Bullen's collection. Maybe the office library "related to typography" that Bullen was able to acquire "in its entirety" relates to the 1906 list of personal books in the printing house. David Mallison's study of Bullen does say that a small reference collection from the De Vinne Press was delivered to Bullen in 1914, but we cannot be sure how this relates to Bullen's statement.[18] One suspects that in touting his collection he allowed facts to give way to bombast, not unusual for the ATF impresario.

Bullen continued with a further account that seems to include slightly less hyperbole:

Under Mr. De Vinne's persuasion the Typothetae of the City of New York had formed the most complete library relating to printing and allied arts in existence prior to 1908. After Mr. De Vinne's death The Typothetae decided to sell its library. The sale was by auction in February, 1924; but before this event, the officials of The Typothetae permitted our Typographic Library to acquire by private arrangement all the books Mr. Bullen considered desirable for our Collection. More than 1000 volumes were thus acquired, many of them very rare, and all desirable. . . .[19]

Bullen had long wished to adorn his ATF Library and Museum with stained glass windows honoring history's major printers. His wish came true in the latter half of the 1920s when windows designed by J. François Kauffman were delivered and installed a few at a time in the ATF Library building in Jersey City. Each one bore the name, device, and active years of the printer. The legend on the De Vinne window said, "America's First Great Printer" (fig. 35). The ATF library collection was deposited at Columbia University in 1936, two years before Bullen died. In 1953 the Avery Corporation, which had purchased the Jersey City building, presented the windows to Columbia.

When it was time to break up housekeeping at 300 West Seventy-sixth Street, 153 decorative objects, mostly nineteenth century, were auctioned by Anderson Galleries on 27 and 28 February 1920. They show the De Vinnes to be typical Victorians with an assortment of Chinese porcelains; busts of classical figures; Limoges, Delft, and Wedgewood vases; and decorative pieces from Italy, Spain, Germany, Japan, etc. It is impossible to say whether these pieces were of personal interest to Theodore De Vinne himself or whether they reflected the tastes of his wife, son, daughter-in-law, or grandchildren, for his was a multigenerational household through his lifetime. Two years before the auction, Theodore B. had offered to the Grolier Club, and the club had accepted, marble busts of Ariosto, Petrarch, and Tasso. These must have been collected by his father, since he didn't seem to know much about them and said they were out of keeping with his other furnishings. In July 1920 Theodore B. and his wife, Lillian, sold the house on Seventy-sixth

Street. It and its neighbors were replaced by an apartment building which, in turn, was replaced by another.

Also in 1920, the De Vinne Press leased portions of the De Vinne Press Building and its annex to Reilly Electrotype Co., a sure sign that declining business was causing vacancies in its once-bustling facilities.

In late 1922 the real estate firm of Rich and McLean placed the following 10-by-16-inch newspaper advertisement:

FOR SALE
AMERICA'S FOREMOST PRINTING HOUSE
THE DE VINNE PRESS

A very unusual opportunity is offered to buy the Printing House founded by the world-famed printer Theodore Low De Vinne, which today continues to hold the same unexcelled and national reputation built up by the founder.[20]

The plant, it went on to say, consisted of a composing room that now included Linotype machines, a job pressroom of eight presses, and a cylinder pressroom of twelve machines, some of which were capable of two-color work. Also included were the pamphlet bindery and electrotype foundry. This was a far cry from the forty-press plant of the 1880s (fig. 36).

FIG. 36. Advertisement of the sale of the De Vinne Press, 1922.

The besieged Bothwell's explanation blamed the liquidation on organized labor and a demand for quantity over quality:

> Labor unions are absolutely prohibitive of fine work. Under their rule the worker becomes a mere machine. We are no longer able to get the type of men suited to our needs. It takes years to develop craftsmen such as our work requires.
>
> There is no longer the great demand for fine printing. Production and quantity are the watchwords today. Business men are educated to buy altogether on price lines. The last thing that people want to pay for today is quality. The demand for fine printing has decreased especially since the war. It seems to have turned the energy of men with money elsewhere than in the direction of fine books.[21]

A debate ensued in the press. Labor unions, trade journals, the Typothetae, newspaper editors, and printers weighed in. Officers of the International Printing Pressmen's Union and the International Typographical Union Local No. 6 disputed the first claim in which Bothwell was adhering to the traditional De Vinne anti-union line.[22] But it was certainly true that the dynamics of hiring and training workmen had shifted in the new century. Updike came to Bothwell's defense:

> Of the conditions that brought this to pass I know too little to be competent to speak. But to any one conversant, even by hearsay, with the handicaps under which printers of the City of New York have of late years been obliged to work it is easy to believe that to persist in the straight paths that were dear to Mr. De Vinne must have been attended with many problems and difficulties. The paralyzing effect of strictly organized union labor has proved a very serious affliction to any New York printing house that held to a certain standard. . . . [I]t is entirely believable that labor conditions were found sufficiently intolerable to supply a valid reason for its closing.[23]

Bothwell's second explanation had two points: Commercial printing was very price conscious, and the book-buying habits of the well-to-do had changed. No one disputed the first point; several commentators confirmed it. To survive and compete, the press would have needed to change the culture engrained in the management that, as the progenitor had set forth in 1883, even on mundane work one paid considerable "attention to little things." And even that might not have been enough to steer the shrinking corporation with its huge plant and attendant overhead and its diminishing clientele into a positive balance sheet.

On Bothwell's second point, many took issue. Bullen and Updike agreed with the editors of the *New York Times* that the number of fine presses and bibliophile clubs indicated "an unabated interest in scrupulous and comely typography."[24] In fact, although the De Vinne Press had done a considerable amount of consciously bibliophilic printing, it was not the lifeblood of the establishment and never had been. Instead, it was trade books and periodicals plus ordinary commercial printing that had kept the machinery humming at 393 Lafayette Street. And this had tapered off for a number of reasons. The Century Company – and, oddly, no one mentioned this – had taken its periodicals and books elsewhere in 1917 after the original principals had faded from the scene and residual loyalties had dissipated. In the same year the Grolier Club had switched to other printers, perhaps signaling a shift in the way the De Vinne Press was perceived by fine printing enthusiasts. Most significantly of all, there was a movement of printing out of New York City. Periodical and book printing – fine or otherwise – was moving to a ring of locations outside the city and, indeed, to other parts of the country, where labor and other costs were lower. This could take place because improved transportation and communication mechanisms rendered printers' proximity to the origin of copy less and less important. In 1860 New York City enjoyed more than one-third of the country's printing business, measured by value of product. By 1900 the city did only one-quarter of the nation's printing and lost ground even more seriously after 1920.[25] In hindsight, it is easy to see that the De Vinne Press was pinched by this simple financial reality that caused many a liquidation or relocation.

The *Brooklyn Daily Eagle* summed up the feeling that pervaded the printing trade: "Sentimentally it is better to see the De Vinne concern vanish gracefully than be lost in the muck of price-competition."[26] The *New York Tribune* printed a lengthy editorial entitled "A Great Printer," which said, in part,

> The withdrawal of the De Vinne Press from the field of American printing and the dispersal of its plant must bring a grievous sense of loss to lovers of good typography. A thousand precious memories are stirred by the news. This famous firm long ago became more than a commercial enterprise; it was an institution the founder of which was not only a business man but an artist. . . .
>
> It was peculiarly as the builder of a tradition that De Vinne functioned. We might name in illustration of his services any one of the fine books he printed for the Grolier Club, models having a tremendous influence upon the work of similar organizations of later origin in this country. . . .
>
> [The Grolier Club's] members would be the first to admit that without De Vinne they could hardly have laid the foundations of their important work. He was their collaborator in a double sense, active in their councils and a masterly maker of their earlier books. It was the club, as a club, that promoted emulation elsewhere, that fathered, as it were, a whole line of ardent bibliophiles, but it owed half the battle to the fact that when it advocated art in bookmaking it could point to things that De Vinne had done for it.[27]

On 10 March 1923 James W. Bothwell, acting as trustee for the nine stockholders, transferred to M. B. Brown Printing and Binding Co. all interest in the De Vinne Press for a purchase price of $150,000.[28] This was less than half the assessed value of a decade earlier. (This figure did not include the buildings or land.) Bothwell became president of the A. W. Stevens Printing Company in Brooklyn; Theodore Brockbank and Charles DeWitt De Vinne – still stockholders at the time of the sale – left the printing business.

The De Vinne Press Building (393–399 Lafayette Street) and the annex (21–23 East Fourth Street) were originally owned jointly by Roswell Smith and Theodore De Vinne in the proportion of three-fourths and one-fourth, respectively, as tenants in common.[29] Article 13 of their 1886 contract had specified that after five years De Vinne would sell his one-fourth to Smith at cost value "on request." In an 1888 codicil to his 1885 will, Smith had referred to that agreement so that his executors would know they could exercise that option if they deemed it in the best interest of his estate. This did not take place until 1929. In late April, the De Vinne heirs, Theodore Brockbank's two children, sold their one-fourth of the property to the Roswell Smith estate, which in turn sold the two lots and buildings to Walter Peek Paper Corporation in 1938.

Despite the death of the founder and the sale of the business, the De Vinne name still resonated in printing circles, and successors to the business used the name in confusing proliferation in the late 1920s and early 1930s. The M. B. Brown Company continued to use "De Vinne Press" as a trade name in addition to its own. In January 1926, several shareholders including one Harry Harris, a principal of M. B. Brown Company, purchased the printing firm Wynkoop Hallenbeck Crawford and incorporated it as De Vinne-Hallenbeck. In December 1933 Harris and others incorporated the De Vinne-Brown Corporation, and in February 1938 they formally merged the M. B. Brown Company into it.[30] New York City telephone directories of the late 1920s and early 1930s illustrate the effort to capitalize on the De Vinne name. Simultaneously they list M. B. Brown Printing and Binding Co. with two addresses (one of them being the old De Vinne Press annex on East Fourth), the De Vinne Press with its original address at 395 Lafayette, the De Vinne Press also at 80 Lafayette, and both Wynkoop Hallenbeck Crawford and De Vinne-Hallenbeck Company at 80 Lafayette as well. This must have been confusing, indeed, for the hapless customer.

Meanwhile, Theodore De Vinne's legacy continued to play itself out at the Grolier Club. After the 1923 sale to Brown, Bothwell had vainly assured the Grolier Club that it could still use the services of the former De Vinne Press:

> The M.B. Brown Printing & Binding Co., of New York, has taken over the building, plant, good will and name of the old Company, and it is the purpose of the new owners to continue the high order of excellence and service maintained by this company for so many years.
>
> While official titles have been changed, the same organization that has been serving you will continue to give you their best efforts in fullest appreciation of your patronage.[31]

In 1924 James Bothwell, no longer a member himself, offered to give the club the chair from the proofreaders' room in the Plantin-Moretus Museum that was "used by Mr. De Vinne for years." It had been presented to De Vinne, according to a brass plate on its back, by his Century Company colleagues in 1886.[32] The club gladly accepted the chair – which clearly does not date from Plantin's own time. It presently resides in the Grolier Club director's office (fig. 37).

There was some sentiment among his old comrades that the club should also have a copy of De Vinne's bronze bust by Chester Beach. It had already received the original plaster cast from T. B. De Vinne

FIG. 37.

The Plantin-Moretus chair De Vinne used in his office at the De Vinne Press, now reupholstered and at the Grolier Club.

in 1918. In 1926 Ira Brainerd, a trustee of the Century Company who was close to De Vinne through the years, organized a subscription to have a fourth bronze bust cast. De Vinne's son joined nineteen other subscribers but, maintaining the characteristic family modesty, wanted to ensure that his participation was given no publicity. Brainerd wrote to club treasurer Robert Jaffray,

> Mr. [T.B.] De Vinne wants it to be very clear that the bust was originally the voluntary action of the [United] Typothetae. . . . The Grolier replica also is not the idea of the De Vinne family. They are glad of spontaneous appreciation of Mr. Theodore Low De Vinne, and Mr. T. B. De Vinne hopes there will be little or no publicity as to his part in it. I write this to oblige him.

That bust resides in the club's library.

Two years later, in 1928, the centenary of De Vinne's Christmas Day birth approached. The club leadership may have already considered some kind of observance, but they were spurred into action when Grolier treasurer Louis I. Haber read a *New York Times* letter to the editor on 9 October 1928 about the upcoming anniversary. He quickly conferred with chairman Harry T. Peters of the Committee on Arrangements and then wrote Granniss suggesting that she reply to the *Times* saying that the club planned an exhibition. "The main thing is get it started before some organization beats us to it," he wrote.[33]

So they set about finding someone to organize the exhibition and to speak at the opening. Henry Watson Kent, the first choice, declined. Kent had been club librarian before Ruth Shepard Granniss and then was elected to membership and took a very active part in the leadership. Kent wrote Peters, "I am perfectly certain that in Miss Granniss' hands the exhibition has every chance to be made as good as it possibly can be made." But there was still the matter of speakers. Kent said it would be a pleasure to talk about De Vinne but he couldn't; he suggested D. B. Updike and James Bothwell. Updike replied that he considered it a great compliment but was not able to undertake such things because of work at the Merrymount Press. Richard Hoe Lawrence, who had been elected a member during the club's first year, was asked to speak about De Vinne and the early years of the club, but he declined as well. Bothwell said he would be glad to do anything *but* speak. Indeed, he proved a crucial resource for the exhibition, supplying unique memorabilia and an institutional memory of the De Vinne Press that he alone possessed. (He would later give the club library much of the memorabilia in the form of a scrapbook.) He sent Granniss a trunk full of books and other items relating to De Vinne's career. Loans came in from Henry Lewis Bullen of the American Type-founders Company, Frederick Melcher of the *Publishers' Weekly*, De Vinne's grandson, and others.

Out of a wide variety of books, periodicals, manuscripts, medals, and assorted memorabilia, Miss Granniss fashioned an exhibition that celebrated De Vinne's many facets. At the opening Ira Brainerd gave a warm and generous summary of De Vinne's life and work. John Clyde Oswald, a De Vinne admirer who published trade journals and books – including reprints of De Vinne's *Practice of Typography* series – offered a somewhat shorter but no less heartfelt tribute. The club's exhibition file notes that ninety-nine attended the opening and that "daily attendance" at this three-week exhibition (16 November through 8 December) was 177. One assumes that this meant the *total* attendance in the days following the opening, not the average daily attendance.[34] In 1929 Bothwell printed the exhibition catalogue at his place of business, the A. W. Stevens Printing Co. in Brooklyn, with a Grolier Club imprint in an edition of three hundred (fig. 38).

Within the printing trade, the one hundredth anniversary of De Vinne's birth was the occasion of enthusiastic, unequivocal tributes to the printer's memory. At its annual meeting in October of that year, the United Typothetae of America had authorized the appointment of a committee to raise funds for a building to house the UTA as a memorial to De Vinne. Fifteen printers promptly pledged $1,000 each. The De Vinne grandchildren, Charles DeWitt De Vinne and Grace De Vinne Goldsmith (Theodore Brockbank having died in 1926), very generously pledged $5,000 each. Sadly, no such

CATALOGUE

OF WORK OF

THE DE VINNE PRESS

EXHIBITED AT

THE GROLIER CLUB

ON THE OCCASION OF THE ONE HUNDREDTH

ANNIVERSARY OF THE BIRTH OF

THEODORE LOW DE VINNE

DECEMBER 25, 1828

WITH ADDRESSES BY

IRA HUTCHINSON BRAINERD

JOHN CLYDE OSWALD

NEW YORK

THE GROLIER CLUB

1929

FIG. 38. Title page of the catalogue from the 1928 Grolier Club exhibit on De Vinne's centennial (9½" x 6¼").

building was ever fully funded and built, for the UTA continued to rent office space in various buildings in Washington, D.C., even after it reorganized as The Printing Industries of America in 1940.

The New York Employing Printers Association (successor to the Typothetae of the City of New York) held a meeting in De Vinne's honor with speeches, among others, by Judge Alfred E. Ommen, counsel of the Employing Printers and longtime legal adviser and confidant of the De Vinne family. Ommen said he had proposed De Vinne for election to the New York University Hall of Fame but found that the interval since death required for eligibility had been extended from ten to twenty-five years so that De Vinne's name had been placed on a list of suggested future candidates.[35] Apparently De Vinne's name was not taken up for nomination at a later date.[36]

The United Typothetae of America designated December 1928 as De Vinne month and devoted its December 24 issue of the weekly *Typothetae Bulletin* to articles about him (fig. 39). Many local Typothetae organizations focused their December meetings on discussion of De Vinne's work. Trade journals ran articles in celebration of the De Vinne centenary.

De Vinne-Hallenbeck distributed a large portrait of De Vinne with a facsimile of his signature: "In honor of the 100th anniversary of the birth of this great American printer, this etching by T. Johnson has been reproduced in daguerreotone by his business successor, The De Vinne-Hallenbeck Co., Inc. New York." This "successor" did not attempt to carry on the grand tradition of De Vinne Press book printing. Judging by two court cases in which De Vinne-Hallenbeck was involved, in 1929 and 1931, it specialized in color lithography for displays and other commercial purposes.[37] A search for books printed by De Vinne-Hallenbeck has yielded very few. Yet the firm did its best to capitalize on the famous name (fig. 40).

By 1935 De Vinne-Hallenbeck had ceased being listed in city directories. It formally dissolved on 6 April 1938. Early in 1940, after losing Tammany Hall favor that had included the contract for printing the *City Record*, De Vinne-Brown "disposed of the major part of its plant at a small fraction of the $750,000 book valua-

FIG. 39.
Cover of the
*Typothetae
Bulletin,* 24
December
1928, one of
many trade-
journal trib-
utes to De
Vinne on the
centennial of
his birth.

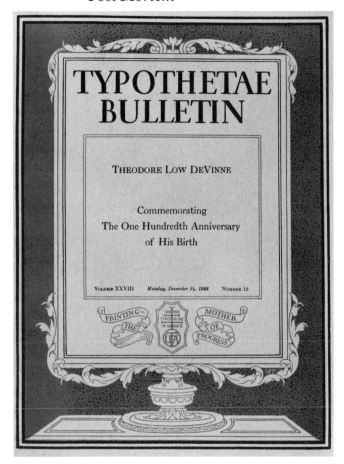

TYPOTHETAE BULLETIN

THEODORE LOW DEVINNE

Commemorating
The One Hundredth Anniversary
of His Birth

VOLUME XXVIII   *Monday, December 24, 1928*   NUMBER 13

PRINTING
THE
UNITED TYPOTHETAE OF AMERICA
MOTHER
OF
PROGRESS

tion"[38] and suspended operations except for a minor ticket printing department.[39] After slightly over a century, the last of the firms associated with Theodore Low De Vinne had come full circle – back to Francis Hart's specialty, job printing for the transportation trade. On 26 December 1940, the day after the 112th anniversary of Theodore De Vinne's birth, the De Vinne-Brown Corporation dissolved. De Vinne would no doubt have been saddened by these opportunistic and inept uses of his name.

Still, the demise of De Vinne's original firm had not detracted from the general high regard in which the founder was held. As

Updike had said in 1923 when the De Vinne Press was put up for sale, Theodore De Vinne's "reputation does not, happily, depend on the later vicissitudes of the establishment the foundation of which he laid with such infinite pains."[40]

IN HONOR OF THE ONE HUNDREDTH ANNIVERSARY OF THE BIRTH OF THIS GREAT AMERICAN PRINTER, THIS ETCHING BY T. JOHNSON HAS BEEN REPRODUCED IN DAGUERREOTONE BY HIS BUSINESS SUCCESSOR, THE DE VINNE-HALLENBECK CO., INC., NEW YORK

FIG. 40. "Daguerreotone" of Thomas Johnson's etching, used by De Vinne-Hallenbeck during the De Vinne centennial.

Legacy

He never posed as a saint. I don't think he would have
liked to be considered one. But his principles were so
straightforward, so sturdy, so uncompromising, that
it would not have taken much "alteration of proof" to
make him at least a superman.

Frank Hopkins, 1936

N O LIFE CAN BE UNDERSTOOD by merely reciting a
chronological tale of events. For De Vinne, a deeper appreciation of his significance requires consideration of the
six primary roles he played: employer, leader of the printing fraternity, printer to Century Company, mechanic, artist, and scholar-
bibliophile. Such analysis confirms Updike's assessment that "the
man was greater than his work." [1]

EMPLOYER

The foundation upon which Theodore De Vinne conducted his
business was a belief in the dignity of physical – particularly skilled
– labor, the mutuality of interest between capital and labor, and the
principles of self-reliance, perseverance, and loyalty. The success
ethic of the nineteenth century was composed of precisely these
ingredients; De Vinne was very much in tune with his times.
Throughout his career, as events and circumstances grew more
complex, there is no evidence that he wavered from this philosophy.

It was a popular notion in America that labor and capital were
two harmonious parts of the same whole. Free-enterprise capital-
ism and a fluid class structure were thought to lead the most dili-
gent of workers into the ranks of the self-employed, the first step
into the highly regarded independent business classes. Buttressed,
no doubt, by his own sober Protestant upbringing, De Vinne found

this promise fulfilled in his own experience; hence his belief that the route to success as a printer – indeed, to the prosperity of the industry – lay in every worker doing his duty faithfully and diligently. Sometimes an employee had to petition for redress if his salary was out of line with his contribution to the printing house, as De Vinne himself had done about 1855 when he felt Hart had not taken suitable initiatives. But even when he was a mere compositor, De Vinne felt his interests closely tied to those of the proprietor of the shop.

His understanding of what corporations now call "human resources" was formed in a time when boys entering the trade might reasonably expect to become master printers, indenturing apprentices of their own some day. Only a minority made it, to be sure, but the path from printer's devil through journeyman to master printer and proprietor was for many years a hoped-for continuum. Because of the peculiarities of the printing industry, this remained a common notion long after it ceased to be so in other trades. Printing-trade workers traditionally considered themselves aristocrats of the labor force (especially compositors once theirs was a specialty that separated them from pressmen). It was a highly skilled trade whose adherents did not have to suffer the ignominy, as did cordwainers, hatters, etc., of having once owned the tools of their trade and then having them supplanted by mechanization. And, in fact, it took a rather small investment to set up as a job printer and enter the ranks of the "employing printers." The custom nature of printed products spared workmen the degradation of becoming operatives on an assembly line. For all these reasons, deference toward and admiration for a benevolent employer came naturally.

For their part, most mid-nineteenth-century New York printing proprietors retained real sympathy for those in stations below them. After all, virtually all of them had come up through the ranks themselves. A study of the biographical details for the most active members of the Typothetae of the City of New York and scattered evidence for less prominent printers show that very few had not followed the same pattern; almost all had served printing apprenticeships. In this setting, the ideal proprietor was a father figure providing for and meting justice to his economic "family." This was clearly a role De Vinne took very much to heart.

He believed strongly that the employees of any printing shop owed more loyalty to the house than to any outside body. De Vinne did not oppose combinations and associations on principle. In fact, he belonged to the General Society of Mechanics and Tradesmen of the City of New York and the New York Typographical Society.[2] He was quite comfortable with the practice of a committee of employing printers meeting with a committee of journeymen and adjusting the standard wages either up or down as the economics of printing in a given city varied. This was an old practice, one predating his entry into management ranks.

What De Vinne could not abide was the growing aggressiveness of trade unions, their insistence that labor interests were opposed to those of management, and their bid for control of matters he considered the proprietor's prerogative. He resented their tendency to demand rather than negotiate wage increases and, most of all, their efforts to establish closed union shops whereby employers were forced to hire only union members.

In the high value he placed on his own authority and the paternalistic manner in which he exercised it, De Vinne was far from unique among businessmen of his generation. In fact, this was the norm. The panoply of examples includes everything from company towns like Pullman, Illinois, and New England mill-workers' dormitories to small workshops in various industries where lifers were kept on staff long after their peak usefulness. Proprietors' motives were said to run the gamut from self-serving exploitation to a religious sense of duty. Where De Vinne belongs on this spectrum is not a simple matter to assess.

There are numerous anecdotes in which he is said to have shown special compassion toward individual employees. For example, *Century* art editor Alexander Drake recalled that De Vinne nearly fired an employee who had made several mistakes on consecutive days but then sent him home with a week's extra pay when he discovered the workman had been nursing a sick wife through the nights.[3] Robert Underwood Johnson, editor of *Century Magazine,* said that De Vinne "succeeded by his personality, firmness, sincerity, and geniality in making his men feel that they were not merely working for a machine, but for a man," and that "respect for him was a commanding motive in the work of his printing-house."[4] Judge Alfred Ommen, De Vinne family legal adviser and counsel to the New York Typothetae, said of De Vinne, "He actively interested himself in the life of his men outside of the plant. He visited them in sickness; he attended the weddings, the christenings and the funerals. . . . As a result there was deep attachment toward him and all his workmen loved him."[5]

These comments on De Vinne as employer are from outsiders who were his peers. Yet his staff often echoed this sort of encomium. Six years after De Vinne's death, composing room foreman Camille De Vèze remembered him this way:

> Theodore L. De Vinne had the genius of surrounding himself with men to whom the reputation of his house and the satisfaction of being associated with it meant more than any financial remuneration ever could, and the loyalty and admiration of these men will always stand as the pedestal on which his own mastership was erected. He was one of the few exceptions to the well authenticated fact that a hero is never a hero to his own valet.[6]

The existence of a "deep attachment" was evidenced on at least two occasions, the employees' response to De Vinne's profit-sharing experiment and their gesture in commemoration of his fiftieth wedding anniversary, though these may well have been choreographed by senior management, not spontaneous sentiments of the rank and file.

De Vinne tried to be both compassionate and strict with his workers, yet deferential to his managers, as shown by a handwritten note of 1896:

> Dear Mr. Bothwell:
>   Mr. Dugan has asked me to use my influence with you for his reinstatement. I told him that I should not interfere with your decision. It might be well however for you to consider his

case again. The man seems ashamed and penitent and promises good behavior. But I leave the case to you who knows all the circumstances.

Yours cordially,
Theo. L. De Vinne[7]

The best sustained, direct testimony we have of what it was like to work for De Vinne comes from Frank Hopkins, employee for ten years during De Vinne's prime. Hopkins spent nine of those years, as he phrased it, "at De Vinne's elbow," during which time he acquired perspectives of both employee and manager.[8]

The salaries, Hopkins recalled, were in line with the standard wages being paid in the industry, but they were not commensurate with the superior abilities and unusually high quality of work expected at the De Vinne plant. Book compositors especially, who worked on piece rates, complained that they could not make decent wages under the exacting rules of composition prevailing in De Vinne's shop. "Sometimes they were awarded an extra price for difficult work. At other times there was nothing to do but make the best of it." To compensate for the disparity between the wages and the quality of work expected, De Vinne would withdraw several thousand dollars every three months or so and divide it among the men he considered the "more deserving." This extra pay was no doubt appreciated, but the system created envy and suspicion. Hopkins felt that "most of the men would have been better satisfied with a straight salary based on their relative importance."

If monetary reward was somewhat lacking at De Vinne's, so, according to Hopkins, was the reward of praise and appreciation from the proprietor. After describing the top twenty-five supervisors, "the gentlemen who made up a working force of rare ability and efficiency with few and inconspicuous exceptions," Hopkins called them the "more or less humble workers behind the scenes."

> No spotlights, no applause, no press notices compensated them for conscientious endeavor. Their reward consisted of a few pitiful greenbacks once a week. And yet they were the backbone of the institution. . . .

There is no room for argument. We were spokes in the great wheel, and if there were no spokes I suppose there would be no wheel. Still, I think a word of credit now and then would have been as grateful to many of the men as a raise in pay.

Hopkins quickly explained or excused most of his other criticisms of De Vinne. For instance, the proprietor frequently threatened to fire workmen who incurred his displeasure. However, Hopkins softened his criticism by saying that De Vinne's bark was worse than his bite. "In all the years I was with him I never knew him to 'discharge a man on the spot,' one of his favorite threats, or to be other than a generous, kindly old friend when he knew all the circumstances." Hopkins said De Vinne was impatient, often wanting things done right away; but this was "a common failing among employers."

Hopkins had ample reason to resent De Vinne but apparently buried any bitterness he felt at being forced to choose between his hobby press and a promising career at De Vinne's. Hopkins reported that the ultimatum to make the choice was delivered in "such a kind, fatherly manner" that he was ashamed of himself and felt as though he had "done something dishonorable." Still, he said, he did not blame De Vinne; he would have felt the same way. In this memoir written from memory shortly before Hopkins died in his seventieth year, he said that he wrote frankly merely to show that De Vinne "was a man of like passions to ours." Hopkins said that De Vinne never posed as a saint. "I don't think he would have liked to be considered one. But his principles were so straightforward, so sturdy, so uncompromising, that it would not have taken much 'alteration of proof' to make him at least a superman."

The extent to which De Vinne received loyalty from his employees was probably due somewhat to this sort of adulation by many members of his staff. In part, his bonus system and profit-sharing plan – when they were in force – no doubt kept many top employees steadfast. Moreover, even if De Vinne did not dispense praise and recognition as lavishly as he might, there was a certain prestige that went along with employment there. As Henry Lewis Bullen put it, "to have learned the printing trade in Mr. De Vinne's office was equal to a diploma from one of our great technical schools."[9] Hopkins testified to the same phenomenon: "It was the ambition of many men in the printing industry to be employed there, not that they were paid better wages than other houses, but because it was an indication of competency to be known as a De Vinne man." (The majority of the workers at De Vinne's printing house were undoubtedly male. The extant records are inadequate to say what the proportions were, but women certainly did composition on *Century Magazine* and *St. Nicholas*. And they were also employed in the bindery.)

It is important to remember that the De Vinne Press was, to a large extent, a family enterprise. The proprietor took his son and grandson into the management. Long ago he had found a place for his sixteen-year-old brother, Daniel, in Francis Hart's shop soon after arriving there himself. Daniel had learned composition and, at some undocumented point, had advanced to foreman of the composing room of Theodore's enterprise. Daniel, it seems, was suited to and content in this role. Hopkins said he had excellent taste in composition and was loyal to his brother's interests. Daniel saved the first sheet printed in the new De Vinne Press Building on 14 April 1886.[10] He was, said one of his apprentices,

> a gentleman of the old school, always dignified and rather reserved with those who were not his intimates. He always inspired respect. This was probably due to the fact that he was a man of large build and always dressed the part of the son of a Methodist clergyman. . . . A momentary hush was noticeable when, at seven o'clock each morning, the top of his silk hat appeared above the railing of the stairs which led to the composing room.[11]

Hopkins noted that Daniel kept his full white beard saturated with Jockey Club cologne (fig. 41). His apprentices often said, "He eats type." He told them always to "think type" and talked about type at home so much that his daughters would ask for so many picas of meat rather than a small or large serving.

Daniel retired in 1904 and was the only brother living when Theodore died. The oldest brother, John Augustus, seems to have lived out his life without leaving much of a trace except the oral tradition that he was an apprentice at the Harpers printing shop. Theodore, the second child, became the head of the family for his generation. Next in birth order were brothers Edwin and Ambrose, who had a blank book and stationery business near the plant at the corner of Murray Street and College Place where Theodore did business for fourteen years. Edwin and his family lived near Theodore in Jersey City for many years. Daniel, the next sibling, was probably closest to Theodore. James Manley, youngest of the brothers, shows up in the records only as an employee of Theodore in the 1870s. The two youngest siblings, Emma and Francis, never married but lived with and cared for their parents. Emma took exception to the way Theodore distributed his estate. She included this article in her will, proved on 29 December 1919:

> *Nineteenth*: I do not give or bequeath anything to the descendants of my brother, Theodore L. De Vinne, deceased, as my said brother provided for them abundantly, leaving the bulk of his property to his son, not fulfilling a promise made by said Theodore L. De Vinne to his brother, Daniel S. De Vinne, thereby seriously affecting the said Daniel S. De Vinne, and also his two sisters.

By the same token, Theodore's will canceled any debts owed him by his brothers, their widows, or heirs. So there may have been considerably more generosity than Emma's acerbic language suggests.

Theodore B. De Vinne may have received the bulk of his father's estate, but James Bothwell was the keeper of the firm's traditions. In fact, the *Typothetae Bulletin* mistakenly referred to Bothwell as "a son-in-law of Mr. De Vinne."[12] In 1901 Bothwell even named one of his own sons Theodore Low De Vinne Bothwell. (One is reminded of a parallel: D. B. Updike's employee and partner, John Bianchi, named a son Daniel Berkeley Bianchi.)

The devotion of key personnel was one of the cornerstones of De Vinne's success; too much reliance on that devotion may also have

FIG. 41. Daniel S. De Vinne, Theodore's younger brother and foreman of the composition department at the De Vinne Press.

contributed to his downfall. In an otherwise very perceptive article, Carl Rollins said, "De Vinne's habit of examining all the evidence, whether the 'four pieces' of the Gutenberg mystery, or the invasion of the photo-mechanical half-tone printing block, gave him a dis-

passionate outlook on the problems of labor-management."[13]
"Dispassionate" may be an apt emotional position in other situations, but labor management is not among them. De Vinne's attitudes toward labor in general and toward employee relations had crystallized early. He was passionately and obstinately opposed to any deviation from his paternalistic ideal. One suspects that bewilderment and sorrow accompanied any deviations as much as rage. "When certain old employees conceived their duty to their Union paramount, and left his employ in a strike," Bullen tells us, "De Vinne shed tears of sorrow at the parting."[14]

De Vinne's obituary in the New York *World* called him "a staunch supporter of every project for the benefit of the working man."[15] Oddly, this bit of journalistic panegyric was not totally inappropriate, certainly not by De Vinne's own reckoning. Hard, honest work; loyalty; respect for rank; and a capacity for delayed gratification had served him well in his own rise to independence. Schooled in a set of values he took to be timeless, De Vinne expected his employees – his household – to share those values, even into a new and changing century.

LEADER

There was no reason to suspect from Theodore De Vinne's modest family circumstances and scant formal education that he would become the best-known practitioner of his calling. Except for some knowledge of Latin and a respect for learning inherited from his father (who was not only a preacher but an erstwhile schoolmaster), De Vinne's first twenty years were much like those of any youngster apprenticed in a trade. He was clever enough to make himself invaluable to Francis Hart, forcing his employer to share the proprietorship, but even this initiative did not presage what was to come.

Nor did some of De Vinne's mature characteristics suggest leadership. Physically he was unremarkable: "slightly under average height, somewhat thick set," wearing the short, full beard that was common in his day. He had a speech impediment that sounded like "huh, huh" with a rising inflection when he paused in conversation.

His friend Ira Brainerd called it "a lovable odd trait." Employee Camille De Vèze noted that De Vinne had for years "schooled himself to overcome this affliction," not entirely successfully, and that De Vinne "often said that the hardest job of his life was suppressing this habit." John Clyde Oswald noted that this "peculiar affectation of voice prevented him from becoming an orator."[16]

The one characteristic on which everyone remarked was De Vinne's modesty. This attribute is not only prevalent in eulogies, where one would expect it, but is also evident time and again in his own correspondence and actions. For instance, when Hamilton Wright Mabie was preparing *The Writers of Knickerbocker New York* for Grolier Club publication, De Vinne had second thoughts about sending Mabie two volumes of his grandfather's poems as an example of bookmaking in New York in 1800, since the gesture might be considered "presumptuous" and a "disposition to gratify family pride."[17] He indicated to Henry Lewis Bullen his "small interest" in collecting critical notices of his work and in having his name in a proposed Hall of Fame in Saint Louis.[18] When a printing machinery manufacturer, as a publicity stunt, promised a cylinder press to the person chosen "printer laureate" by popular vote, De Vinne demurred at the introduction of his name into the contest and specifically asked W. W. Pasko to cease all efforts in his behalf.[19] In his writings De Vinne declined to take credit for the innovations and improvements in printing others have associated with him.

De Vinne, in short, does not seem to have been a charismatic figure. *Century Magazine*, in its loving and reverent obituary, admitted that De Vinne "had little of the magnetism of a leader among men, and less taste for exercising such influence."[20] The only thing, superficially at least, that distinguished him from his fellows was his habit of wearing a velvet beret, styled after the medieval craftsman's cap; and that may be more attributable to his love of history than to personal vanity. Indeed, it is not known how much he used it, but he is depicted wearing it in several late portraits and the Chester Beach bust.[21] He also wears it on the obverse of a medal designed by J. P. Brennen and commissioned by the United Typo-

FIG. 42. Medal commissioned by the United Typothetae of America.

thetae of America for presentation to subsequent UTA presidents and other worthies, whose names were inscribed on the reverse (fig. 42).

How, then, did this ostensibly ordinary man become the acknowledged leader of the printing industry in New York – indeed its most prominent national figure?

In the first place, he was an ombudsman to the trade. He perceived the value of trade cohesiveness early in his career. While still in his thirties, he emerged as leader of New York printing proprietors. The considerable effort he invested in organizing and nurturing the Typothetae of the City of New York – and the spread of this concept into other cities – naturally propelled him into a position of prominence.

De Vinne was both a spokesman and a vigorous worker behind the scenes, influencing policy and lending his pen to the various Typothetae causes. He was particularly outspoken on the two matters of greatest concern to the industry: labor relations and price maintenance.

Legacy

One of the Typothetae's staunchest resisters of the closed shop, he chaired the Typothetae "emergency committee" in 1887 when the first closed-shop strike occurred. He customarily exerted his personal efforts toward arbitration to avert strikes, as in this 1887 instance when he called in State Arbitrator F. F. Donovan or in 1896 when he sought the assistance of civic reformer and labor arbitrator Seth Low (no relation) to avoid a strike over the nine-hour day.[22]

It was the question of prices for printed products that had caused the formation of the Typothetae in the first place; and that problem, eclipsed by labor from time to time, was the organization's constant concern. De Vinne worked for price maintenance throughout his career, focusing on the two troublesome areas: how a printer calculated prices based on his own in-shop costs, and how, in the face of free-market competition, printers kept prices at acceptably high and profitable levels.

A second explanation for De Vinne's leadership position was the didactic nature of so much of his work: he was an educator of novices. The four-volume *Practice of Typography* is the most obvious and enduring example. In light of the nineteenth-century decline of the apprenticeship system, these practical treatises, which were reprinted for two decades after their initial appearance, served as dependable textbooks for the ambitious beginner. Many of his articles also had the patient tone of the teacher. Whether the subject was lithography (where the title actually said, "for the Use of Novices"), or type measurement, or history, De Vinne's purpose was to share a knowledge gained through experience and study.

The third way in which De Vinne rose to a position of unusual influence was through the volume and breadth of his writings. His dozen books and more than one hundred articles could not have escaped the notice of anyone familiar with printing trade literature during his lifetime; his later works reached a more general, sophisticated public.

His written works fall into five major categories. In addition to the instructional manuals, he wrote other technical but less pedagogical pieces to share his notions with printers in general. There are also many works having to do with printing aesthetics, business management, and the history of printing. In addition, he contributed book reviews, addresses, and letters to the editor that are impossible to reduce to a category.

Even though the bulk of his articles did appear in printing trade journals, a wide assortment of other periodicals carried and sought pieces by De Vinne. In addition to writing for *Century*, he appeared in the pages of magazines devoted to literature and publishing: *Biographer, The Book-Lovers Almanac, Current Literature, The Literary Collector, The National Journalist for Editors*, the *New York Times Saturday Review*, and *The Publishers' Weekly*. He wrote for technical publications outside the field of printing: *The Manufacturer and Builder* and *Scientific American*; New York daily newspapers – the *Journal*, the *Evening Post*, and the *Tribune*; and weekly papers – *The Independent, The Nation*, and *The Outlook*. His writing, therefore, had much to do with making him not only an authority figure within the industry but also a national representative of the printing trade to those outside it.

The fourth reason for De Vinne's prominence was simply the success of his business. The De Vinne Press Building itself was a powerful symbol of his leadership. Even today this massive edifice is not dwarfed by more modern buildings in its vicinity. From the late 1880s into the new century, one can imagine the pride with which men and women entered its doors to be part of the work force. Henry Lewis Bullen and Frank Hopkins spoke of the shop's reputation among New York journeymen. While immigrant compositor Gregory Weinstein was working at William Martin's in the 1880s, he complained of lack of leads, quads, and spaces; the proprietor replied, "Where do you think you are? In a De Vinne shop or government printing office?"[23]

De Vinne's visibility as printer to the Century Company should not be underestimated. Among printers, and to a considerable extent outside the trade as well, his name rode the crest of *Century Magazine*'s popularity, a prominence sustained by his printing of their many books and, notably, *The Century Dictionary*. His friendship with and printing for book connoisseurs of his day (Samuel P. Avery, William Loring Andrews, Archer M. Huntington, John Pierpont Morgan, and the like – not to mention his membership in numerous bibliophile organizations) added to his success in ways mere financial gain could never have done. Ira Brainerd focused on the two connections De Vinne had that may have outweighed all the others to explain his prominence: "Probably through the Grolier Club and the Century Company, for both names were widely broadcast, De Vinne did for his craft more than any one man of his day; he inspired the artist and he stimulated the public, and the two were got nearer together."[24]

Fifth, and finally, De Vinne rose to leadership because he sincerely idealized the printing craft. "Master of its history," Bullen said, "he appreciated the greatness of his occupation, and made it respected by others."[25] In its obituary of De Vinne, *Century Magazine* noted that all the "articles of great force and attractive substance" that he had contributed to that magazine "were written in the interest of his cause, the proficiency and honor of his calling."[26] Following his father's footsteps, Theodore Low De Vinne was an evangelist, preaching the gospel of loyalty within the shop and to the industry, attention to mechanical detail, readable products, and respect for history. One of the most charming manifestations of his idealization of printing was the admirable characteristics he concentrated on when writing about Caxton, Moxon, Plantin, Aldus, and other worthies among his forebears. De Vinne always had in his mind the goal of returning "the printer of good books [to] the place he once had as a member of the learned professions."[27]

PRINTER TO THE CENTURY COMPANY

It was widely known that Theodore De Vinne, supreme commercial printer of his day, was "Printer to the Century Company," as the terra cotta legend near the front door of the De Vinne Press Building announced. With the acquisition of their business, De Vinne's firm aligned itself with what would become one of the culturally significant and commercially successful enterprises of its day. It was a happy arrangement, allowing De Vinne the freedom and financial security to pursue the many activities that caught his interest. Century Company printing alone, Frank Hopkins observed, would have supported a thriving business.

Nearly everyone agrees that at the peak of their relationship there was some sort of symbiosis at work between Century and De Vinne. The parallel with the bond forged between English publisher William Pickering and the Whittinghams of the Chiswick Press has been noted by more than one commentator. The publishers aspired to the best quality; De Vinne rose to – even welcomed – the challenge. On another level, De Vinne contributed to and reveled in the intellectual camaraderie he enjoyed with Century editors and executives. It fed and stimulated his natural curiosity. He even toured Europe with his Century colleagues. In the words of Ira Brainerd,

> Such clients as Roswell Smith and his lieutenants were the very sort that fitted De Vinne, for they were trained and cultured men, abreast of the times and ambitious; no printer with ideals and experience and a hunger for progress in the craft and in business could ask better.[28]

Frank Hopkins said that the company of these high-class gentlemen reflected as much glory on the De Vinne Press as the press brought to them.

Carl Rollins noted more recently that "the success of the Century Company's publications was due to an unusual degree of sympathy and intimacy between printer and customer."[29] There is evidence, however, that Century officers may have considered themselves De Vinne's "employers" rather than his "customers."[30] There was an internal Century Company story that at some early meeting Roswell Smith had said, "Do you know, Mr. De Vinne, what I am proposing to do? I am proposing to make you the foremost printer of your time." William W. Ellsworth, who had spent his entire working life at Century and who was related to Roswell Smith by marriage, went even further and said that "Roswell Smith made out of a blank-book manufacturer an expert who wrote . . . many books on typography."[31]

Ellsworth's hyperbolic comment was off the mark; De Vinne was considerably more than a stationer and had already started studying and writing when the relationship with the magazine publisher was initiated. What Smith did do was provide a steady volume of business and make possible a facility in which to produce it – no insignificant gesture. Ellsworth also claimed that De Vinne had wanted to name his press "The Roswell Smith Press" when he acquired the balance of it from the Hart estate. This notion seems improbable, despite De Vinne's close and deferential relationship with Smith.

De Vinne and Smith were nearly the same age (De Vinne being three months older) but there was ample reason for deference. Their acquaintance began when De Vinne was still Hart's junior partner – a craftsman with minimal formal education. Roswell Smith had studied English at Brown and had read law, establishing himself in its practice and amassing enough capital to launch a magazine.

At the same time, deference seemed to flow both ways. In time the Century staff "high and low" showed De Vinne great respect, and he was recognized as "an important member, indeed as a comrade" of the "circle who built St. Nicholas and Century." When De Vinne received honorary degrees from Columbia and Yale Universities in 1901, *Century* editors could hardly contain their pride in "our printer."[32]

Even though De Vinne may have been somewhat more reserved than the top personnel at the Century Company, there was much about them to which he could relate. President Roswell Smith was a leader of the Congregational Club, though he remained a member of the Presbyterian church where his good friend, the Rev. S. D. Robinson, was pastor. He began every staff meeting with a prayer. In any crisis, he simply did his best and then trusted to Providence – much like De Vinne. His first editor, Josiah Gilbert Holland, was, in essence, a lay preacher. Holland's successor, Richard Watson Gilder, was, like De Vinne, the son of a Methodist minister; and Gilder maintained a strong personal piety even after becoming an agnostic in later life. At times, the meetings of the Century staff must have resembled a family at worship. As for De Vinne, if he continued the religious tradition of his father, he was a rather undemonstrative parishioner; none of the pieces written about him mention church participation. But his *modus vivendi* (being a model Old Testament patriarch and always going the New Testament extra mile) suggests that he had internalized the values of evangelical Protestantism and had no difficulty communicating, if not communing, with the Century officers.

Century Magazine's obituary of Theodore De Vinne was full of loving praise for the integrity, skill, and ingenuity of a longtime comrade. There was no hint that the publishers had grown dissatisfied with his firm. Ira Brainerd, Century trustee at the time of De Vinne's death and one of his pallbearers, could have shed light on the relationship but instead called it a "great friendship, close and tested, of nearly forty years." Frank Hopkins said, tantalizingly, in his memoirs that there was a story behind De Vinne's relationship with the Century Company "too long to detail here."[33]

Speculation aside, Theodore De Vinne's partnership with the Century Company was central to the development of his career. Being printer of *Century Magazine* helped build his prestige within the printing fraternity while his articles in that magazine introduced him to the general reading public; as Century's business expanded, it provided steady, long-term employment of his facilities; the De Vinne Press Building was financed largely by the president of Century; association with the Century crowd provided a background and social context in which De Vinne worked; printing for the Century Company made it both possible and imperative that De Vinne experiment with new techniques and materials; and, finally, the erosion of that special relationship led, in part, to the demise of his printing house. As dedicated as he was from the outset, he may well have been able to achieve financial and technical success through other means – even without Roswell Smith. (Indeed, as noted earlier, he was creatively expanding his business and establishing a customer base before that relationship began.) But, as it happened, De Vinne truly was "Printer to the Century Company."

MECHANIC

All printing, of no matter what quality, combines technical skill and aesthetic judgments. Strictly speaking, the two cannot be separated; mechanical expertise always affects physical appearance, and design requirements often inspire technical innovation. De Vinne himself said, "There is no good art that is not based upon good mechanics."[34] Or, as John Kristensen more felicitously paraphrased it at the 1999 annual conference of the American Printing History Association, "There is no art without craft."

Everyone agrees on one point: De Vinne's reputation rested largely on the technical excellence of his work. His greatest overall contribution was to take emerging mass-production techniques and adapt them to finer work. At his death, it could be said legitimately that, with the single exception of machine composition, "there is no department of printing, as now practiced, that does not owe something substantial to the persevering industry and insight of Mr. De Vinne."[35]

It is not a simple matter to document precisely what innovations should be credited to him. His personal style was so modest that his many writings on technological change omit what part he had played. There is no better example of this than an article he wrote for *Century Magazine*, titled "The Printing of 'The Century,'" whose unassuming tone caused Richard Watson Gilder to comment on the editorial page,

> The progress made during the lifetime of *The Century* [in its mechanical development] has been owing very largely to [Mr. De Vinne's] own skill, energy, and patience in experiment. In the interesting article he has written, nothing is said of this; but it would ill become us not to make here and now such public acknowledgment.[36]

If one reason for De Vinne's reticence was his innate modesty, another was his belief that invention and innovation are impossible until the underlying arts are in place, so that one development depends upon and is encouraged by many others – indeed that technological progress as an organic, evolutionary, almost inevitable force punctuated by occasional flashes of human cleverness. Late in life he expressed an interest in writing an article on this theme titled "The Age – Not the Man – Invents."[37]

The office in which De Vinne acquired the rudiments of his trade was rudimentary indeed. Yet he took his training to heart and years later referred to his apprenticeship fondly; it had provided a solid basis for his career. His first technical challenge as a journeyman was the struggle to get better work out of Hart's cylinder press. Contemporary sources agree that "fine printing on cylinder presses was considered impossible [until the Hart firm] persisted in experiments, and finally discovered how to make a form ready and produce good job work [on the cylinder] without needless wear of type."[38]

Two other advances in printing methods with which De Vinne was associated – advances that were necessary for the production of high-circulation periodicals – were the shift from dampened to dry paper and from soft to hard packing. He admitted that his *Scribner's* was the first magazine to develop this new, speedier method of production and that its example was "ably followed by *Harper's*, the *Cosmopolitan*, and others." However, rather than indulge in self-praise, he described this innovation as a natural outgrowth of other developments. In the decades of the 1840s, he said, the Yankee and Gillman card presses took card printing away from the handpress. Soon the Ruggles and Gordon presses revolutionized other kinds of job printing. They not only printed faster than handpresses but better; and the best results were obtained by printing on dry, rather than dampened, paper and against the hard packing of glazed mill boards, rather than woolen or other elastic surfaces. "This method of printing on dry paper was afterward utilized on cylinder-presses," De Vinne wrote, "and applied with great success to fine woodcuts. The success of American magazines is largely due to the dry-paper method of printing illustrations."[39]

It was the printing of illustrations, of course, that allowed De Vinne to leverage Hart & Co. out of the ranks of mere job printers. His meticulous printing of wood engravings (although he deplored the effort and expense) became an important element of his reputation. And openness to automated techniques kept him in the forefront.

The mere volume of his business, particularly the monthly periodicals and the mammoth dictionary, fed De Vinne's interest in more powerful and efficient presses. As a result, he experimented with existing equipment and inspired press manufacturers – particularly R. Hoe & Co. – to make modifications, all the while focused on maintaining the quality of presswork on which his reputation depended.

All his life De Vinne was curious about technological advances and looked for ways to apply them to his work. He marveled at the power of electricity, for instance. In 1903 he recalled,

> About sixty years ago, during my last term at school, I attended its lectures on natural philosophy, and there saw for the first time what we now would call a crude electrical apparatus. I wondered, as did my schoolmates, at the incessant but fruitless activity of the machine. One of us asked the teacher if it were not possible to put this activity to some practical use. The teacher said, as yet, . . . we must consider this and other exhibits of electrical apparatus as scientific toys without practical value.

Within a few decades electrical generators sent light, heat, and power to whole cities. And, in his own printing house, every day a "humming little dynamo" generated an "unseen power which was liberating atoms of copper finer and purer than those obtained by fire heat." [40] Indeed, electrotype plates – essential in an age of large editions – provided an economical surrogate for delicate wood engravings, saved type from wear, freed up composed type for other use, and waited in storage to be used for reprints. In his constant search for better, more efficient uses of existing technology, he speculated about the creation of an electrotype plate that contained the full page rather than just the text block.

A much better way would be to fasten the electrotype shell in a steel mold, to exhaust the air from that mold and to cast the plate to the exact size, including head margin, with the bevels, so that the plate would be as finished as a type when that comes from a mold. I do not see my way clearly to do it, but I believe it will be done before the century is out.[41]

As one would expect, he also innovated in the composing room. Consider his type stands that brought many cases to the compositor's reach for such complex works as the *Century Dictionary*. When he pictured them in *Modern Methods of Book Composition* in 1904, he labeled the illustrations merely "The De Vinne stand" and "The De Vinne case." Whereas he gave explicit personal credit in the text of *Modern Methods* to John Polhemus and Thomas Rooker for innovations they had made in type stands and cases, only in the index was he bold enough to say "De Vinne, Theodore Low, dictionary stand and cases designed by." Perhaps he felt his credit for this invention had been established adequately in the trade.

Mechanical typesetting was the one technical advance during his lifetime for which he showed little enthusiasm. The De Vinne Press had typesetting machinery at least from 1891 on,[42] and he did include a chapter on machine composition in his 1904 *Modern Methods of Book Composition* (contributed by Philip T. Dodge, president of the Mergenthaler Linotype Company). He even wrote a testimonial letter for the Mergenthaler, which they printed as a broadside.[43] But De Vinne acknowledged the limitations of these machines that could "do no more than set type. They cannot read proof, correct, make up, impose, do stone-work, or even set up the more difficult kinds of book composition, which are done now by hand as they have been for more than four hundred years."[44] Machine composition did create a shortcut, but the more important judgments of composition still depended on human expertise.

Despite this reservation, he was a great promoter of mechanization. He held that "a needless magic surrounds the phrase handmade" – that the result, not the method of manufacture, determines the quality and worth of any object. He disagreed with John Ruskin and William Morris that handwork would redeem the laborer. Far from threatening the status of workers, he believed machines actually improved their lives by releasing them from the drudgery of heavy and monotonous work, by lowering prices, and by increasing production, efficiency, and ultimately wages.[45]

Schooled in hand methods but open to the efficacy of the machine, De Vinne could contemplate with apparent equanimity a day when the printing business as he knew it – even his revered hand-set type – would no longer exist. He wrote with remarkable prescience in 1894:

> It may be that in the coming century all our children will be taught shorthand along with the Roman alphabet. It may be that the authors of books, or editors of newspapers, instead of writing out their copy, may talk to the phonograph, and this phonograph may be transmuted by typewriters into a readable shorthand, and this shorthand may be photo-engraved and electrotyped and set to press and printed without the use of a single type. Stranger things have happened. I can even imagine the possibility of the web press and all forms of presswork being abolished and the typewritten copy printed by some cheap and quick system of photography.[46]

ARTIST

It is difficult to consider De Vinne's work without peering backward through the twentieth-century fine-printing movement. And those who have expected America's most prominent nineteenth-century commercial printer to exhibit private-press sensibilities have been disappointed. This biography tries not to use that yardstick but instead to measure De Vinne's achievements against his own goals and the work of his contemporaries. Writing about the 1865–1915 period – almost exactly the years of De Vinne's maturity – Howard Mumford Jones said, "In sum, the period did not exist as an imperfect prophecy of the twentieth-century; it lived in its own right."[47] It is in this spirit that we can most fairly discuss De Vinne's aesthetics.

To modern connoisseurs, relatively few of De Vinne's books beg to be fondled or enshrined. But when the book collector's interest begins to flicker, that of the social historian is kindled. How is it that this practical printer grew to care so much about the aesthetics of the printed page? What motivated him to lobby his fellow printers to avoid Victorian excesses and study historical models? Most of all, why did he step out of the workaday path followed by other members of his age cohort in the nineteenth-century printing trade?

Biographical study of the two dozen most prominent New York City book-and-job printers of De Vinne's generation shows notable similarities: modest family circumstances, apprenticeships in small northeastern towns before coming to New York City, working as journeymen printers while saving money to open their own businesses, building their shops into companies that produced comfortable livelihoods.[48] They included such printers as Corydon A. Alvord, R. Harmer Smith, Wesley Washington Pasko, John Polhemus, Joseph J. Little, Charles H. Cochrane, Douglas Taylor, Charles Francis, Martin B. Brown, John F. Trow, John J. Hallenbeck, and Howard Lockwood. If their names strike no chord with the reader, it is not because they are absent from the record; it is because they left printing very much as they found it. Howard Lockwood did publish several printing trade journals, and Pasko edited the 1894 *American Dictionary of Printing and Bookmaking* (which cribbed copiously from a willing and supportive De Vinne). But not one of them took serious interest in printing aesthetics.

As for the pantheon of American fine printing, one has only to look at their dates to see that this was the generation *after* De Vinne's: D. B. Updike (1860–1941), Frederic W. Goudy (1865–1947), Will Bradley (1868–1962), Bruce Rogers (1870–1957), John Henry Nash (1871–1947), W. A. Dwiggins (1880–1956), Carl P. Rollins (1880–1960), T. M. Cleland (1880–1964), and Will Ransom (1883–1949). It is ahistorical to expect Theodore De Vinne (1828–1914) to foresee how this "heroic generation," to use Susan Thompson's term,[49] would be transformed by the example of William Morris – or to be in sympathy with that generation's interpretations.

It may be instructive to review what De Vinne said on the subject of printing aesthetics – a particularly recurrent theme in his later writings. First of all, he recognized the difficulty of establishing a set of universal, timeless criteria for judging printed works.

> Who is the judge of good taste? When the critic says that a title [page] is in bad taste, to what court of last resort can he appeal? The good taste of the last is the bad taste of this century, yet there are mannerisms of early printers, subsequently discarded for their gross impropriety, that are now in favor as exhibits of the highest taste.[50]

Or, on another occasion,

> [T]he number of persons who are continually creating something new is as great as it was in the days of St. Paul, when some Greek put up a tablet to the unknown God. In art, science, philosophy, architecture, music, and almost every manifestation of human development there are strivings for some unknown god of good taste. And that brings us back to the question: What is good taste? Every century sees some changes in type. Some are for the better, some are not. But the desire for something new, something in fashion, is always present.[51]

De Vinne recognized a distinction between fads and more lasting principles. He believed "that printing is the architecture of words, and that it should be controlled by rules of symmetry and proportion that govern all kinds of construction, and that never will go out of fashion."[52] He admitted to Robert Underwood Johnson that to many printers he was "more than a heretic on the subject of advanced or artistic typography."[53]

Central to De Vinne's canon of good taste were the related laws of simplicity and legibility. "I believe that simplicity is beauty," he said. "I believe that the plainest types are the most beautiful types."[54] Simplicity meant the restrained use of display, that is, employing spare decoration or none at all to accompany a text, avoiding the combination of numerous unrelated typefaces in one work, and steering clear of the ornamental display faces so frequently used in Victorian times.

Regarding the first of these issues, that of decoration (as distinct from illustration), De Vinne advised young printers that a book's design (though he did not use that word) should agree with its subject matter. A book "addressed to the thinking and reasoning faculties of a mature reader" should have no decoration at all. Books for young students could have the severity of typography modified, still without decoration, however. "Bold display, eccentric lettering, and fanciful arrangements are attractive in certain kinds of job-work, but they are out of order in any book intended for a permanent place on the library shelf." Only books "classified under the name of light reading, not intended for study, but for amusement or information" should receive decoration. "Even when ornament is ordered," he advised, "there should be a leaning toward simplicity. Appropriateness should be considered. Eccentricities that are pleasing in one book may be positively tawdry in another." Above all, "types that represent words and thought must have first place; ornamentation of any kind should be subordinate."[55]

It was characteristic of job work in De Vinne's day to combine as many different faces of type as possible to attract attention. Sometimes this "jobishness" found its way onto title pages, a practice that De Vinne – in his maturity – abhorred. Even in advertising, however, he urged that both type and style be plain. "Now and then one may make a hit by some audacious arrangement, but where one succeeds ten fail."[56] "The advertiser who uses a harlequin typographic dress to attract notice," he warned, "will discover sooner or later that he drives away more buyers than he draws to him."[57]

Ornamented typefaces were particularly subject to De Vinne's disdain. Are letters "weights, measures of defined and unvarying value to be known at a glance," he asked, "or are they bits of putty, to be molded by caprice or ignorance into fantastic forms of uncertain meaning?" His whole life centered on arranging type. "I should know all the letters, but I have to confess that I stumble often over mysterious characters that I never have seen before, and hope never to see again."[58]

De Vinne felt that for the text of a book, the foremost purpose of any printing was to convey the author's thoughts. Hence, legibility was primary. This was why he despised ornamented and fanciful faces and cared not at all for gothic, black-letter types (which held sway in Germany for centuries). It was also the reason he preferred certain roman types over others and the typographic style he dubbed "masculine" over a more delicate "feminine" style. De Vinne used this gender nomenclature as early as 1873.[59] Twenty years later, keeping to this theme, he explained in some detail that by masculine he meant, "all printing that is noticeable for its readability, for its strength and absence of useless ornament," and that feminine printing was that "noticeable for its delicacy . . . as well as for its profusion of ornamentation."[60] In some of De Vinne's earliest writing he complained, "We have carried the refinements of letter cutting almost to invisibility; the hair-line of modern type is really an illustration of the mathematical axiom that a line has extension but no width."[61] For a collection of pieces by members of the Authors Club, De Vinne constructed a dialogue in which "Senex" and "Juvenis" debate the merits of old-style and modern types.[62] Senex, expressing De Vinne's point of view, says that Bodoni's "faultless curves, sharp lines, and exact angles . . . were disfigurements made at the expense of readability. Types are made to be easily read, not to show the skill of the designer. When they fail in readability the fault is fatal."[63]

De Vinne said he objected to delicate modern faces not only on practical grounds (they were harder to read) and on aesthetic grounds (their weakness was not pleasing to his eye) but also on technical grounds. Previous printing methods – damp paper and elastic impression surfaces – resulted in a deeper bite and thickened the thin strokes of the letter. Modern printing did no such thing; it required type with thicker, not thinner, hairlines to achieve the same results. Punch-cutters, he noted, disregarded the changes in printing methods and strained "after the hair-line that stops just before invisibility"; then pressmen added to the problem by inking with the hardest rollers and giving the scantest possible impression.[64] Noting that the thin lines on the type wore badly, he said that letterpress printers had no business imitating copperplate engraving or lithography. He quoted Ruskin to the effect that, once properly trained, one should do only what can be done easily.

A shallow reading of De Vinne's statements might lead one to conclude that he disliked modern types. Nothing could be further from the truth. It was only the extreme moderns (or moderns badly printed) that displeased him. In practice, he had a fondness for the style of modern that modified the stark angularity and verticality of Continental faces. Most notably, he liked Scotch-face and its variants that in more recent times have been classed as "English moderns" (perhaps more appropriately "British" or "English-language moderns"). Scotch-face was an American term given to types from designs originating in William Miller's foundry in Edinburgh and Alexander Wilson's foundry in Glasgow in the early nineteenth century. The style, produced in various weights and widths by several American founders, gained considerable prominence and was used regularly at the De Vinne Press.

In his 1885 lecture at the Grolier Club, De Vinne described the salient features of the Scotch-face: "The hair-line serif was connected to the body-mark by means of a bracket-like curve, supported by a sloping shoulder, which gave it strength, while it did not rob it of its old lightness and delicacy; . . . the letters were more closely fitted and more compact."[65] He had sung the praises of Scotch-face type in his earliest writing, saying that it was the perfect combination of strength and delicacy.[66] The main thing that differentiates the English modern from the French and Italian modern faces, aside from its prominent brackets, is its more molded shape with thick-thin contrast strong but not abrupt.

Markers that distinguish modern from old-style faces include the curved up-tail on the "R," the tail of the "Q" looped on its left side, prominent beaks on such capitals as "E," "F," "L," and "T," the "C" with no serif on the bottom and almost closed, the bar on the "e" dropped to the middle, the bowl of the "a" enlarged and the letter nearly closed, and round rather than tear-drop-shaped terminals on letters such as the "f" and "r." De Vinne included a simplified chart in his *Plain Printing Types* (fig. 43). (Beatrice Warde gave De Vinne credit for perpetuating "old-style" and "modern-face" nomenclature to describe physical characteristics of type styles rather than to denote their periods of origin.)[67]

"Scotch-face" today usually refers to a narrow face with heavy

F I G . 4 3 .

Modern and
old-style type,
as illustrated
by De Vinne in
*The Practice of
Typography:
Plain Printing
Types*, p. 189.

Old-style and Modern-face   189

A A	a a	N N	n n
B B	b b	O O	o o
C C	c c	P P	p p
D D	d d	Q Q	q q
E E	e e	R R	r r
F F	f f	S S	s s
G G	g g	T T	t t
H H	h h	U U	u u
I I	i i	V V	v v
J J	j j	W W	w w
K K	k k	X X	x x
L L	l l	Y Y	y y
M M	m m	Z Z	z z

capitals that appear prominent in a page of text, but in the nineteenth century the term was used in a more inclusive sense. De Vinne acknowledged this by writing, "The name of Scotch-face was then given by printers, too often inexactly, to every face in which bracketed serifs were joined to sharp hair lines or graceful curves."[68]

De Vinne's 1891 type specimen, *The Roman and Italic Printing Types in the Printing House of Theodore L. De Vinne & Co.*, presents pages of text in the faces he considered "suitable for books, magazines, pamphlets, catalogues, and circulars." It shows "old style and modern cuts of letter" on opposing pages (in different sizes, leaded and not, of different weights and widths) without a hint of any value judgment – except that the face chosen for the title page is *modern*.[69]

De Vinne had a special fondness for Lindsay, a compressed Scotch-face he used frequently for both titles and text; it serves as his last word on the subject, since he chose it for *Notable Printers*. In his own Century Expanded type, even though contrast between thick and thin is moderate (a characteristic he generally preferred for text types), his affinity for Scotch-face type (as the term was used then) is evident. It is particularly apparent in the capitals (fig. 44).

Updike used Scotch-face, calling Alexander Wilson's types "a very

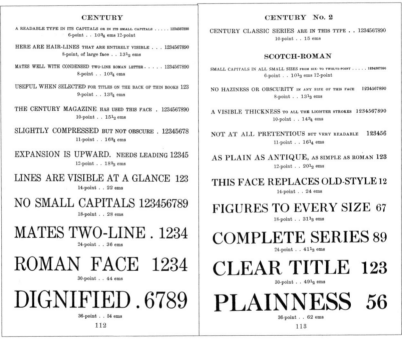

FIG. 44. Century and Scotch-face type from *Types of the De Vinne Press*, 1907, pp. 112, 113.

handsome and serviceable letter."[70] A tally of the types he chose for his work shows that he began to use Scotch-face in 1897 and Monotype Scotch-face in 1935, and that together they were second only to Caslon in prominence among the books he designed.[71] Yet he avoided the high-contrast types De Vinne often employed. This difference in taste may be one reason Updike said that De Vinne "belonged, perhaps, too much to the school of Didot and had too little sympathy with the good elements in that 'revival of printing' which took place during the latter part of his career."[72]

To be sure, De Vinne arrived at his aesthetic convictions over a period of time, saying later in life, "In my youth, I have had the taste that I now condemn."[73] Indeed he did. A selection of title pages he is known to have created shows the evolution of his aesthetic choices. First is the one he composed as an apprentice, *An Outline History of Orange County* (1846-47). The title page copy had some seventy-five words, which the teenager had arranged using numerous typefaces to look much like an advertising broadside of the day.[74] More than half a century later he offered the *Orange County* title page as a model to be avoided[75] (fig. 45).

In *The Invention of Printing* (1876), when he was supplying his own copy, the two-color title page still has a needless verbosity, but it shows at least that De Vinne had learned in the quarter century since *Orange County* how to emphasize the important words typographically (fig. 46). Still, the multiplicity of faces, including some he would later excoriate, places it squarely in its Victorian context.

A decade later, in *Historic Printing Types* (1886), published by the fledgling Grolier Club, he approached the sparer style that would be his choice going forward: one face (or two very similar ones) in three or four sizes to distinguish the importance of various words, symmetrically composed in all capitals (fig. 47). For the text he chose the Lindsay type. The title page is in a compatible but less narrow English modern. For *Title-Pages As Seen by a Printer* (1901) he used his own Renner type and composed the title page in the same style, using the Grolier Club's arms and printing the title of the book in red (fig. 48). The title page of his 1907 type specimen,

AN OUTLINE

HISTORY OF ORANGE COUNTY,

WITH AN

ENUMERATION OF THE NAMES

OF ITS

TOWNS, VILLAGES, RIVERS, CREEKS,

LAKES, PONDS, MOUNTAINS, HILLS AND

OTHER KNOWN LOCALITIES,

AND THEIR

ETYMOLOGIES OR HISTORICAL REASONS THEREFOR;

TOGETHER WITH

LOCAL TRADITIONS

AND SHORT

BIOGRAPHICAL SKETCHES

OF

EARLY SETTLERS, ETC.

BY SAM'L W. EAGER, ESQ.,
MEMBER OF THE HISTORICAL ASSOCIATION OF NEWBURGH, AND
CORRESPONDING MEMBER OF THE HISTORICAL SOCIETY
OF THE STATE OF NEW YORK.

NEWBURGH:
S. T. CALLAHAN,
1846-7.

Reduced facsimile.

FIG. 45. A title page De Vinne composed as an apprentice, here identified as a model to be avoided, *Treatise on Title-Pages*, 1902, p. 216.

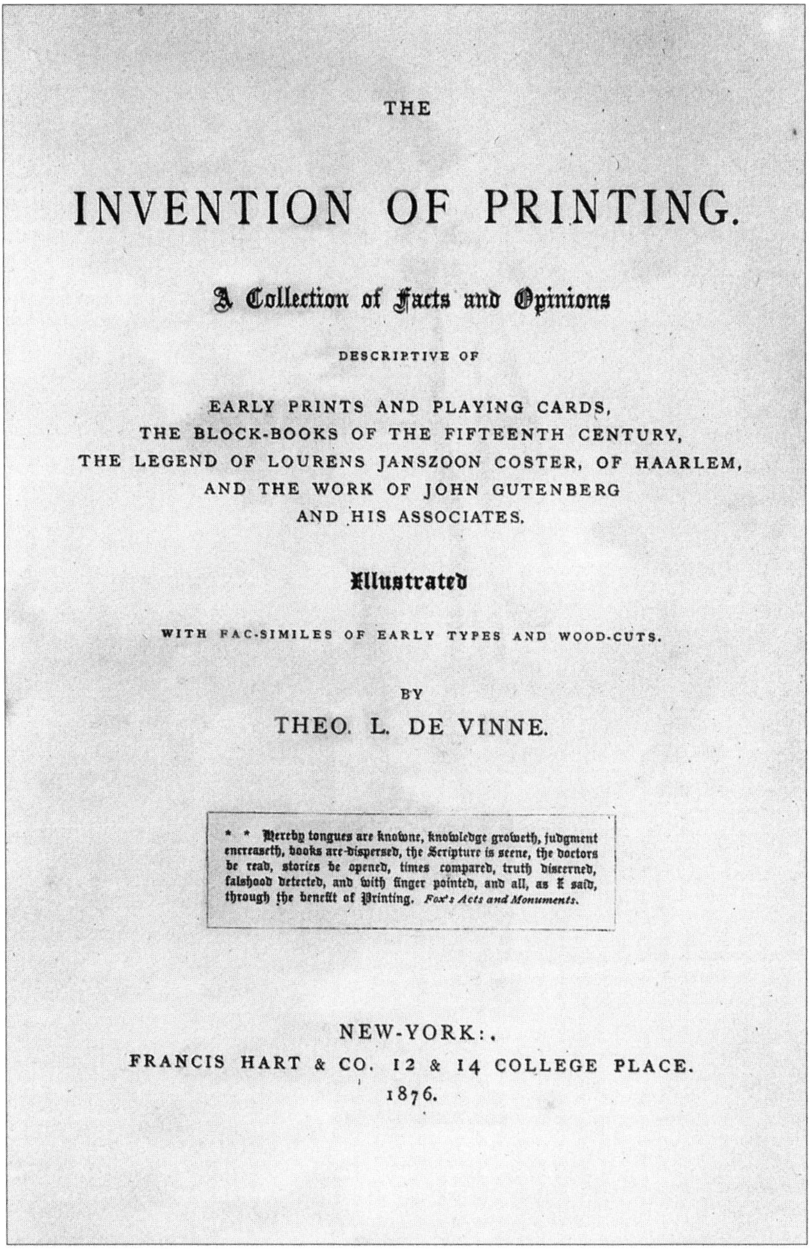

THE

INVENTION OF PRINTING.

A Collection of Facts and Opinions

DESCRIPTIVE OF

EARLY PRINTS AND PLAYING CARDS,
THE BLOCK-BOOKS OF THE FIFTEENTH CENTURY,
THE LEGEND OF LOURENS JANSZOON COSTER, OF HAARLEM,
AND THE WORK OF JOHN GUTENBERG
AND HIS ASSOCIATES.

Illustrated

WITH FAC-SIMILES OF EARLY TYPES AND WOOD-CUTS.

BY

THEO. L. DE VINNE.

> * * Hereby tongues are knowne, knowledge groweth, judgment encreaseth, books are dispersed, the Scripture is seene, the doctors be read, stories be opened, times compared, truth discerned, falshood detected, and with finger pointed, and all, as I said, through the benefit of Printing. *Fox's Acts and Monuments.*

NEW-YORK:
FRANCIS HART & CO. 12 & 14 COLLEGE PLACE.
1876.

FIG. 46. Title page of *The Invention of Printing*, 1876 (9⅜" x 6½"). "Invention of Printing," "Illustrated," and the rule around the Fox quote are in red ink. The "ghost" is offset from the frontispiece depicting "Thorwaldsen's statue of John Gutenberg."

HISTORIC

PRINTING TYPES

A LECTURE

READ BEFORE THE GROLIER CLUB OF NEW-YORK, JANUARY 25, 1885,
WITH ADDITIONS AND NEW ILLUSTRATIONS

BY

THEO. L. DE VINNE

NEW-YORK
THE GROLIER CLUB
MDCCCLXXXVI

FIG. 47. Title page of *Historic Printing Types*, 1886 (10" x 8", untrimmed).

Types of the De Vinne Press: Specimens for the Use of Compositors, Proofreaders and Publishers, returned to the austere arrangement of English modern type, but the effect was softened by the three-color depiction of his printer's device and a frontispiece of the charming and familiar wood engraving of the De Vinne Press Building (plate 8). Similarly, for the Grolier Club's *Scarlet Letter* he chose Lindsay for the text and a title page that was by now practically a De Vinne standard (fig. 49).

As De Vinne said, "One has to study a good many titles, and make many failures before he learns that simplicity is the highest beauty in type."[76]

Perhaps it was natural for De Vinne, who had so much to say about typefaces, to try his hand at type designing. Joseph Blumenthal has written that Century and Renner "seem not to have weathered the tests of fickle time." This is certainly true of Renner, but Century and its progeny have enjoyed a remarkable longevity. De Vinne's considerable writings on type and his attempts to create new faces himself made him an authority in his day. This fact and the durability of the Century type family notwithstanding, type design is not an important element in his reputation today. As Blumenthal aptly summed it up, "There have been relatively few great type designers in the five centuries of the printed book [and] De Vinne, with all his gifts, is not one of the elect."[77]

De Vinne had a wide assortment of customers. Besides the Century Company, whose business kept his presses humming for so many years, a number of other publishers came to him from time to time when there was a limited or otherwise important edition in the offing: Dodd, Mead & Co.; Doubleday; E. P. Dutton; Charles E. Peabody & Co. of Boston; Stone & Kimball of Chicago; Way & Williams, also of Chicago; and even the once-estranged Charles Scribner's Sons, who had their own printing plant but used De Vinne often for finer work. In addition to publishing firms, there were numerous museums, universities, churches, and other cultural institutions that used De Vinne's well-known services. At least two dozen private societies (largely but not exclusively bibliophilic)

TITLE-PAGES
AS SEEN BY A PRINTER

WITH NUMEROUS
ILLUSTRATIONS IN FACSIMILE
AND SOME OBSERVATIONS ON THE EARLY
AND RECENT PRINTING OF BOOKS

BY

THEODORE LOW DE VINNE

THE GROLIER CLUB
OF THE CITY OF NEW YORK
MCMI

FIG. 48. Title page of *Title-Pages As Seen by a Printer*, 1901 (9½" x 6½", untrimmed). "Title-Pages As Seen by a Printer" is in red ink.

THE SCARLET LETTER

BY NATHANIEL HAWTHORNE

ILLUSTRATED BY

GEORGE H. BOUGHTON

THE GROLIER CLUB
OF THE CITY OF NEW YORK
1908

FIG. 49. Title page of *The Scarlet Letter*, 1908 (11" x 7 ½", untrimmed). The title and the Grolier Club's arms are in red ink.

entrusted their publications to his press. He printed many volumes for private individuals, including Archer M. Huntington and William Loring Andrews. Herman Melville took his *John Marr* to De Vinne in 1888 for an edition of twenty-five copies.

The works De Vinne printed for this diverse clientele exhibit no consistent style – not even the conservative one he clearly preferred. There are several reasons for the disparity between his products and his own inclinations.

In the first place, he thought of himself as a "contracting printer" who produced printed material to order. His earliest advice to the person in a printing office taking orders was to let the customer make his own decisions about type, paper, and style.

> Never try to alter or even direct a customer's choice unless specially requested. . . . Let him make his own decision.
>
> If the [customer's] directions are possible of execution, they should be obeyed. The fact that they are inconsistent with a compositor's notions of good taste is quite immaterial. The customer has a right to have his work done in any style he chooses, whether it is tasteful or absurd.[78]

These words are found in that part of De Vinne's *Printers' Price List* where he warned novices about the expense of alterations in proof; it was clearly more economical to suit the customer at the outset. Deference to the customer's wishes remained a constant theme. For example, he advised some changes in the spacing of headings when he saw proofs of a volume of the Doubleday Elizabethan Shakspere [*sic*] series; nevertheless, he told Bothwell, "If author and publisher approve I withdraw objection."[79] Only rarely throughout his career did he suggest that the printer take a less passive role and "try to control the undisciplined taste of his customer."[80]

At one time, De Vinne said, he dreamed of having in his shop only types of which he approved, but he found he had to stock the very faces he condemned "in order to cater to a variety of tastes."[81] Despite clearly stated preferences, his press was not about to lose any business because of a narrow point of view. And, indeed, his type specimens show that Victorian excesses were as available from his shop as from any other. A few months after Francis Hart's death

Legacy

De Vinne produced *Specimens of Old Style Types in the Printing-Office of Francis Hart & Co.* (September 1877), consisting of various sizes of Bruce No. 20 and Bruce Old Style No. 15. This was followed in 1878 by *Specimens of Pointed Texts and Black Letters* and in 1880 by *Specimens of Script and Italic,* the three parts forming one continuously paginated whole of 251 pages. There was nothing exceptional or unexpected in any of these, but in 1883 there appeared *Specimens of Some of the New and Quaint Types Recently Added to Stock . . .,* and this was an extensive sixty-two-page selection of the lavishly ornamented faces De Vinne denounced. Undoubtedly, many were intended only for job work. His 1897 *Old Faces of Roman and Medieval Types Lately Added to the De Vinne Press* (forty-seven pages) included Jenson and Satanick, proof that he did not want to lose out on the William Morris vogue. The title page was set in the Arts-and-Crafts block style (fig. 50). As if to drive the point home, the wrapper has a white-on-black foliated pseudo-Morrissian border (fig. 51).

In the fifty-three-page *Styles of Types for Books and Advertisements Now in Service at the De Vinne Press* of 1905, his Renner face had the pride of place: fourteen pages of examples, including italic and bold, plus running titles throughout in Renner italic. No other face got more than four pages and most were accorded two. But the remarkable aspect of this specimen book is the appearance of drapery borders on the wrapper cover (fig. 52) and some of the Renner sample pages (fig. 53) as well as elaborate gold borders inside the wrappers. Incongruously, the title page is again in the block style of the Arts-and-Crafts book (with a red foliated rectangle initialed "FWG," which can only be Frederick W. Goudy) (fig. 54). This specimen is an excellent illustration of De Vinne's reluctance to impose his taste on his customers.

The 442-page specimen book of 1907, *Types of the De Vinne Press: Specimens for the Use of Compositors, Proofreaders and Publishers,* took the type-specimen genre to a new level. While being an extensive roster of typefaces available at the press, it was also a compendium of typographic information. For years De Vinne

233

OLD FACES OF
ROMAN
AND MEDIEVAL TYPES LATELY ADDED TO THE DE VINNE PRESS

PRINTED AT THE DE VINNE
PRESS, No. 12 LAFAYETTE
PLACE ... NEW-YORK ... 1897

FIG. 50. Title page of the 1897 De Vinne Press type specimen (9½" x 6½"). The shaded box is in light brown ink.

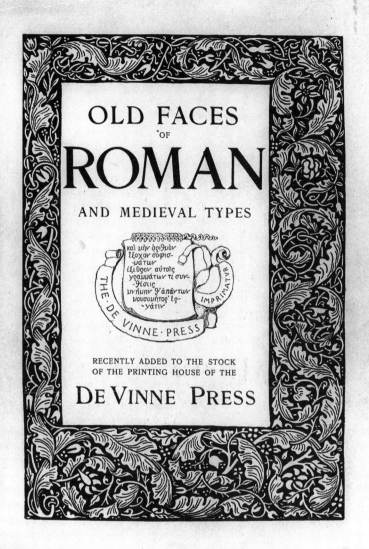

OLD FACES

OF

ROMAN

AND MEDIEVAL TYPES

καὶ μὴν ἀριθμὸν
ἔξοχον σοφισ-
μάτων
ἐξιῦρον αὐτοῖς
γραμμάτων τί συν-
θέσις
μνήμην θ'ἀπάντων
μουσομήτορ' ἐρ-
γάτιν

THE·DE·VINNE·PRESS

IMPRIMATVR

RECENTLY ADDED TO THE STOCK
OF THE PRINTING HOUSE OF THE

DE VINNE PRESS

FIG. 51. Cover of the 1897 De Vinne Press type specimen.

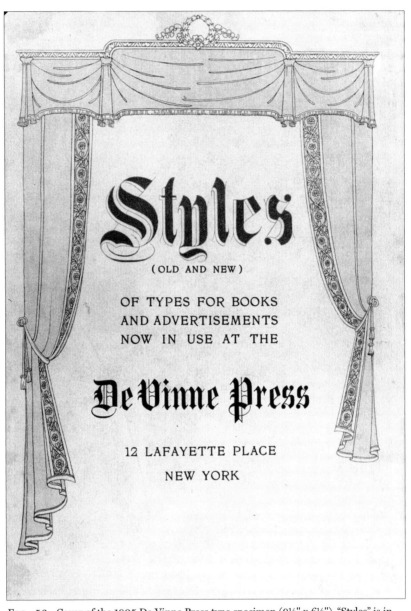

FIG. 52. Cover of the 1905 De Vinne Press type specimen (9½" x 6½"). "Styles" is in red ink; the curtains are brown and pale green.

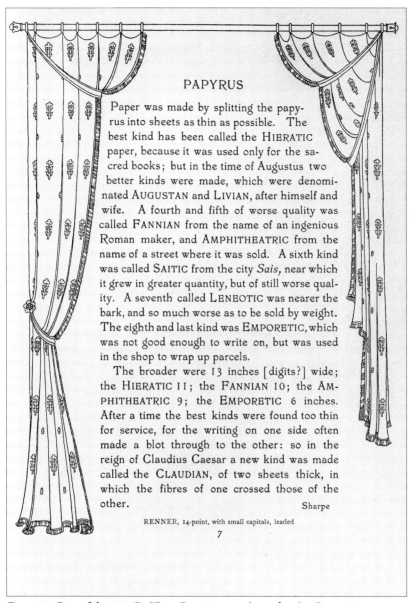

PAPYRUS

Paper was made by splitting the papyrus into sheets as thin as possible. The best kind has been called the HIERATIC paper, because it was used only for the sacred books; but in the time of Augustus two better kinds were made, which were denominated AUGUSTAN and LIVIAN, after himself and wife. A fourth and fifth of worse quality was called FANNIAN from the name of an ingenious Roman maker, and AMPHITHEATRIC from the name of a street where it was sold. A sixth kind was called SAITIC from the city *Sais,* near which it grew in greater quantity, but of still worse quality. A seventh called LENEOTIC was nearer the bark, and so much worse as to be sold by weight. The eighth and last kind was EMPORETIC, which was not good enough to write on, but was used in the shop to wrap up parcels.

The broader were 13 inches [digits?] wide; the HIERATIC 11; the FANNIAN 10; the AMPHITHEATRIC 9; the EMPORETIC 6 inches. After a time the best kinds were found too thin for service, for the writing on one side often made a blot through to the other: so in the reign of Claudius Caesar a new kind was made called the CLAUDIAN, of two sheets thick, in which the fibres of one crossed those of the other.   Sharpe

RENNER, 14-point, with small capitals, leaded

7

FIG. 53. Page of the 1905 De Vinne Press type specimen showing Renner type.

had collected quotations having to do with books and printing; these he had used in previous type specimens. But this one drew more than ever upon his own great storehouse of knowledge of typographic history.

De Vinne said a printer should flatly refuse, without apology or explanation, to print anything scurrilous, fraudulent, or otherwise morally or legally questionable, a principle Hopkins said De Vinne followed religiously. However, he apparently never refused work simply because the requested style offended him. He suggested another solution instead: the printer could omit his imprint.[82]

A second reason it is difficult to identify a "De Vinne style" is that he had no qualms about delegating responsibility. Although he was very active up through the 1880s, by the mid-1890s he was no longer spending a full day at the office even when he was in town. During much of its heyday – although certainly produced by the staff he had personally trained – the press's works, as Hopkins testified, were sometimes seen by the proprietor only after completion.

De Vinne's ideas were formed in a period before the profession of "book designer" was established. Both the term and the concept were still developing; even the private presses initially used the expression "supervisor" rather than the more autocratic "designer." In commercial printing, design was a group responsibility with printer, publisher, and author each having a voice. Indeed, art-conscious bibliophilic societies such as the Grolier Club designed their publications in committee. However, the trend toward one-person design was certainly discernible, and De Vinne was not in sympathy if that meant an outside "expert" was going to dictate to the printer. He looked askance at the "typographic designer . . . who claims that he is a qualified artist with type."[83]

Thirdly, De Vinne believed that no printer, type designer, or other participant in the creation of a book should impose his personality upon the work, the main objective of which was to convey the author's thoughts. This conviction certainly set him apart from the turn-of-the-century private-press movement in which artistic expression was paramount and the text was often entirely subordinate.

STYLES

OF TYPES FOR BOOKS
AND ADVERTISEMENTS
NOW IN SERVICE AT

No. 12 LAFAYETTE PLACE
IN THE CITY OF NEW YORK

FIG. 54. Title page of the 1905 De Vinne Press type specimen. The foliated box is in red ink.

Finally, there is no "De Vinne style" (apart from "good, honest and plain workmanship") because he did not view artistry as separate from good technique. Indeed, he would object to our considering him separately as mechanic and artist. "Art is one of the most flexible words in the English language," he said. He looked forward to the day when "the making of a good book, *from the mechanical point of view* [emphasis added], will be regarded as an achievement quite as worthy as the painting of a good picture" – when Venus will be "wedded, not to Apollo the poet, but to Vulcan the mechanic."[84]

De Vinne was a careful printer. He would not have endorsed (or perhaps even understood) this distinction made later by Stanley Morison:

> The *fine* printer begins where the careful printer has left off. For "fine" printing something is required in addition to care – certain vital gifts of the mind and understanding. Only when these are added to a knowledge of the technical processes will there result a piece of design, i.e., a work expressing logic, consistency and personality.[85]

If De Vinne's work leaves no clear, consistent style to be followed, the thrust of his life was nevertheless an argument against the excesses of his predecessors and contemporaries. How he arrived at those notions, so contrary to the prevailing practices, bears some examination. He was trained in the debased mid-nineteenth-century style known to his master, small-town printer S. T. Callahan. His judgment on the questions of ornamentation and elaborate display apparently began to take shape while he was still apprenticed in Newburgh, New York. Writing in the early 1890s, he said "some forty-five years ago" Newburgh native Andrew Jackson Downing (landscape gardener and arbiter of taste on domestic architecture) had drawn a pen across a title page of a catalogue the young De Vinne had composed, giving him these words of advice: "Let me give you a good rule, my lad; it is an old architect's rule, which will hold good forever. You may ornament construction; you must not construct ornament."[86]

Another influence nudging De Vinne away from the excesses of his day was his early habit of referring to older printing. While still an apprentice, he had begun to examine every old book he could get his hands on. His lifelong habit of collecting and studying models of his forebears helped him form judgments as to what had lasting appeal.

A more specific influence was the Chiswick Press. Through both his admiration for the work done during the Pickering-Whittingham period and his friendship with the later managing partner Charles T. Jacobi, De Vinne absorbed and incorporated ideas of restraint and appreciation for old-style type. Although De Vinne met Jacobi (a younger man by twenty-five years) only in the 1890s during a trip to Europe when his notions were well formed, Jacobi reported that De Vinne had long been an admirer of the Chiswick Press. He said De Vinne visited him on subsequent trips to London and that they corresponded almost up to the time of De Vinne's death in 1914.[87]

De Vinne also made his affinity with the Chiswick style clear in his own writings.[88] Aside from any transfer of ideas about printing, there are a number of interesting parallels between the two houses. Printer Charles Whittingham (1795–1876) was proud of his thorough knowledge of the particulars of printing and never hesitated to let his men see him "at case." His workmen were craftsmen rather than run-of-the-mill journeymen. He owned one of the best printer's libraries in Europe. He brought John Wilkins, who had been his overseer and his apprentice, into partnership to manage the press (similar to James W. Bothwell's history). He had a long, friendly, productive relationship with publisher William Pickering (the equivalent of Roswell Smith). And he "made his business his pleasure."[89] The correspondence between these facts and those of De Vinne's career is obvious.

A further reason De Vinne leaned toward simplicity had to do with business considerations. He opposed elaborate job composition not only because it tended to be tasteless but also because it was expensive: "Twisted brass rules, curved lines, and the eccentric arrangements of ornamental letters and borders that make job work so horribly expensive, are not in good taste." Further, he asked, "Are we not worshipping false gods? Are not compositors more anxious to show their own skill and ingenuity than to carry out the intent of a book or pamphlet? Are we not making printing needlessly expensive?"[90]

Finally, the style of printing he advocated was, quite simply, consistent with his personality. Nurtured by humble Methodist tradition, it emphasized utility and the lack of display for its own sake. Printing was fundamentally a service – a means of conveying the thoughts of the author to the reader. This was to be accomplished by using the most practical available method; relief printing needed to concentrate on what it could do well. The best printing was the most readable printing (a principle he no doubt believed in more than ever as his own eyesight dimmed).

As difficult as it is to assess De Vinne's work without considering the products of the private press movement that blossomed toward the end of his life, it is inappropriate to expect De Vinne – a distinctly nineteenth-century person – to share or anticipate the sensibilities of this later generation of artists in the book. He said himself, "I am not an amateur nor a theorist, nor a reformer nor a teacher of new notions about typography. I am a pupil of the old school."[91] As such, he viewed the world "over the top of his type-case," as William Dana Orcutt phrased it, and that view was necessarily restricted.[92]

Although De Vinne did not lead the way aesthetically into the new century, fine-printing practitioners who followed him tended to appreciate the benign influence of his conservative proselytizing as valuable groundwork. Peripatetic California fine printer John Henry Nash claimed significant direct inspiration from De Vinne during the three years he spent in New York City after the 1906 San Francisco fire.[93] (And when he later assembled a typographic library modeled on Bullen's American Type Founders Library and Museum, De Vinne was among the printers, including the likes of Gutenberg and Bodoni, of whom Nash commissioned Henry Raschen to paint oil portraits for his offices in San Francisco.)

Updike likewise included a portrait of De Vinne and an image of the De Vinne Press Building in his elaborately decorated offices. And as late as 1940, the year before his death, Updike was still quoting De Vinne on the principles of appropriate typographic design.[94] Even though he found De Vinne's aesthetic powers of discrimination limited, he revered De Vinne for his historical knowledge and technical expertise. Stanley Morison felt Updike owed a significant debt to De Vinne.[95]

In 1933 typographer Frederic W. Goudy reprinted De Vinne's Senex and Juvenis piece of 1896. In his introduction, Goudy said,

> If I were asked to say what I think has been the greatest single influence in my work as a type designer I would be hard put to find a satisfactory reply; but there is no doubt in my mind that the principles set forth in this article and in his book "Notable Printers of Italy during the 15th Century" have certainly loomed large in crystallizing the character of my types. The consistency of thought he displayed, his sound knowledge of old types, his fairness in the consideration of each moot point, the simple yet lucid presentation of his ideas and opinions interested me; they influenced my own thought, and in turn are reflected in my work.

Goudy conceded that in his "more mature consideration" of the Senex-Juvenis debate he felt that Senex should have stressed the need for "greater grace and beauty in types" but that "readability is of course to be considered above every other quality, because, failing that it fails utterly, regardless of every other excellence."[96]

British typographer Stanley Morison cited De Vinne as an early influence on his own thought and said that De Vinne, "as a distinguished printer, type-designer and historian of the printing craft, was responsible for bringing back the realisation in America of the need for care and skilful application of the craft to produce good books." Morison's biographer, James Moran, noted the presence of De Vinne's spirit in Morison's much-reprinted "First Principles of Typography." Nothing could be more in tune with De Vinne's priorities:

> Typography is the efficient means to an essentially utilitarian and only accidentally aesthetic end, for enjoyment of patterns is rarely the reader's chief aim. Therefore, any disposition of printing material which, whatever the intention, has the effect of coming between author and reader is wrong.[97]

Few fine commercial printers' careers parallel De Vinne's sufficiently to suggest close comparison. Walter Gilliss (1855–1925) and Daniel Berkeley Updike (1860–1941) are the best candidates. Both produced a more consistently well-designed body of imprints, yet neither operated on De Vinne's scale. Updike's Merrymount Press seldom employed more than thirty people at one time[98]; at its peak, the De Vinne Press had as many as three hundred employees. Even if De Vinne had wished to maintain strict design control, it would have been difficult on that scale. Updike, who shared none of De Vinne's deep knowledge or love of the printing process itself, operated on the premise that he would only work within the range of what appealed to his finely tuned taste, hence the greater aesthetic consistency of his oeuvre. Although both men were autodidacts passionately interested in the history of typography, the two could hardly have been more different in background and temperament. De Vinne and Updike were, respectively, low-church Methodist and Episcopalian; son of an immigrant father and descendant of a prominent Providence family; an apprentice to a very physical trade at fourteen and a self-chosen designer of printed matter at age thirty-three from experience in publishing; eager participant in the evolution of printing technology and fundamentally uninterested in the printing process itself; one who plugged away at the duties ahead and a proponent of working hard while having fun (the origin of the Merrymount Press's name); and, again, born in 1828 and 1860. It hardly seems surprising that the bodies of work they left behind differ substantially.

Gilliss was in the first batch of non-founding members to be elected to the Grolier Club in February 1884. Later that year he began a five-year partnership with fellow Grolierite Arthur B. Turnure, printing *The Art Age*, one of the first periodicals to encompass the graphic arts. The Gilliss Press shared the Grolier Club's incidental and job printing with De Vinne. But Gilliss also established a book-printing business. He printed catalogues for the Metropolitan Museum of Art. He developed a friendship with William Loring Andrews and took up the printing of the great bibliophile's works after De Vinne had printed the first six. Like De Vinne, Walter Gilliss was fully aware of the enthusiasm Morris set in motion, but he maintained his own established conservative style. Certainly his modest body of work was more distinguished than the wide-ranging output of the De Vinne Press; yet Gilliss did not make a business success of his enterprise, being forced to auction most of his equipment in 1908. He went on to a successful career as a typographic adviser to Doubleday, Page & Co. and other publishers and continued to produce books with the Gilliss Press imprint, including a number for the Grolier Club.

Gilliss also wrote about printing but without De Vinne's depth. The two men were colleagues in the Typothetae, where Gilliss took special interest in De Vinne's Moxon reprint project. In 1924 the *New York Times* covered the Grolier Club's "printer's series" in which the club published six books (1921–1924), each the work of a noted American printer or designer. Gilliss, then the club secretary, wrote an impassioned letter to the *Times* objecting to its lack of mention in the article of "the great De Vinne".

> It was due in great measure to the knowledge and skill of Mr. De Vinne as a Printer and his prestige as a leader of the Printing Art in this country that the publications of the Club from the time of its founding in 1884 began to claim wide attention, and it was largely through the commanding position in the trade which he held so long, that the revival of printing which was begun by him, and continued by his followers (largely exemplified by the publications of the Club), that the Printing Art in this country stands where it does today.[99]

It has been said of English artist Eric Gill that he "was a child of his time, naturally formed by the aesthetic background of his youth and early manhood. So, indeed, one could say of all the great designers and typographers of the 1920s and 1930s."[100] So, indeed, one could say of De Vinne. Yet he revolted against the direction nineteenth-century typography had taken and tried to turn it back to earlier and superior models. That was no insignificant contribution to the art of printing.

SCHOLAR AND BIBLIOPHILE

Despite the investment of energy in building up a business, leading New York City's master printers, experimenting with new techniques, codifying trade practices, and campaigning for his conservative code of printing aesthetics, De Vinne found time to indulge in one more passion. He had a deep interest in the history of printing and an urge to share his findings. Approximately one quarter of his published pieces had to do with printing history. In part, De Vinne's interest in early printing was a pragmatic one, not a mere antiquarian interest, and it could not have been stated more clearly than in A. W. Pollard's comment quoted by De Vinne in the preliminaries of *Notable Printers of Italy*: "As a rule we should go to the old printers not so much for models to be slavishly followed as for ideas which can be adopted and improved by modern appliances and modern skill."

Research into typographical history may have been so integral to his outlook on life that it fit seamlessly into his demanding work week. Finding time to write, on the other hand, must have been a challenge to this busy proprietor, especially during the opening hands-on decades of his career. At age thirty-five, in one of his first historical articles, De Vinne pinpointed the moment when this consuming interest began. It dated, he said, from his apprenticeship days when he was obliged to carry copy to an author who fancied himself a connoisseur of books and discussed his acquisitions with the boy. From that time, said De Vinne, "I have been curious in old books, and have never neglected an opportunity of inspecting a bookstall, or of ransacking an old library, and have held many talks with bookish men." He had also "waded through volume after volume of old histories of printing."[101]

Although his formal education was meager, De Vinne came to the task of writing printing history reasonably well equipped. In order to study original sources, he taught himself French, Italian, and German (although he disliked black-letter type so much that he had other people read German aloud to him). He had a systematic intellect, the means to acquire or borrow the pertinent material, and a passion for his subject.

His major historical work, the 1876 *Invention of Printing*, has been discussed above. In it, like his other works of scholarship, he had no desire to be esoteric. He was addressing his fellow printers and the intelligent general public, deliberately avoiding "personal controversies, prolix descriptions of books, extracts in foreign languages, and the verbal criticisms which are of interest to librarians and book-collectors only," as he said in the prospectus.

It was while writing about his printing forebears that De Vinne revealed his passion most eloquently. In 1878 he contributed one of his several pieces to *Scribner's*. In "The First Editor" he told the story of Aldus Manutius, who as a forty-year-old scholar opened a printing office to edit and publish the major Greek and Latin texts. As with Caxton, De Vinne admired Aldus's motives: "He went to printing, because he believed it was his appointed work; it was in the line of his duty as an educator of the people. His way to the teaching of a larger school . . . was through the door of a printing office."

A decade later, in 1888, De Vinne again contributed a piece on the history of printing to *Century Magazine*. "A Printer's Paradise: The Plantin-Moretus Museum at Antwerp" was an account of De Vinne's visit to the museum, enriched with historical information about Christopher Plantin's business that was gleaned in part from archives the museum conservator and scholar Max Rooses made available to him. As he had with Caxton and Aldus, De Vinne took notice of Plantin's personal characteristics, expressing pride in the way Plantin kept his business records, his forbearance in hard times, and his ultimate prosperity as a printer and publisher. The Grolier Club made this *Century* article its eighth official publication, entitled *Christopher Plantin and the Plantin-Moretus Museum at Antwerp*.

Several other works, such as *Plain Printing Types* and *A Treatise on Title-Pages*, had significant sections that drew upon De Vinne's historical scholarship. Other pieces included the 1880 *Scribner's Monthly* article on "The Growth of Woodcut Printing," the first half of which was given to a discussion of the art prior to its mid-nineteenth century revival, after which he shifted into a technical exposition of his overlay methods.

An 1874 trade journal piece, "Old Specimen Books," demonstrated that his interest in the history of his craft was not confined to antiquarianism; he was also curious about the more recent past. This article was a contribution toward an inventory of American type-specimen books. De Vinne described the earliest he was aware of, an 1817 D. & G. Bruce specimen. At the end of the article he noted the discovery of a still earlier one – an 1815 Bruce specimen. Three even earlier ones would be discovered by later printing historians,[102] but De Vinne can only be commended for his instinct to assemble and preserve the artifacts for future historical inquiry, even if his information was incomplete.

De Vinne's last major writing effort, brought to completion when failing eyesight, general declining health, and the loss of his wife all provided a discouraging backdrop, was the 1910 *Notable Printers of Italy During the Fifteenth Century*. It and his 1876 *Invention of Printing* stand as worthy bookends to the rest of his scholarly writing.

In addition to creating original works, there were two instances in which De Vinne organized the reprinting of classics of printing history literature. The first was the Grolier Club's initial publication, *A Decree of Star Chamber*. The second came in 1896 when De Vinne convinced the Typothetae of the City of New York to publish a reprint of Joseph Moxon's *Mechanick Exercises*. As a contribution to historical studies it succeeded; as a fund-raiser for the Typothetae it failed.

Such was De Vinne's scholarly reputation at home and abroad that the Englishmen Bigmore and Wyman chose De Vinne, in addition to Frederik Muller of Amsterdam and Theodor Goebel of Stuttgart, to "examine the proofs and supply corrections and additions" for their three-volume *Bibliography of Printing* (1880–86).[103]

It was natural that De Vinne should turn to writing. Not only was there the example of his father, but there was also the strong author-printer tradition before him. This was particularly true in

England where, for example, John Nichols (1745–1826) had written some sixty books, and where a mere list of the books of Charles Knight (1791–1873), noted Bigmore and Wyman, "occupies above a score of folio pages in the Catalogue of the British Museum."[104] De Vinne's contemporary, William Blades (1824–1890), was also prolific. Interestingly, they were on opposite sides of the Coster-Gutenberg debate. De Vinne's dispassionate, prosaic examination of the evidence contrasts with Blades's agitated score keeping to show which legend had suffered the greatest scholarly blows.[105]

In America, too, some practitioners have also been writers: Isaiah Thomas, Joel Munsell, and typefounder Thomas Mackellar, for instance, as well as De Vinne's contemporaries in the New York City commercial printing environment: Charles Cochrane, W. W. Pasko, and the like. In the next generation D. B. Updike would write his masterful treatise on printing types. None, however, matched De Vinne's scope or quantity. In an era before the writing of history was professionalized and institutionalized, "amateur" historians carried on a strong tradition of examining evidence about the past, and to this De Vinne added a very respectable corpus of work. In addition to citing some seventy standard works on printing history, his writing also abounds with classical and literary allusions – Horace, Byron, Ruskin, Shakespeare, and (not surprisingly) John Wesley.

While a few minor trade journal articles appear to have been written in haste, his printing manuals and works on history show a thorough, organized (if sometimes ponderous) approach. James Bothwell indicated the care De Vinne gave to his more important writings:

> [He] wrote his manuscript in long hand, revised it, had it typed, revised again, and had a fresh copy typed. This he corrected and put in the compositor's hands. Here he parted with his own counsel and had successive proofs and changes, costing, for example, in the case of "Plain Printing Types," double the original composition.[106]

He did the same with the other three *Practice of Typography* volumes – labeling them "pre-edition," "unpublished," or "proof copy." Economy was not the point when it came to improving the text of his own works. If anything, he was excessively cautious. He circulated the finished-looking, bound versions to friends, colleagues, and staff, asking for corrections. On at least one volume, *Modern Methods of Book Composition*, he offered his staff financial incentives: a dollar for identifying minor errors and ten dollars for "serious" errors. Judging by the marked-up copy belonging to De Vinne Press stalwart Camille DeVèze and the notes therein in De Vinne's hand,[107] staff members took up the challenge more eagerly than the author had intended, marking every hint of a broken piece of type as well as more important imperfections. DeVèze complained, "I received $50.00 though I found at least 10 serious [errors]."

In the spring of 1894 De Vinne sent J. W. Phinney a proof copy of *Plain Printing Types*, asking him to review the section on typefounding history. In their very cordial exchange of letters on historic types, De Vinne had to follow up twice, finally offering to go to Boston and "take down the needed corrections from your spoken words." He said, "I do not want to publish anything that is not true. I would much sooner be found fault with for omissions than for errors."[108]

In May of 1901 he thanked literature professor Brander Matthews for corrections on the "dummy" of *Correct Composition*, electrotyped and published later that year. In November of 1902 De Vinne wrote,

My Dear Mr. Matthews:

I thank you much for kind words and needed corrections. I have already ordered changes made in the plates [of the 1902 second printing], though I am not at all sure that my book will go into a third edition. It's some satisfaction, however, to feel that I have tried to be exact and that I have had good helpers.

Yours cordially,[109]

Here De Vinne was assuming his characteristic modest pose; some of the four volumes of *The Practice of Typography* were reprinted four times, some five.

In terms of practical printing we cannot say of De Vinne as he did of Caxton, "He bent himself to his work, and never relaxed till death overtook him,"[110] for De Vinne turned most of his printing over to others during the last two decades of his life. Yet if we take his real vocation to be the promotion of the typographic art and its history, this accolade comes closer to fitting him. His correspondence with Henry Lewis Bullen in his last years shows that as late as three months before his death he was still interested in scholarship: conferring with Horace Hart of the Oxford Press about a manual on English typography, finding portraits of French typefounders for Bullen's collection, making lists of topics he had not been able to cover in his writings, and generally encouraging the growth of the typographic Library and Museum of the American Type Founders Company.[111]

It is entirely fitting to recognize De Vinne as a scholar. With little formal education, he schooled himself very thoroughly in his specialty, and when there was no clear demarcation between professional and amateur scholarship, he felt comfortable tackling the big questions. He read the existing scholarly thought. He made a thorough study of printing artifacts and drew conclusions from their internal evidence. He felt, rightly, that his experience as a practical printer gave him insights not available to academic theorists. He never claimed the title of "scholar printer," a term used so loosely at times that it refers to nearly everyone who both wrote and printed. He preferred to call his own work "useful summaries," even when he contributed original analyses and insights.

Given De Vinne's preoccupation with practical printing and his obsession with its history, it would have been impossible for him not to have been a book collector. He obviously enjoyed and used the books he acquired, identifying them with his bookplate – designed, like the De Vinne Press device, by architect George F. Babb and engraved by Edwin Davis French, the foremost American bookplate artist of the time.[112] For a motto De Vinne chose a quotation from Horace – one of the most famous from ancient literature: "Aere perennius." Horace said that in his own poetry he had built a monument "more enduring than bronze." De Vinne most certainly intended the phrase to mean printing or books in general – not his own corpus (fig. 55).

We do not need to adopt G. Thomas Tanselle's engagingly inclu-

Fig. 55.

De Vinne's bookplate, bearing a quote from Horace: "More enduring than bronze."

sive definition of collecting – the "accumulation of tangible things"[113] – to call De Vinne a book collector, for he collected very consciously and thematically. There were, of course, presentation copies and other gifts he did not choose. But his working library reflected De Vinne's need to study firsthand his antecedents' products, to keep abreast of new approaches in typographic design, and to participate in the scholarship of the history of printing.

It is instructive that De Vinne wrote nothing about collecting and appeared to care little about how his books looked on the shelf. Ira Brainerd called it "a worker's library."[114] This, in fact, was what separated him from many Grolier Club members in his later years. De Vinne was a bibliophile – a lover of books, but not a lover of collecting. His library, a trove of evidence about past practices, was essentially a reference collection from which he could pursue his studies and collect his data. Collecting was handmaiden to scholarship.

Conclusion

THEODORE LOW DE VINNE lived a long, rich life immersed in the practice of typography – a field he took on with thoroughness and devotion. When employee Camille De Vèze asked him why he didn't write an autobiography, the self-effacing dean of American printers replied that he doubted anyone would be interested. The present author hopes this long-overdue study of his life proves the contrary. Had he possessed Benjamin Franklin's temerity and written his own epitaph, it would have begun with Franklin's opening, "He was a printer." But, given his reluctance to proclaim his own accomplishments, De Vinne would have stopped with those four words.

The decline and ultimate demise of his printing house notwithstanding, he was a successful businessman. He started without inheritance or family advantages and with little education. He served the required apprenticeship and went on to become the most successful commercial printer of his generation. He achieved enough financial security to indulge his typographic hobbies while leaving a comfortable inheritance to his descendants. A sense of personal integrity, often laced with deference, characterized his business dealings. Inside his printing establishment, paternalism and anti-unionism were constant themes. Although not charismatic in the usual sense, he somehow inspired great loyalty among his employees, even though their monetary rewards were not equal to the superior performance expected of them. When the founding father-figure ceased to be a daily presence, the center began to give way. It was never his intention to establish a printing dynasty. At the age of eighty-three, when he vetoed an infusion of outside capital, he said calmly that it was no disgrace to lose at business. Success in business did not define his personal sense of worth; it was certainly not the primary ingredient firing his imagination.

De Vinne had many circumstances in his favor. He put his native intelligence to good use, and he bolstered it with lifelong self-education and sustained application. He was lucky: an open field was chosen for him at age fourteen, and he was near enough to the nation's printing capital to take up a career there. After the Civil War, with paper becoming cheaper and book publishing acquiring a surging national market, the publishing business gradually settled in New York where there were opportunities for enterprising printers. By the end of the century, 20 percent of the country's printing and publishing workers were employed in the city, a figure not equaled even by the next three cities combined (Chicago, Philadelphia, and Boston).[1] Add to that the fact that printed products, in all their infinite variety, formed the very lifeblood of commerce and culture during his lifetime; printing was *the* medium. It is no surprise that a general-audience periodical such as *Scientific American* addressed and supported this important technology – or that the editors sought out De Vinne as industry spokesman.

Another happy condition of De Vinne's career years was that every aspect of printing technology, after remaining stable for four centuries, began to change rapidly. He was an eager participant in these technological shifts, always trying to get better results from the latest improvements, always pressing for the modifications he thought might enhance quality and performance.

A further advantage De Vinne possessed (and of which he may not have been aware) was the hunger and motivation of the self-made man. That hunger, in truth, was a valuable commodity – a luxury. Ironically, one can pass along to one's children and grandchildren all manner of material comforts, as he did, but usually not that special "hunger."

De Vinne maintained a wide circle of friends, colleagues, and professional acquaintances. His fellow printers, as epitomized by the local and national Typothetae, approached him with unabashed adulation – not inappropriate, given the prodigious energies he spent on their behalf. But the record also shows considerable respect from and camaraderie with a variety of customers. He traveled and socialized with Century Company personnel, although one can hardly imagine him sitting very long in Richard Watson Gilder's salons, reading poetry and discussing the eternal verities. The theory, practice, and history of printing remained the essential lubricants in most of his relationships. He carried on correspondence – or had a face-to-face relationship – with virtually all the major contemporary figures in the book arts in America as well as many in England.

A considerable mythology arose around De Vinne both during his life and afterward. He has even been given credit for the age-old saying that printing is "the art preservative of all arts."[2] De Vinne never sought personal fame, but somehow it grew up around his activities. In American society at large, he accepted his role as the printing industry's representative; he did so with outward grace but inward discomfort. The bust, the etched portrait, the medals, and the posed photographs – the De Vinne iconography that flourished even during his lifetime – were at odds with his personal modesty. Yet he cooperated. Trade journals craved pictures of the aging De Vinne, such as the one at his desk with the iconic beret atop his head (fig. 56). He sits in the chair from the Plantin-Moretus museum (retouched in this halftone). Over his left shoulder hangs the thirty-by-forty-inch engrossed testimonial presented by his employees at the April 1892 profit-sharing dinner. On the far wall, to the viewer's left, is the 1891 Grolier Club etching of Léopold Flameng's 1890 painting "Aldus in His Printing Establishment at Venice Showing Bindings to Grolier."

At some point De Vinne apparently decided to stem the flow of these images. A photographic portrait printed in a 1901 trade journal bears the caption, "From the last photograph he will ever have taken," and has a foliated border that must have embarrassed him (fig. 57).

While uniformly praising his presswork, twentieth-century commentators have said that De Vinne's printing was more admirable in its mechanical execution than in its artistic conception; that few of his books will ever rank highly among typographic specimens treasured by collectors; that his work exhibited simplicity, restraint, directness, and utility but lacked grace and charm; and that,

FIG. 56. De Vinne at his desk, posing in his beret. *Inland Printer*, April 1899, p. 35.

although widely read and certainly exposed to the best the past had to offer, he lacked both originality and infallible taste.[3]

De Vinne was well aware of the aesthetic shifts in printing at the turn of the twentieth century. But he did not embrace or approve of the "transition of book-making from a trade to an art," as William Dana Orcutt described what Morris set in motion.[4] De Vinne anticipated Beatrice Warde's "crystal-clear goblet" sentiments by half a century.[5] He maintained that books were containers and vehicles for the thoughts of their authors, not opportunities for designers to display themselves. His desiderata were legibility and clarity, qualities he found primarily in traditional roman types, conservatively arranged. A recovered Victorian, he adopted the creed, "Simplicity is beauty." Many of the principles he espoused were incorporated in the work of the next generation. He led the way out of the Victorian wilderness, even if he did not cross over to the promised land.

It is not De Vinne's actual printing as much as his writing that secures him a place in history. Intended mostly to educate, his work addresses virtually every aspect of typography and its history. He had a gift in the use of language. As Brander Matthews phrased it, De Vinne's writing style was "as clear and as simple, as firm and as vigorous, as [was] his press-work as a printer."[6] Moreover, his analyses were deep and insightful.

One must agree with Carl Rollins that De Vinne was not a genius but was "a commonplace man endowed with certain gifts of which he made full use." These gifts included dogged persistence and a clear head. De Vinne was "a thoroughly adjusted man, at peace with his times and his profession."[7]

While De Vinne did not endorse books as objets d'art, he did believe that "meritorious printing" was a worthy branch of the fine arts. And he believed that good workmanship was the underpinning of beautiful printing – that there is no art without craft.

FIG. 57.

De Vinne's "last photograph": Frontispiece of the October 1901 issue of *The Western Printer*.

PLATE 1A.
Hart & Co. business card, ca. 1858–1871, in full Victorian dress.

PLATE 1B.
Theodore L. De Vinne & Co. business card, ca. 1886–1906, in a more restrained design.

The De Vinne Press.
—
THEO. L. DE VINNE & CO.

PRINTERS,

12 LAFAYETTE PLACE,

NEW-YORK.

PLATE 1C.
Medal designed for the 1902 United Typothetae of America convention in Pittsburgh. Gutenberg views a roster of printing luminaries including De Vinne.

259

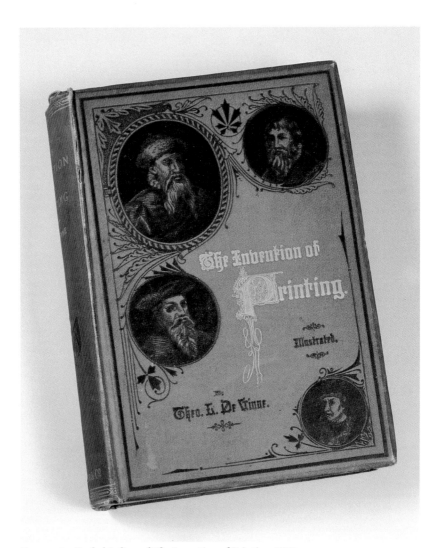

PLATE 2. Trade binding of *The Invention of Printing*, 1877.

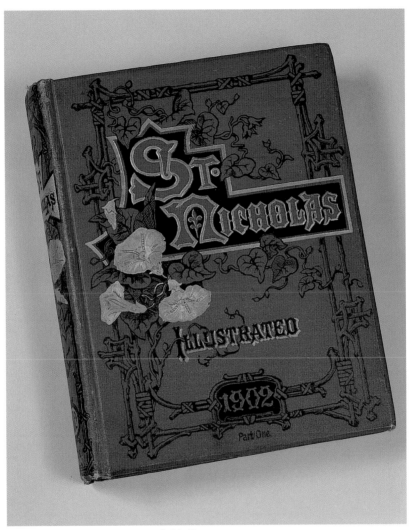

PLATE 3. *St. Nicholas*, in its trade binding.

A
DECREE OF STAR CHAMBER
CONCERNING PRINTING.

MADE JULY 11, 1637.

REPRINTED BY THE GROLIER CLUB, FROM THE
FIRST EDITION BY ROBERT BARKER, 1637.

PLATE 4. Title page of *A Decree of Star Chamber Concerning Printing*, 1884 (9" x 6½").

PLATE 5. *The Century Dictionary* (1889–91) in the original twenty-four parts (13" x 10").

I

THE PRISON-DOOR

THRONG of bearded men, in sad-colored garments, and gray, steeple-crowned hats, intermixed with women, some wearing hoods, and others bareheaded, was assembled in front of a wooden edifice, the door of which was heavily timbered with oak, and studded with iron spikes.

The founders of a new colony, whatever Utopia of human virtue and happiness they might originally project, have invariably recognized it among their earliest practical necessities to allot a portion of the virgin soil as a cemetery, and another portion as the site of a prison. In accordance with this rule, it may safely be assumed that the forefathers of Boston had built the first prison-house somewhere in the vicinity of Cornhill, almost as seasonably as they marked out the first burial-ground, on Isaac Johnson's lot, and round about his grave, which subsequently became the nucleus of all the con-

59

PLATE 6. *The Scarlet Letter*, 1908, decorated initial on the opening page of the first chapter.

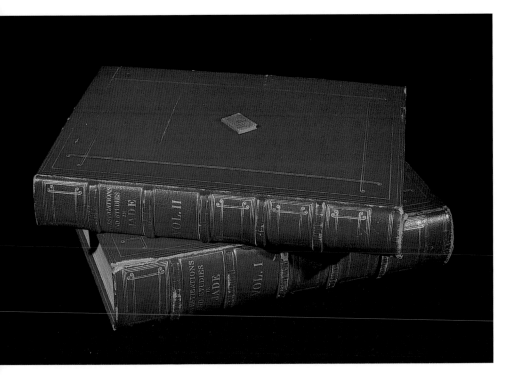

P LATE 7. The smallest and largest books from the De Vinne Press: *Brilliants: A Setting of Humorous Poetry in Brilliant Type*, 1888 (2¼" x 1½"), on top of *The Bishop Collection: Investigations and Studies in Jade*, 1906 (25" x 18½").

TYPES

OF

THE DE VINNE PRESS

SPECIMENS
FOR THE USE OF COMPOSITORS
PROOFREADERS AND
PUBLISHERS

395 LAFAYETTE STREET, NEW YORK
1907

PLATE 8. Title page of the 1907 De Vinne Press specimen book (9½" x 6").

Appendix A

A CHECKLIST OF
THEODORE LOW DE VINNE'S
PUBLISHED WRITINGS

Previous bibliographies of De Vinne's writings have been based on a list compiled by Alexander Washington Collins (1870–1918), a Pittsburgh compositor who took great interest in everything associated with De Vinne. On Christmas Day 1910 he presented the bibliography to De Vinne in the form of a broadside. Collins also assembled a collection of De Vinne's periodical articles into a volume bound with a special title page. It was No. 182 in the auction of Collins's library by Anderson Galleries on 24 April 1922 and No. 88 in the 1928 Grolier Club exhibition; its subsequent whereabouts are unknown. Collins presented a similar compilation to De Vinne. It was No. 486 in the 1920 De Vinne auction where Henry Lewis Bullen purchased it for his American Type Founders Company Typographic Library and Museum. After the ATF collection reached Columbia University Libraries, the volume was "withdrawn" on 15 August 1960. It bears the inventory marks of the Chiswick Book Shop and of Jack Golden and was recently purchased from a dealer by the author.

Collins's bibliography of De Vinne's writings appeared in the *American Printer* (58 [March 1914]: 95–96) shortly after De Vinne's death. The Grolier Club yearbook for 1914 included the Collins bibliography with some corrections and additions compiled by Ruth Shepard Granniss, who acknowledged the assistance of Collins, Henry Lewis Bullen of the ATF, James Bothwell of the De Vinne Press, and the Chief Bibliographer of the Library of Congress. That version appeared in the 1915 memorial volume, *Theodore Low De Vinne, Printer* and, with six additions, in the 1968 *Theodore Low De Vinne*, Typophile Chap Book 47, 1:39–61.

The following checklist includes De Vinne's monographs, contributions to monographs, periodical articles, letters to editors, published speeches, and other miscellaneous published material. Titles appear under the year of first publication. Entries are in chronological order within the year, as best it could be determined. Previously listed works that the author has not been able to examine are marked "unconfirmed." Just over half of the items below have not appeared in earlier lists.

De Vinne's writings are followed by a checklist of his firm's type specimens, arranged chronologically.

1859

"A Portrait and a History." *Printers' Miscellany: A Practical Exposition of Types and Presses* (New York) 1 (April 1859): [1–3]. Regarding a Hoe cylinder press.

[Untitled article regarding] Scotch-face type, the history of letter forms, and the development of typefaces. *Printers' Miscellany* (New York) 1 (July 1859): [1–4].

These two articles were added to the De Vinne bibliography by Granniss. In his American Type Founders card catalogue, Bullen named De Vinne as the editor of this periodical (which appeared only in April, July, and December of 1859). No articles are signed, but this in-depth July piece on typefaces is clearly his voice. The "Portrait" and all the other articles may have been written by him as well.

1863

Prices for Printing Adopted by the Employing Printers of the City of New York, in Convention, January 20th, 1863. 12 pp.

A similar compilation (25 pp.): 2 February 1864 (proof copy) and 11 February 1864 (final "authentic" copy). There were probably others.

"Work for the Several Unions: The Apprenticeship System." *Printer* (New York) 4 (June 1863):166–67. Report of the Committee on the Apprenticeship System of the Associated Employing Printers of the City of New York, signed by C. A. Alvord, P. C. Baker, John F. Trow, and Theo. L. De Vinne.

1864

"The Profits of Book Composition." *Printer* (New York) 5 (January 1864): 38–40. Letter to the editor, signed "Brevier."

Reprinted in pamphlet form, New York: Employing Printers of New York, 1864. 33 pp.

"Our Fathers in the Art: They builded wiser than they knew; they founded an order that will be honored when the claims of noble birth shall be forgotten." *Printer* (New York) 5 (April 1864):68–69. Response to a toast at the second annual dinner of the Employing Printers of the City of New York, 29 February 1864.

Checklist

"Mediaeval Printing." *Printer* (New York) 5 (April 1864): 65–67. The substance of a paper read before the New York Typographical Society, 20 February 1864.

Reprinted in *Printers' Journal* (New York) 1 (18 June 1866): 138–40 and (2 July 1866): 149–51.

"Fust and Gutenberg." *Printer* (New York) 5 (August 1864): 118.

"The Strike, from an Employer's Point of View." *Printer* (New York) 5 (September 1864): 136–37. Letter to the editor, signed "Brevier."

"Trade Unions. 'Strike! but hear.'" *Printer* (New York) 5 (October 1864): 145–48; (November 1864): 161–64; (December 1864): 178–80.

1865

"Trade Unions." *Printer* (New York) 6 (January 1865): 7. Letter to the editor.

"News from Abroad." *Printer* (New York) 6 (February 1865): 24. Letter to the editor, signed "Brevier." Regards some erroneous statements in the *Printers' Journal* (London) concerning the relations between employers and employees in New York's printing industry.

"Labor and Trade Unions." *Printer* (New York) 6 (August 1865): 102–4. Letter to the editor.

1867

The Practice of Lithography for the Use of Novices. New York: R. Hoe & Co., 1867. 21 pp.

1869

The Printers' Price List: A Manual for the Use of Clerks and Book-Keepers in Job Printing Offices. New York: Francis Hart & Co., 1869. 168 pp. "Proof copy" precedes title.

[Second edition.] New York: Francis Hart & Co., 1871. 459 pp.

[Facsimile of second edition.] New York: Garland Publishing, 1980. Introduction by Irene Tichenor.

"Gutenberg, 1400–1468." *Eclectic Magazine of Foreign Literature, Science and Art* (New York) n.s. 10 (July 1869): 114. [Unsigned article attributed to TLD by Collins.]

1871

"Speed in Composition." *Printing Gazette* (Cleveland) 6 (1871). Twelve monthly articles:

"Speed in Type-Setting – How Acquired." (January): 1–2.

"The Defects of and Improvements in Type Cases." (February): 1–3.

"The Defects and Irregularities of the Lower Case." (March): 1–3.

"Attempts to Simplify Justification and Spacing." (April): 1–2.

"Logotypes and Combination Types." (May): 1–2.

"Beniowski's Case and Logotypes." (June): 1–2.

"Improved Methods of Making Combination Types." (July): 1–2.

"Type-Setting and Distributing Machines." [Part 1 of 3] (August): 1–2.

"Type-Setting and Distributing Machines." [Part 2 of 3] (September): 1–2.

"Type-Setting and Distributing Machines." [Part 3 of 3] (October): 1–2.

"The Alden Type-Setting and Distributing Machine." (November): 1–2.

"Type-Setting Machines." (December): 1–3.

"Giambattista Bodoni." *Printers' Circular* (Philadelphia) 6 (March 1871): 8–9.

"About Margins." *Printers' Circular* (Philadelphia) 6 (May 1871): 106–8; (June 1871): 148–50; (July 1871): 202–3; (August 1871): 244–45; (September 1871): 292–95.

"How He Collected His Bill." *Proof Sheet* (Philadelphia) 4 (May 1871): 90–91. Reprinted in *Printing History* 3.2, no. 6 (1981): 30–32.

"Low Prices and Ruinous Competition." *Typo* (Syracuse) 1871 [unconfirmed]. Quoted in *Printing Gazette* (Cleveland) 6 (September 1871): 6.

"A Perfect Specimen of American Book-Making." *New York Semi-Weekly Tribune* (8 August 1871): 6. Regards the illustrated catalogue of Mallory, Wheeler & Co., of New Haven. [Unsigned but probably by De Vinne; appears in his envelope marked "Some of My Contributions to Periodicals," De Vinne Papers, Rare Book and Manuscript Library, Columbia University.]

1872

Record of the Proceedings and Ceremonies Pertaining to the Erection of the Franklin Statue in Printing-House Square, presented by Albert De Groot, to the Press and Printers of the City of New York. New York: F. Hart & Co., 1872. 104 pp.

The State of the Trade: Observations on Eight Hours and Higher Prices, Suggested by Recent Conferences between the New-York Typographical Union and the Employing Book and Job Printers of that City. New York: Francis Hart & Co., 1872. 44 pp.

"The Tariff on Types." *New York Tribune* (6 March 1872): 9. Letter to the editor. Reprinted in *Printing Gazette* (Cleveland) 7 (March 1872): 1–2; and in *Proof Sheet* (Philadelphia) 5 (March 1872): 67–68.

"About Cheap Types." *Printers' Circular* (Philadelphia) 7 (April 1872): 46–47. Reprinted in *Printing Gazette* (Cleveland) 7 (May 1872): 2.

"William Caxton." *Printers' Circular* (Philadelphia) 7 (September 1872): 241–43; (October 1872): 281–83; (November 1872): 321–23; (December 1872): 353–55.

Checklist
1873

"The Cost of Printing." *Quadrat* (Pittsburgh) 1 (June 1873): 49. Letter to the editor.

"The Mazarin Bible." *Printers' Circular* (Philadelphia) 8 (September 1873): 233–35.

1874

"Old Specimen Books." *Printers' Circular* (Philadelphia) 9 (April 1874): 45–47.

1876

The Invention of Printing: A Collection of Facts and Opinions Descriptive of Early Prints and Playing Cards, the Block-Books of the Fifteenth Century, the Legend of Lourens Janszoon Coster, of Haarlem, and the Work of John Gutenberg and his Associates. New York: Francis Hart & Co., 1876. 8vo. 556 pp. Published in five parts and in publisher's cloth and half-morocco bindings.

This first printing appeared in more than one form. Copies have been noted in which some gatherings incorporate corrections of some of the errors listed in the "Additional Notes and Corrections." Some of these copies have 1876 on the title page, and others have 1877. Other anomalies have also been found. See Appendix B for a discussion of this work's publishing history.

"Second Edition" [i.e., second printing]. London: Trübner & Co.; New York: Francis Hart & Co. 1877. 8vo. 557 pp.

"Second Edition" [i.e., third printing]. New York: Francis Hart & Co.; London: Trübner & Co., 1878. 8vo. 557 pp.

[Fourth printing: facsimile of the partially corrected form of the 1876 printing.] Detroit: Gale Research Co., 1969.

[Second edition.] New York: George Bruce's Son & Co., 1878. 168 pp. Text is set in various type sizes, printed on one side of the sheet, forming part of Bruce's specimen books of 1878 and 1882.

[Excerpt.] Oscar Jolles, trans. *Der Schlüssel zur Erfindung der Typographie.* Berlin: H. Berthold, 1921. 25 pp. 400 copies.

"John Gutenberg." *Scribner's Monthly* 12 (May 1876): 73–85.

"Type." *The American Cyclopaedia: A Popular Dictionary of General Knowledge.* 16 vols. New York: Appleton, 1873–76. 16: 92–94.

1877

The Greeley Monument: Unveiled at Greenwood, December 4th, 1876. New York: Francis Hart & Co., 1877. 34 pp. Compiled by De Vinne.

1878

"On the Bodies of Type." *Caslon's Circular* (London), published in eight install-
ments: 4 (April 1878): [1]–[2], 4 (July 1878): [2], 4 (October 1878): [2], 5
(January 1879): [2], 5 (April 1879): [2], 5 (July 1879): [2], 5 (October
1879): [2], 6 (January 1880): [2].

"Woodcuts: Concerning the Taking of Proofs and Prints." *Printing Times and
Lithographer* (London) n.s. 4 (15 October 1878): 197–99; (15 November
1878): 221–22.

1879

"A Printer on the Limitations of Engraving on Wood." *Printing Times and
Lithographer* (London) n.s. 5 (15 March 1879): 45–47; (15 April 1879):
69–70; (15 May 1879): 94–96.

1880

"The Growth of Woodcut Printing." *Scribner's Monthly* 19 (April 1880):
860–74; 20 (May 1880): 34–45.

Reprinted in *Theodore Low De Vinne*. Typophile Chap Book 47. New York:
Typophiles, 1968, 2: 61–132.

1881

"The First Editor." *Scribner's Monthly* 22 (October 1881): 889–98.

Reprinted as *Aldus Pius Manutius*. San Francisco: Grabhorn Press for the
Book Club of California, 1924, [31] pp. 250 copies.

Reprinted in *Theodore Low De Vinne*. Typophile Chap Book 47. New York:
Typophiles, 1968, 2: 139–71.

Reprinted, New York: Targ Editions, 1983. 39 pp. 250 copies. Printed by
Leslie Miller at the Grenfell Press with woodcuts by Antonio Frasconi.

1882

"England's First Printer." *Critic: An Illustrated Monthly Review of Literature,
Art, and Life* (New York) 2 (28 January 1882): 20–21.

1883

*Manual of Printing Office Practice: Office Manual for the Use of Workmen in
the Printing House of Theo. L. De Vinne & Co., 63 Murray Street, New York.*
1883. 42 pp.

Excerpt reprinted (without attribution) in *Art Age* (New York) 1 (January
1884): 55, 65–67 and (February 1884): 70, 71, 73, 74.

Excerpt reprinted in *British and Colonial Printer and Stationer and
Booksellers' Circular* (London) 18 (14 April 1887): 1-2, (21 April): 3, 6, (28
April): 2-3, (5 May): 2-3, (12 May): 2-3, (19 May): 1-2, (26 May): 2-3.

Checklist

[Second edition.] New York: Press of Ars Typographica, 1926. 52 pp. Introductory note by Douglas C. McMurtrie.

Second edition reprinted. Forest Hills, N.Y.: Battery Park Book Company, 1978.

1884

"Throwing In." *Art Age* (New York) 1 (January 1884): 54. Letter to the editor regarding the printers' responsibility to keep type standing for subsequent printings.

[Preface, 6 pp.] *A Decree of Star Chamber Concerning Printing. Made July 11, 1637.* New York: Grolier Club, 1884. 148 copies on Holland paper, 2 copies on vellum. "Reprinted . . . from the First Edition by Robert Barker, 1637." First publication of the Grolier Club.

1885

"On the Printing of 'The Century.'" *Century Magazine* 30, n.s. 8 (September 1885): 808–9.

"The Only Remedy." *American Bookmaker* (New York) 1 (November 1885): 158. Letter to the editor regarding uniform type bodies.

Reprinted in *American Printer* (New York) 50 (July 1910): 608.

1886

"Concerning French Types." *American Bookmaker* (New York) 1 (February 1886): 47–48. Letter to the editor.

"Coöperation." *Century Magazine* 32, n.s. 10 (July 1886): 403–4.

Historic Printing Types: A Lecture Read before the Grolier Club of New York, January 25, 1885, with Additions and New Illustrations. New York: Grolier Club, 1886. 110 pp. 200 copies on Holland paper, 2 copies on vellum. According to the 1914 Grolier Club *Yearbook*, "a few extra copies, printed on plain paper for Mr. De Vinne's personal use, have the imprint of The De Vinne Press."

Specimens of Historical Printing Types, Printed (But not Published) as Illustrations to a Discourse by Theodore L. De Vinne, Before the Grolier Club, January 28, 1885. [17] pp.

Lecture abstracted in the club's *Transactions* 1(1885): 32–37.

1888

"A Printer's Paradise: The Plantin Moretus Museum at Antwerp." *Century Magazine* 36, n.s. 14 (June 1888): 225–45.

Reprinted with additions and notes as *Christopher Plantin and the Plantin-Moretus Museum at Antwerp.* New York: Grolier Club, 1888. 98 pp. 300 copies on paper; 3 copies on vellum.

Reprinted as *The Plantin-Moretus Museum, A Printer's Paradise.* San

Francisco: Grabhorn Press, 1929. 54 pp. 425 copies.

[Untitled extract.] Antwerp, August 1950. 40 copies. [Copy in Rosenwald Collection at Library of Congress.]

Century article reprinted in *Theodore Low De Vinne*. Typophile Chap Book 47. New York: Typophiles, 1968, 2: 1–53.

"A Just Employer." *Century Magazine* 36, n.s. 14 (September 1888): 791. Eulogy of Samuel D. Warren, papermaker.

[Presidential address.] United Typothetae of America. *Proceedings of the Second Annual Meeting*, 1888, pp. 6–14.

Reprinted in *American Bookmaker* (New York) 7 (October 1888): 100–102.

Brilliants: A Setting of Humorous Poetry in Brilliant Types. New York: De Vinne Press, 1888. 58 mm. xv, 96 pp. Compiled by De Vinne. His preface, pp. vii–xv, discusses famous miniature books and types.

Reprinted, 1895.

Upon Small Types, preface to *Brilliants*. Brooklyn: Traders Press, 1969. xiv, 27, [6] pp., 58 mm. 500 copies. Preface by Jack R. Levien.

1889

"Do Machines Hurt a Trade?" *Manufacturer and Builder* (New York) 21 (June 1889): 138.

[Remarks on copyright.] United Typothetae of America. *Proceedings of the Third Annual Meeting*, 1889, pp. 40, 49–53.

Reprinted as "International Copyright." *Publishers' Weekly* 36 (12 October 1889): 538–39.

Also printed as three-page leaflet [n.p., n.d.].

1890

"Printing as a Profession for Young Men." St. Louis *Republic* [unconfirmed].

Reprinted in *St. Louis Stationer* 2 (February 1890): 69, 71.

[Copyright League report.] United Typothetae of America. *Proceedings of the Fourth Annual Meeting*, 1890, pp. 65, 75–79.

"Report of the Committee on Uniformity in the Bodies of Type." United Typothetae of America. *Proceedings of the Fourth Annual Meeting*, 1890, Appendix A, pp. 1–8.

"New Fixtures for the Composing Room." United Typothetae of America. *Proceedings of the Fourth Annual Meeting*, 1890, Appendix C, pp. 1–12.

"A Specimen Book Which Will Prevent the Repeated Composition of Lines of Type. . . ." United Typothetae of America. *Proceedings of the Fourth Annual Meeting*, 1890, Appendix D, pp. 1–4.

"The Printing of 'The Century.'" *Century Magazine* 41, n.s. 19 (November 1890): 87–99.

Checklist

1891

"Typography in Advertisements." *Printers' Ink* (New York) 4 (7 January 1891): 3–4.

Excerpt reprinted in *Printers' Ink* (New York) 86 (26 February 1914): 27–28.

[After-dinner remarks at Typothetae dinner] in John Polhemus. *My First Vacation and Welcome Home.* New York: John Polhemus Printing Company, 1891, pp. 7–13.

"Concerning Estimates." United Typothetae of America. *Proceedings of the Fifth Annual Meeting,* 1891, pp. 223–27.

1892

"Blades's Pentateuch of Printing." *Nation* (New York) 54 (7 January 1892): 15–16. Book review.

[Speech regarding unions, in response to a resolution in support of the Pittsburgh Typothetae.] United Typothetae of America. *Proceedings of the Sixth Annual Meeting,* 1892, pp. 111–19.

Reprinted in *American Bookmaker* (New York) 15 (September 1892): 92–93.

"Masculine Printing." United Typothetae of America. *Proceedings of the Sixth Annual Meeting,* 1892, pp. 163–73.

Reprinted in *American Bookmaker* (New York) 15 (November 1892): 140–44.

1893

"Does Composition Pay?" *American Bookmaker* (New York) 16 (February 1893):60–63.

[Speech at the annual Franklin dinner.] "Typothetae of New York: Celebrating Franklin's Birthday." *American Bookmaker* (New York) 16 (February 1893): 81–82.

"On Type Measurement." *American Bookmaker* (New York) 16 (June 1893): 205–8.

"Do You Know the Letters?" in *Liber Scriptorum.* New York: Authors' Club, 1893, pp. 192–99.

1894

"Machinery in Printing." *Canadian Printer and Publisher* [unconfirmed].

Reprinted in *American Bookmaker* (New York) 19 (September 1894): 66–68.

"The Advance in Printing." United Typothetae of America. *Proceedings of the Eighth Annual Convention,* 1894, pp. 199–204.

Reprinted in *Engraver and Printer* (Boston) 7 (January 1895): 4–6.

"American Machinery v. British." *British and Colonial Printer and Stationer and Booksellers' Circular* (London) 34 (22 November 1894): 5. Letter to the editor.

1895

"American Printing" in Chauncey Mitchell Depew, ed. *1795–1895: One Hundred Years of American Commerce*. 2 vols. New York: D.O. Haynes & Co., 1895, 1: 314–19.

[To Chicago Society of Proofreaders.] *Proofsheet* (Chicago) 1 (March 1895): 109–10. Letter dated 24 January 1895.

"The French Method of Making Book Margins." *Engraver and Printer* (Boston) 7 (March 1895): 52–53. Letter to the editor.

"Some Questions and Answers." *Proofsheet* (Chicago) 1 (July 1895): 213–15. Letter to the editor.

1896

"The 'Century's Printer' on the 'Century's Type.'" *Century Magazine* 51, n.s. 29 (March 1896): 794–96.

Reprinted with slight modifications in *Specimens of the Century Romans: Designed by Theodore L. De Vinne and Cut by the American Type Founders Company for the Century Magazine*. American Type Founders, n.d.

Reprinted in *Theodore Low De Vinne*. Typophile Chap Book 47. New York: Typophiles, 1968, 1: 63–73.

"Mr. Theo. L. De Vinne on Plain Printing." *Printers' Register – Supplement* (London) 35 (6 May 1896): iii–iv (also numbered 211–12). Quotes letter to Cooper and Budd, printer and publisher of George Joyner's *Fine Printing*, which inspired De Vinne's comments.

Preface and Notes. *Moxon's Mechanick Exercises: Or, the Doctrine of Handy-Works Applied to the Art of Printing; a Literal Reprint of the First Edition Published in 1683*. 2 vols. New York: The Typothetae of the City of New York, 1896, 1: ix–xviii, 2: 399–430.

"The Old and the New" in *Book-Lovers Almanac for the Year 1896*. New York: Duprat & Co., © 1895, pp. 41–49.

Reprinted as *The Old and the New: A Friendly Dispute Between Juvenis and Senex*. Marlborough, N. Y.: Village Press, 1933. [16] pp. 300 copies. With a note by Frederic W. Goudy.

Reprinted with Goudy's title and notes in Paul A. Bennett, ed. *Books and Printing: A Treasury for Typophiles*. Cleveland: World Publishing Co., 1951, pp. 274–80.

Revised edition, 1963.

"Cost of Improvements." United Typothetae of America. *Proceedings of the Tenth Annual Convention*, 1896, pp. 79–84. [Paper read in De Vinne's absence.]

"Hints on Book-Making." *Independent* (New York) (10 December 1896): 2–3.

Checklist

1897

"The Printing of William Morris." *Book Buyer* (New York) 13 (January 1897): 920–23.

"The Adaptability of Paper." *Bookman* (New York) 5 (May 1897): 222–24.

Reprinted in *Inland Printer* (Chicago) 23 (May 1899): 51–53.

"The Printing of Books." *Outlook* (New York) 57 (4 December 1897): 805–9.

1899

"Some Further Views on a Printing Combination as Applied to New York." *Printer and Bookmaker* (New York) 28 (August 1899): 259–60.

"The Printer's Art." United Typothetae of America. *Proceedings of the Thirteenth Annual Convention*, 1899, pp. 258–60. Response to a toast.

Reprinted [a slightly different rendering] in *Printer and Bookmaker* (New York) 29 (October 1899): 91.

"Changed Conditions in the Printing Trade." *Printer and Bookmaker* (New York) 29 (December 1899): 185–86.

1900

"Fifty Years of Printing." New York *Tribune* (25 March 1900): 6.

Reprinted in *American Printer* (New York) 30 (May 1900): 138–40.

"The Gutenberg Anniversary." *Outlook* (New York) 65 (5 May 1900): 31–37.

Reprinted in *American Printer* (New York) 30 (June 1900): 218–21.

The Practice of Typography: A Treatise on the Process of Type-Making, the Point System, the Names, Sizes, Styles and Prices of Plain Printing Types. New York: Century Co., 1900, c1899. 403 pp.

Reprinted, New York: Century Co., 1902 and 1910.

Reprinted, New York: Oswald Publishing Co., 1914, printed at the De Vinne Press.

Reprinted, New York: Oswald Publishing Co., 1925.

"The Art of Gutenberg." New York *Journal* [unconfirmed].

Reprinted in *American Printer* (New York) 30 (August 1900): 341.

"A Book That Won the Grand Prize." *New York Times Saturday Review* (27 October 1900): 736–37.

"Color-Printing in 1866." *Inland Printer* (Chicago) 26 (October 1900): 49, 50.

1901

"Fads in Printing." *American Printer* (New York) 31 (January 1901): 326–27.

"Fads in Typography." *Inland Printer* (Chicago) 26 (January 1901): 601–4.

"Printing in the Nineteenth Century." New York *Evening Post* (12 January 1901): 8–9.

Reprinted in *American Printer* (New York) 32 (March 1901): 33–37.

Excerpt reprinted as "Perfecting the Press" in *Current Literature* (New York) 30 (May 1901): 533–35.

Reprinted in *The Nineteenth Century: A Review of Progress*. New York: G. P. Putnam's Sons, 1901.

Excerpt reprinted as "Perfecting the Press" in *Scientific American, Supplement* No. 1380 (14 June 1902): 22121–22.

Reprinted, New York: Lead Mould Electrotype Foundry, 1924. 16 pp. 575 copies, 425 of which were presented to members of the American Institute of Graphic Arts.

Excerpt reprinted in Rauri McLean, ed. *Typographers on Type*. London: Lund Humphries, 1995, pp. 7–10.

"Fiftieth Wedding Anniversary of Mr. and Mrs. Theodore L. De Vinne." *Inland Printer* (Chicago) 26 (February 1901): 785. An address delivered to employees.

Title-Pages As Seen by a Printer, with Numerous Illustrations in Facsimile, and Some Observations on the Early and Recent Printing of Books. New York: Grolier Club, 1901. 370 pp. 325 copies. [See also *The Practice of Typography: A Treatise on Title-Pages . . .* (1902).]

Excerpt reprinted as "The Kelmscott Style" in *Bibliographer* (New York) 1 (January 1902): 1–10.

"Some History of Taste in Typography." *Inland Printer* (Chicago) 27 (May 1901): 189–91.

"To Produce Artistic Printing." *American Printer* (New York) 32 (September 1901): 41, 43.

"The Union Label from the Employer's Standpoint." *Union Label Magazine* (Boston) [unconfirmed].

Reprinted as "Logic, Law and the Union Label" in *American Printer* (New York) 33 (October 1901): 122, 124–25.

Review of George Washington Moon. *The Oldest Type-Printed Book in Existence. Nation* (New York) 73 (24 October 1901): 324–25. [Collins attributed this to De Vinne. It is unsigned, and the table of contents does not list authors of reviews.]

The Practice of Typography: Correct Composition, a Treatise on Spelling, Abbreviations, the Compounding and Division of Words, the Proper Use of Figures and Numerals, Italic and Capital Letters, Notes, etc., with Observations on Punctuation and Proof-Reading. New York: Century Co., 1901. 476 pp.

Reprinted, New York: Century Co., 1902 and 1904.

Reprinted, New York: Oswald Publishing Co., 1914, 1916, 1921, printed at the De Vinne Press.

Checklist

"About Large Types." *Literary Collector* (New York) 3 (December 1901): 65–69.

"Printing Sixty Years Ago." Columbia Typographical Union. *Third Year Book.* (Washington, D.C., December 1901): 27, 29, 31, 33.

1902

"Samuel Putnam Avery: An Appreciation." *American Printer* (New York) 33 (January 1902): 377–79.

[Franklin Day address before the Typothetae of the City of New York, 17 January 1902.] *American Printer* (New York) 33 (February 1902): 451–54.

The Practice of Typography: A Treatise on Title-Pages, with Numerous Illustrations in Facsimile, and Some Observations on the Early and Recent Printing of Books. New York: Century Co., 1902. 485 pp. [Expanded version of *Title-Pages as Seen by a Printer* (1901).]

Reprinted, New York: Century Co., 1904.

Reprinted, New York: Oswald Publishing Co., 1914, printed at the De Vinne Press.

Reprinted, New York: Haskell House, 1972.

"The Chap-Book and Its Outgrowths." *Literary Collector* (New York) 5 (November 1902):1–5.

1903

"About Pages and Margins." *Printing Art* (Cambridge) 1 (April 1903): 27–31; (May 1903): 59–65.

"The Drugulin Specimen Book of Foreign Languages." *American Printer* (New York) 36 (May 1903): 255. Book review.

"A New Edition of the 'Inferno' Described by Mr. De Vinne." *New York Times Saturday Review of Books* (16 May 1903): 338. Letter to the editor.

"A Morning with Theodore L. De Vinne." *Scientific American*, Printing Number, 89 (14 November 1903): 339.

Reprinted in *Inland Printer* (Chicago) 32 (January 1904): 596–97.

Reprinted in *Theodore Low De Vinne.* Typophile Chap Book 47. New York: Typophiles, 1968. 1:75–83.

"Typographical Effect." *Independent* (New York) 55 (19 November 1903): 2723–25.

Quoted in *Printers' Ink* (New York) 46 (6 January 1904): 34.

Reprinted, Indianapolis: Studio Press, 1917. [8] pp.

1904

"About Sizes of Books." *Printing Art* (Cambridge) 4 (September 1904): 13–18; (October 1904): 73–77.

The Practice of Typography: Modern Methods of Book Composition, a Treatise on Type-Setting by Hand and by Machine, and on the Proper Arrangement and Imposition of Pages. New York: Century Co., 1904. 477 pp.

> Excerpt reprinted as "Head-Bands and Tail-Pieces" in *Printing Art* (Cambridge) 3 (July 1904): 149–53. [By "special arrangement with Mr. De Vinne and Century Co.," this appeared before publication of the book.]
>
> Reprinted, New York: Century Co., 1910.
>
> Reprinted, New York: Oswald Publishing Co., 1914 and 1921, printed at the De Vinne Press.
>
> *Book Composition . . . Chapters from De Vinne's 'Modern Methods of Book Composition'* revised and arranged by J.W. Bothwell, The De Vinne Press, New York. (Typographical Technical Series for Apprentices. pt. 2, no. 20) Chicago: United Typothetae of America Committee on Education, 1918.

"Attractiveness in Books." *Independent* (New York) 57 (15 December 1904): 1374–77.

1905

"Samuel Putnam Avery." *New York Genealogical and Biographical Record* 36 (January 1905): 1–4.

> Reprinted in *Editorials and Resolutions in Memory of Samuel Putnam Avery.* New York: privately printed, 1905, pp. 69–76. 100 copies.

[Presidential address.] *Officers, Committees, Constitution, Annual Reports, etc.* New York: Grolier Club, 1905, pp. 79–86.

"The Printer's Province." *Printing Art* (Cambridge) 5 (May 1905): 129–31.

"Learning the Trade." *Printing Art* (Cambridge) 6 (December 1905): 209–12.

> Reprinted as pamphlet, Bronx, N.Y., 1927. [10] pp.

1906

[Presidential address.] *Officers, Committees, Constitution, Annual Reports, etc.* New York: Grolier Club, 1906, pp. 79–87.

[Introduction to] Frederick H. Hitchcock, ed. *The Building of a Book.* New York: Grafton Press, 1906, pp. 1–3.

> "Second edition, revised and enlarged," New York: Bowker, 1929.

"To the Compositor." *Printing Art* (Cambridge) 7 (May 1906): 160.

"Good Taste in Typography." *Printing Art* (Cambridge) 8 (October 1906): 100.

1907

[Letter]. *American Printer* (New York) 45 (September 1907): 41–42. Letter to the editor regarding the eight-hour movement.

1909

The Linotype As I Have Found It. New York, ©1909. Broadside. A testimonial letter from De Vinne to the Mergenthaler Linotype Company regarding the use of their machines at the De Vinne Press; printed at the De Vinne Press [unconfirmed].

1910

Notable Printers of Italy During the Fifteenth Century, Illustrated with Facsimiles from Early Editions and with Remarks on Early and Recent Printing. New York: Grolier Club, 1910. 210 pp. 300 copies on American paper, 3 copies on Imperial Japan paper, 97 additional copies printed for De Vinne's personal use with the De Vinne Press imprint.

Reprinted, Mansfield Center, Conn.: Martino Publishing, 2003.

"A Typographical Study in Retrospect." *American Printer* (New York) 50 (July 1910): 602.

1911

"Giambattista Bodoni." *Printing Art* (Cambridge) 17 (June 1911): 277–82.

"The Printing of Wood-Engravings." *Print-Collectors' Quarterly* (New York) 1 (July 1911): 365–80.

"About Cheap Books." *American Printer* (New York) 53 (November 1911): 313–14.

Date unknown

The following are in the De Vinne Papers, Rare Book and Manuscript Library, Columbia University:

[Speech to the] National Editorial Association. Printed in "The Mechanical Department" column of the *National Journalist* [undated clipping].

[Review of] J. Luther Ringwalt. *American Encyclopedia of Printing* [unidentified galley proof].

"French and American Bodies of Type" [unidentified clipping].

"Competent Proofreaders" [unidentified clipping].

TYPE SPECIMENS

Specimens of Old Style Types in the Printing Office of Francis Hart & Co. (1877). 63 pp. Part 1 of 3.

Specimens of Pointed Texts and Black Letters in the Printing Office of Francis Hart & Co. (1878). Pp. 69–158. Part 2 of 3.

Specimens of Script and Italic Types in the Printing Office of Francis Hart & Co. (1880). Pp. 167–251. Part 3 of 3.

Specimens of Some of the New and Quaint Types Recently Added to Stock in the Printing Office of Theo. L. De Vinne & Co. (1883). 62 pp.

Specimens of Black-Letter in Stock at the De Vinne Press (1887). 12 leaves.

The Roman and Italic Printing Types in the Printing House of Theodore L. De Vinne & Co. (1891). 145 pp.

Old Faces of Roman and Medieval Types Lately Added to the De Vinne Press (1897). 47 pp.

Styles of Types for Books and Advertisements Now in Service at the De Vinne Press (1905). 52+[1] pp.

Types of the De Vinne Press: Specimens for the Use of Compositors, Proofreaders and Publishers (1907). 442 pp.

Specimens of Machine Faces in Use at the De Vinne Press (1908). 85 pp.

Specimens of Writing Types of the Style of the Louis Quatorze Period, in the Printing House of the De Vinne Press (n.d.). [14] pp.

Appendix B

FURTHER NOTES ON *THE INVENTION OF PRINTING*

THE INVENTION OF PRINTING is the one book among De Vinne's writings whose publication history is sufficiently curious to deserve a deeper discussion. While trying to sort through its different printings and editions, one is reminded of Updike's comment in the preface to the 1937 printing of his *Printing Types*. The title page nomenclature for different "editions" of a work, he said, "supplies a basis for that kind of confusion so exciting to collectors, so puzzling to bibliographers, so annoying to publishers, and to the printer of no significance at all."

What emerges in the case of *The Invention of Printing* is an author-printer-publisher eager to lay his findings before his audience and to fill existing demand. After the work came out in parts but before its second printing, this apparently meant correcting some minor errors, using up existing sheets wherever possible, and binding in a modified "Additional Notes and Corrections" at the end. The question of what title page to attach seems to have been a somewhat relaxed matter.

The first printing of *The Invention of Printing* (which, to review, appeared in five parts at six-week intervals beginning in December 1875) consisted of 541 pages of preliminaries and text. There followed three pages of "Authorities Consulted," an eight-page index, and two pages of "Additional Notes and Corrections," bringing the total (with two blank pages) to 556 pages. Before all five parts had appeared, De Vinne must have begun to receive comments and to review the text again himself, hence the notes and corrections at the end of Part 5. The title page of this printing bore the imprint of Francis Hart & Co. But some copies of this first printing now in England also have "London: Trübner & Co.," undoubtedly hand-stamped, on the title page. One of them, at the St. Bride Library, was William Blades's copy and has various De Vinne materials pasted in.

With the fifth part there came two items to be bound into the front of the completed volume: a table of contents and an illustrations list, the page numbers on which could not be known until the entire book was typeset. In addition, there were two cancels, or substitutions, with instructions to the binder. The cancel containing pages 43–46 enabled De Vinne to revise his discussion on page 44 of the decline of books and reading in the sixth century so as to include a quotation from Henry Hallam's 1853 *View of the State of Europe*

During the Middle Ages, which De Vinne apparently felt expressed the state of affairs better than he had. To accomplish this, he rewrote the paragraph and moved some text to footnotes, whose smaller type allowed him to fit everything on the new page without affecting the following page. This eliminated the need for new electrotype plates for page 45 and beyond. The other cancel contained pages 369, 370, 375, and 376. The objective of this substitution was to correct the year of Gutenberg's birth, given on page 376, from "1498 to 1499" to "1398 to 1399." This typo was simply too egregious to let stand, acknowledged only by an entry in the corrections list.

A special printing was anticipated at one point, for the inside of the wrapper for Part 5 promised the following:

> Large Paper Copies. At the request of several subscribers, a quarto edition of the Invention of Printing, leaf not less than 9½ by 12½ inches, will be published during the summer of 1877. This edition will be limited to fifty copies. Price per copy, in paper covers, $12.00.

No evidence has come to light that this quarto was ever published. However, further octavo printings did appear in 1877 and 1878.

The 1877 printing has a new title page of which the lower half (at least) was reset to include the words "second edition" in roman capital letters. The boxed quotation from Fox's *Acts and Monuments* was reset to correct some awkward spacing, and the imprint places Trübner & Co. ahead of Francis Hart & Co. There is no copyright statement on the verso of the title leaf (as there had been in the 1876 printing). All eleven corrections listed at the back of the first printing were made in the text; in each case, rewording was used so that the correction would be limited to one page (and one electrotype plate). Four notes were dropped from the "Additional Notes and Corrections," four notes and one correction were added and seven notes modified after the 1876 printing; as a result, this section took up three pages, bringing the total (with blank versos before Authorities and Index) to 557 pages. The "Authorities Consulted" pages are the same except that two authors (Danou and Nichols) are given fuller names than in the 1876 printing.

In 1878 another printing appeared with the same preliminaries, text, and end matter as the 1877 printing but with a new title page and with the 1876 copyright statement restored on its verso. On the title page, "second edition" is in gothic type rather than in roman, and the imprint gives Francis Hart & Co. first and Trubner [no umlaut] & Co. second. A close, side-by-side comparison of the three printings confirms that, while the paper and structure of the gatherings are the same in all, they represent three separate printings from the plates, since signature marks (that is, those that survived trimming) vary slightly in their placement.

On the Invention of Printing

The original decorated trade bindings appear to have been produced in several shades of brown or gray cloth, although age has made the spines almost a uniform olive. Examined copies of the 1878 printing still in their trade bindings lack the black ruled border of the cover illustration on earlier printings examined.

We now turn back to the 1876 printing of which at least one variant form appeared (in addition to that created by the cancels described above). Several copies have been found in which some of the corrections noted at the end of the 1876 printing have been made in the text. (Those on pages 24, 34, 65, 98, 104, 111, 150, and 412 were made in type, and those on pages 177 and 180, which involved only one character each, were scraped off and corrected with pen. The one called for on page 299 was somehow missed, for it was neither corrected in the text nor listed in "Additional Notes and Corrections" in this variant form.) We can be confident that this is, indeed, an interim form falling between the publication in parts (completed in 1876) and the 1877 printing, since in the matter of notes and corrections this version sometimes agrees with the 1876 printing and sometimes with the 1877. But there are no new corrections called for or changes made in the notes beyond those given at the end of the 1877 printing (and carried forward into the 1878 intact). This form of the first printing sometimes has 1876 on the title page, as in one in the private collection of David Rose, and sometimes 1877 on the title page, as in a copy at the Grolier Club. (The Gale facsimile is from this interim version, but Gale did not reproduce an original title page or indicate what copy was used.)

Anomalies do not stop there. Copies at Columbia University and the Free Library of Philadelphia match the 1878 printing in all respects except that the title page does not include the name of Trübner. And the Fales Collection at New York University has a copy that matches the 1876 printing except that it has the title page of the 1878 printing. (Could De Vinne have had some remaining original sheets that he decided to distribute in 1878?)

To De Vinne, it seems, the differences among these printings were minor, and he did not hesitate to distribute them with a variety of title pages. (Indeed, that is why bibliographers consider them all the same edition; they are printed from substantially the same setting of type.) More curiosities could probably be discovered upon examining more copies. A close comparison of copies whose signature marks have not been trimmed off might also allow the matching of sheets from some of the "anomalies" with sheets of the full printings. For purposes of this biography, these kinds of extended searches have not been undertaken.

By comparison, the second edition of *The Invention of Printing* – at least based on the seven copies examined – exhibits a rather boring uniformity. Printed by Francis Hart & Co. but copyrighted (1878) by George Bruce's Son &

Co., this edition was composed in Bruce types of decreasing sizes (from great-primer down to diamond), printed on one side of the sheet, and bound with folds at the top edges. As the type became smaller, the text was printed in two text blocks per page and later in four blocks. Each page bears the notation, "George Bruce's Son & Co., Type-Founders, No. 13 Chambers-Street, New-York," making it an impressive promotional tool for the Bruce firm. Most of the illustrations are grouped at the end, rather than throughout the text as in the first edition. The list of authorities, in diamond (4½-point) type, is that of the first edition (with Danou and Nichols identified only by surname). But in the notes and corrections, De Vinne took the opportunity to add eleven further notes – some of them quite lengthy – beyond those of the second and third printings of the first edition. Bruce distributed this work with its type specimens of 1878 and 1882 (where one often finds it bound in) and, very likely, separately as well. Certainly, separately bound copies are in existence today.

This analysis is based on an examination of thirty-nine copies (identified here by parenthetical letters)* in the following twenty-one institutions and private collections: British Library (b, d, e); Columbia University (b, f, h); Free Library of Philadelphia (e, f, g); Grolier Club (c, e, h); Guildhall Library, London (d); Library Company of Philadelphia (a); Library of Congress (b, [e] no longer with title page); New-York Historical Society (b); New York Public Library (b [two copies], e); New York University, Fales Collection (f); New York University, Institute of Fine Arts (d); Parsons School of Design (g); Pierpont Morgan Library (b); Pratt Institute (b); Princeton University (e, g); Queens Borough Public Library (e); St. Bride Library, London (b [two copies], d, h); University of Pennsylvania (d); collection of David Rose (c); collection of Stephen O. Saxe (b, h); author's collection (b, c, d).

* a = 1876, Hart & Co., in original parts.
  b = 1876, Hart & Co., bound as intended
  c = interim printing (matching Gale reprint)
  d = 1877, Trübner and Hart
  e = 1878, Hart and Trubner
  f = anomalies discussed in the preceding paragraphs
  g = distributed with Bruce type specimen, 1878
  h = distributed with Bruce type specimen, 1882

Appendix C

A CORE DE VINNE COLLECTION

THIS IS A VERY PERSONAL LIST of twenty-five items that I believe best illustrate the work and career of Theodore Low De Vinne.

The most important fruits of his insatiable historical appetite were (1) *The Invention of Printing* (1876), clothed in period dress and written amid the very demanding process of building up a business, and (2) *Notable Printers of Italy During the Fifteenth Century* (1910), published under the lukewarm auspices of the Grolier Club when he was infirm but determined and had, at least, the club's indomitable librarian, Miss Granniss, for moral support and bibliographical assistance. His 1896 reprint of Joseph Moxon's *Mechanick Exercises* (3) is an eloquent example of De Vinne's proselytizing to raise historical awareness among printers; his extensive preface and notes show the depth of his passion. This work also represents his leadership in the New York Typothetae, which served as publisher, although De Vinne assumed the financial risk himself.

Most essential in the practical printing department is (4) his highly influential four-volume *Practice of Typography*, first editions in 1900, 1901, 1902, and 1904; for today's reader it is full of detail about the printing process at the turn of the century. Representing his early, aggressive work for the printing industry – and, again, shedding considerable light on the trade – are (5) the 1871 second and more informative edition of *The Printers' Price List* (available in facsimile) and (6) *The State of the Trade: Observations on Eight Hours and Higher Prices* (1872). For insight into the way he ran his own business, there is (7) the *Manual of Printing Office Practice*, virtually unobtainable in the original pocket-sized 1883 edition, but subsequently printed in a larger format with an introduction by Douglas C. McMurtrie.

As for type itself, which was of more consuming interest to De Vinne than any other single topic, (8) the 1907 *Types of the De Vinne Press: Specimens for the Use of Compositors, Proofreaders and Publishers* stands out among his eleven specimen books. This 442-page opus, in addition to being what the subtitle claims, reveals his own considerable learning on the subject of types. Furthermore, it is a handsome volume. In his 1885 lecture, *Historic Printing Types*, published in 1886 (9), he revealed to his new Grolier Club colleagues what would be his perennial focus at the club.

Periodicals were a significant part of De Vinne's business. The core collection needs an example of (10) *Scribner's Monthly*; an ideal issue would be October 1881, which contains De Vinne's article on Aldus Manutius, "The First Editor," reprinted several times. Desired examples of *Century Magazine* cannot be reduced to fewer than three containing articles that he wrote: (11) June 1888 for "A Printer's Paradise: The Plantin Moretus Museum at Antwerp," reprinted by the Grolier Club and others; (12) November 1890 for "The Printing of 'The Century,'" with its description and wood-engraved illustrations of life inside the De Vinne Press Building; and (13) March 1896 for "The 'Century's Printer' on the 'Century's Type,'" in which he discussed the new typeface that had made its first appearance in the November 1895 issue. Not to be overlooked is the supreme children's periodical of the era, (14) *St. Nicholas*. Any six-month volume, especially in its red, black, and gold trade binding, would be a fine representative.

A collection of books he printed should include the volume on which he did composition and presswork as an apprentice, (15) *An Outline History of Orange County* (1846–47) by Samuel W. Eager. Later he was able to convert the design of his title page from chagrin to instruction. Many De Vinne Press imprints suggest themselves for inclusion. Perhaps the most underrated among bibliophiles is (16) *The Century Dictionary*, for the production of which De Vinne designed an elaborate type stand and built an addition onto the De Vinne Press Building. A monument to commercial printing, the dictionary is especially desirable in its original twenty-four parts in their Century trade binding. Given the importance of wood engravings to De Vinne's early fame and success, the collection would be well served by (17) the four-volume *Battles and Leaders of the Civil War*, which the Century Company published in 1887 from articles written for their magazine by generals on both sides of the Civil War. Without the seventeen hundred wood engravings, its words would have been much less compelling. The incredible, nuanced detail with which Timothy Cole delivered artworks of Europe to the *Century Magazine*'s audience can best be represented by (18) one or more of the five compilations: *Old Italian Masters Engraved on Wood . . .* (1892) or French masters (1896), Dutch and Flemish masters (1901), English masters (1902), or Spanish masters (1907).

Since De Vinne suggested the Grolier Club's first publication, wrote a preface, and printed it, (19) *A Decree of Star Chamber Concerning Printing* (1884) would be ideal.

The Episcopal *Book of Common Prayer* (1892 and 1893), given its interesting production history, has a place on the list. It is as close as any book comes to the De Vinne house style. Most appropriate would be (20) the octavo printing, without the added borders that, even Updike admitted, compromised its "chilly" integrity.

Several volumes *about* De Vinne round out the core collection. The tribute volume published after his death, (21) *Theodore Low De Vinne, Printer* (1915), printed in his Renner type and bound in its modest brown paper over boards, befits his personality even while it fails to convey the full importance of his contribution to printing history. The 1929 *Catalogue of Work of the De Vinne Press Exhibited at the Grolier Club* (22) gives a fuller picture. The 1920 Anderson Galleries sale catalogue (23) is essential to understanding the reference collection with which De Vinne surrounded himself. The ruminations of one of De Vinne's most promising employees, Frank Hopkins, provide insight into the De Vinne Press's inner workings, including the bitter-sweet circumstances of Hopkins's leaving the press: (24) *The De Vinne and Marion Presses* (1936). The Typophiles' 1968 two-volume Chap Book 47 (25) reprints several important articles, including Carl P. Rollins's perceptive 1950 essay on De Vinne from *Signature*; De Vinne's two-part article, "The Growth of Wood-Cut Printing," from the April and May 1880 issues of *Scribner's Monthly*; and several of the articles mentioned above.

This list has many shortcomings: none of the small, utilitarian volumes printed by Francis Hart & Co. when De Vinne was trying to get a foothold in the book-printing business; inadequate representation of the bibliophilic printing he did beyond the Grolier Club; not enough of the workaday trade editions he turned out for Century and other publishers. But a core collection is merely a place to begin.

NOTES

Abbreviations in Notes

Bothwell Scrapbook, GC James W. Bothwell, compiler, *Newspaper Tributes to the Memory of Theodore Low De Vinne* [scrapbook, ca. 1840–1928], Grolier Club

Century *Century Illustrated Monthly Magazine*

Choate De Vinne Papers, Andrew Mellon Library, Choate Rosemary Hall, Wallingford, Conn.

DeV Memorabilia, GC Theodore Low De Vinne Memorabilia Collection, 1850–1914, Grolier Club

DeV Papers, AAS Theodore Low De Vinne Papers, American Antiquarian Society

DeV Papers, CU Theodore Low De Vinne Papers, Rare Book and Manuscript Library, Columbia University

DeV Photographs, GC Theodore Low De Vinne Photograph and Memorabilia Collection, 1897–1924, Grolier Club

GC Publications Committee on Publications records, Grolier Club

NYPL New York Public Library, Astor, Lenox and Tilden Foundations

Scribner's *Scribner's Monthly: An Illustrated Magazine for the People*

TLD Theodore Low De Vinne

CHAPTER 2

1. Information relating to the Reverend De Vinné, unless otherwise noted, is from *A Memorial of the Reverend Daniel De Vinne* (New York: printed for the family, 1883).

2. Daniel S. De Vinne to Henry Lewis Bullen, 18 March 1914, DeV Papers, CU. Bullen reprinted the letter, attributing it to Theodore, in the *Inland Printer* 83 (August 1929): 104.

3. Abel Stevens, *History of the Methodist Episcopal Church in the United States of America* (New York: Carlton & Porter, 1867), 422.

4. *A Memorial of Joanna Augusta De Vinne* (New York: printed for family friends only, 1888), 13.

5. According to one authority, these two amounts had the purchasing power in 2003 of $104,429 and $115,534, respectively. John J. McCusker, "Comparing the Purchasing Power of Money in the United States (or Colonies) from 1665 to 2003." Economic History Services, 2004, http://www.eh.net/hmit/ppowerusd/.

6. Daniel De Vinné, *The Church and Slavery: A Historical Survey of the Methodist Episcopal Church in Its Relation to Slavery* (Boston: D. S. King, 1844), reprinted as *The Methodist Episcopal Church and Slavery: A Historical Survey of the Relation of the Early Methodists to Slavery* (New York: F. Hart, 1857); and *A History of the Irish Primitive Church Together with the Life of St. Patrick, and His Confession in Latin, with a Parallel Translation* (New York: Francis Hart & Co., 1870).

7. "Theodore L. De Vinne & Co. – Late Francis Hart & Co., a Notable New York Printing House," *Paper World* 6 (March 1883): 2.

CHAPTER 3

1. TLD, "Printing Sixty Years Ago," in Columbia Typographical Union, *Third Year Book* (Washington, D.C.: 1901), 27.

2. Theodore Brockbank De Vinne to J. W. Phinney, 7 June 1894, DeV Papers, AAS.

3. Equivalent in purchasing power to $167,440 in 2003. John J. McCusker, "Comparing the Purchasing Power of Money in the United States (or Colonies) from 1665 to 2003." Economic History Services, 2004, http://www.eh.net/hmit/ppowerusd/.

4. Circular in Bothwell Scrapbook, GC.

5. A platen applies pressure over the entire rectangular bed of composed type at one time. On a cylinder press, the cylinder rolls the sheet of paper over the type and puts pressure at any one instant only on a narrow band of type.

6. TLD, "Printing Sixty Years Ago," 31; "Printing in New York," 6, manuscript draft, DeV Papers, CU; "Fifty Years of Printing," *American Printer* 30 (May 1900): 138.

7. Correspondence with Hart is found in the De Vinne Papers at Choate.

8. Equivalent to $287 in 2003. McCusker, "Comparing the Purchasing Power."

9. In 1928 Alfred E. Omen recalled her as "an English woman" (*Printing* 46 [22 December 1928]: 14). This does not seem consistent with the fact that her parents and several adult siblings lived in Hudson, Wisconsin, where she visited them in 1858 and 1873. Her letters to Theodore mention that her father missed his "old home in Connecticut" and wished he could buy it back (DeV Memorabilia, GC).

10. Full-page ad, in a scrapbook of the R. Hoe & Co. Collection, Manuscripts Division, Library of Congress. It appears on the verso of a Hoe advertisement.

11. *Catalogue of the Printers' Free Library, under the Direction of the New York Typographical Society* (New York: Baker, Godwin & Co., 1852 and 1855).

12. Richard L. King, "The Book Collections of the New York and San Francisco Mercantile Libraries," *Business History* 20 (January 1978): 42.

13. Henry Lewis Bullen, "Theodore Low De Vinne, Printer," *American Bulletin* 3 (April 1914): 8; Ruth Shepard Granniss, "American Book Collecting and the Growth of Libraries," in Hellmut Lehmann-Haupt, *The Book in America* (New York: R. R. Bowker, 1939), 370.

14. TLD, "Giambattista Bodoni," *Printers' Circular* 6 (March 1871): 8; "The Mazarin Bible," *Printers' Circular* 8 (September 1873): 234.

CHAPTER 4

1. Bothwell Scrapbook, GC.

2. Equivalent to $333,430 in 2003. John J. McCusker, "Comparing the Purchasing Power of Money in the United States (or Colonies) from 1665 to 2003." Economic History Services, 2004, http://www.eh.net/hmit/ppowerusd/.

3. All information in this chapter regarding the Hart-De Vinne partnership, unless otherwise noted, is from the De Vinne Papers at Choate.

4. Because of the daily newspaper's perishable nature and the short intervals between copy preparation and production deadlines, newspaper publishers tended to run their own printing plants. Some large book publishers eventually had their own plants or at least composing rooms. The balance of the printing trade (which did custom work for a variety of customers) formed the book-and-job branch.

5. This article is undeniably De Vinne's voice. The other pieces are probably his writing as well; no articles are signed.

6. TLD, speech at the annual Franklin dinner, "Typothetae of New York: Celebrating Franklin's Birthday," *American Bookmaker* 16 (February 1893): 81.

7. United Typothetae of America convention souvenir, 1896.

8. TLD, "The Profits of Book Composition," *Printer* 5 (January 1864): 38–40. "Brevier" was the name of a small type size that would become 8-point in the American point system, adopted near the end of the century.

9. Prospectus in DeV Papers, CU; Ira Brainerd, "Theodore Low De Vinne: The Printer, the Author, the Man," *Printing Art* 35 (May 1920): 202. For a fuller discussion of *The Printers' Price List*, see the author's introduction to the 1980 reprint by Garland Press.

10. The *Printer* was founded in 1858 as an independent trade periodical and was effectively the organ of the National Typographical Union from 1859 until editor Greason "became thoroughly disenchanted with the union linkup of his paper" in 1866. Greason subsequently reprinted some of De Vinne's articles. David P. Forsyth, *The Business Press in America: 1750–1861* (Philadelphia: Chilton Books, 1964), 241.

11. Meetings in 1849 had led to the formation of the New York Printers' Union, which joined with those of other cities to become the National Typographical Union in 1852 – the earliest permanent labor union in the country. In 1869 it encompassed Canada and became the International Typographical Union, or ITU, of which the New York local was "Big Six." In 1864, believing their needs were not being met in the compositor-dominated Typographical Union, pressmen organized their own union, becoming in 1889 the International Printing Pressmen's Union. Similar exoduses from the ITU created unions for bookbinders, stereotypers and electrotypers, and photoengravers.

12. TLD, *The State of the Trade* (New York: Francis Hart & Co., 1872), 6, 32, 43.

13. TLD to Francis Hart, 22 September 1872, Choate.

14. TLD to Francis Hart, 29 September 1872, Choate.

15. "The De Vinne Press," *American Bulletin* n.s. 5 (September 1910): 7. The medal was part of the Grolier Club Exhibit honoring De Vinne's centenary. Grolier Club, *Catalogue of Work of the De Vinne Press* (New York: Grolier Club, 1929), 31. See also Carl Purington Rollins's discussion of the 250-page Alden Typesetting and Distributing Machine Co. prospectus which Hart & Co. printed in 1865 in "Theodore Low De Vinne," *Signature* n.s. 10 (1950): 7–8.

16. "Theodore L. De Vinne & Co. – Late Francis Hart & Co., a Notable New York Printing House," *Paper World* 6 (March 1883): 2.

17. TLD, "Color Printing in 1866," *Inland Printer* 26 (October 1900): 49; and Choate.

18. There were several methods at this time for creating line blocks in relief so they could be printed by letterpress along with type. See section 33 a-g of Bamber Gascoigne, *How to Identify Prints* (New York: Thames and Hudson, 1986).

19. *New-York News-Letter* 1 (May 1868): 8.

20. "TLD & Co.," *Paper World*, p. 3; Henry Lewis Bullen, "Theodore Low De Vinne, Printer," *American Bulletin* 3 (April 1914): 7.

21. Choate.

22. Robert Underwood Johnson, *Remembered Yesterdays* (Boston: Little, Brown, 1925), 109.

23. Henry Lewis Bullen, "How Theodore Low De Vinne Became America's Most Famous Printer," *Inland Printer* 69 (July 1922): 517.

24. Equivalent to $1,333,234 in 2003. McCusker, "Comparing the Purchasing Power."

25. TLD, "Mediæval Printing," *Printer* 5 (April 1864): 65.

26. TLD, "Fust and Gutenberg," *Printer* 5 (August 1864): 118.

27. TLD, "Giambattista Bodoni," *Printers' Circular* 6 (March 1871): 8–9; TLD, "Giambattista Bodoni," *Printing Art* 17 (June 1911): 277–82.

28. TLD, "William Caxton," *Printers' Circular* 7 (October 1872): 282.

29. Susan Otis Thompson, preface to *Caxton: An American Contribution to the Quincentenary Celebration*, Typophile Chap Book 52 (New York: Typophiles, 1976), x.

30. TLD, "England's First Printer," *Critic* 2 (28 January 1882): 20–21.

31. TLD, "Blades's Pentateuch of Printing," *Nation* 54 (7 January 1892): 15–16. De Vinne did not approve, however, of the *Pentateuch* itself, which was completed by others and published posthumously (Blades died in 1890) and "gives no new information, nor does it present all the old facts that are really needed in an epitome of typographic history."

32. *The Quadrat* 3 (June 1875): 88.

33. TLD to Joel Munsell, DeV Papers, CU. The letter is dated "11 January 1875," but the content could only have been written in January 1876. So this must have been a case of that error one makes by continuing to write the old year when barely in the new one.

34. Chain lines, visible in the texture of handmade paper and caused by the large wires going across the mesh in the bottom of the paper mold, can be simulated in machine-made paper.

35. TLD, *The Invention of Printing* (New York: Francis Hart & Co., 1876), 15.

36. Ibid., 12.

37. Review in "Culture and Progress" column, *Scribner's* 16 (August 1878): 594.

38. Typothetae Minutes, 3:307, Typothetae Papers, Rare Book and Manuscript Library, Columbia University.

39. Otto W. Furmann, *Gutenberg and the Strasbourg Documents of 1439* (New York: Press of the Woolly Whale, 1940), 117.

40. Trübner published William Blades's 1877 *Biography and Typography of William Caxton, England's First Printer* and advertised both it and the Trübner/Hart *Invention of Printing* at the 1877 Caxton Celebration.

Advertising flier, loose in *The Invention of Printing* at University of Pennsylvania Furness Art Library.

41. TLD, "John Gutenberg," *Scribner's* 12 (May 1876): 73–85.

42. TLD, "The Mazarin Bible," *Printers' Circular* 8 (September 1873): 234.

43. TLD, "The Gutenberg Anniversary," *Outlook* 65 (5 May 1900): 31–37; and "The Art of Gutenberg," *American Printer* 30 (August 1900): 341.

44. TLD, review of George Washington Moon, *The Oldest Type-Printed Book in Existence, Nation* 73 (24 October 1901): 324–25.

45. TLD to J. W. Phinney, 19 March 1896, DeV Papers, AAS.

46. Paul Needham, preface to Janet Ing, *Johann Gutenberg and his Bible*, Typophile Chap Book 58 (New York: The Typophiles, 1988), 16.

47. Lecture demonstration sponsored by the Bibliographical Society of America and the American Printing History Association, Grolier Club, New York, 22 January 2001.

48. Probated 15 June 1877, Liber 68, p. 259, Surrogate's Court, Kings County, New York.

49. $90,000 in 1877 was equivalent to $1,571,886 in 2003. McCusker, "Comparing the Purchasing Power."

50. "TLD & Co.," *Paper World*, 2.

Chapter 5

1. Samuel C. Chew, *Fruit Among the Leaves* (New York: Appleton-Century-Crofts, 1950), 68.

2. John Tomsich, *A Genteel Endeavor: American Culture and Politics in the Gilded Age* (Stanford: Stanford University Press, 1971), 121.

3. L. Frank Tooker, *The Joys and Tribulations of an Editor* (New York: Century, 1924), 121.

4. Arthur John, *The Best Years of the Century* (Urbana: University of Illinois Press, 1981), 77.

5. Eric De Maré, *The Victorian Wood-Block Illustrators* (London: Gordon Fraser, 1980), 178.

6. William James Linton, "Art in Engraving on Wood," *Atlantic Monthly* 43 (June 1879): 705–15; and *The History of Wood-Engraving in America* (Boston: Estes & Lauriat, 1882), 69–71.

7. De Maré, *Victorian Wood-Block*, 7.

8. TLD, "Fads in Typography," *Inland Printer* 26 (January 1901): 602. In Arthur Warren's biography of uncle and nephew Whittingham (printed by De Vinne "without whose wise and generous counsel," Warren says, he could not have produced the work), he expressed doubt about the veracity of family tradition that would have Whittingham as the originator of overlays, citing De Vinne's reservations on the matter. *The Charles Whittinghams, Printers* (New

York: Grolier Club, 1896), 293.

9. TLD, "American Printing," in Chauncey Mitchell Depew, ed., *1795–1895: One Hundred Years of American Commerce* (New York: D. O. Haynes & Co., 1895), 1:318.

10. TLD, "Color-Printing in 1866," *Inland Printer* 26 (October 1900): 49; "Mr. Theo. L. De Vinne on Plain Printing," *Printers' Register – Supplement* 35 (6 May 1896): iii; "Woodcuts: Concerning the Taking of Proofs and Prints," *Printing Times and Lithographer* n.s. 4 (15 October 1878): 197–99, (15 November 1878): 221–22; "A Printer on the Limitations of Engraving on Wood," *Printing Times and Lithographer* n.s. 5 (15 March 1879): 45–47, (15 April 1879): 69–70, and (15 May 1879): 94–96; "The Growth of Woodcut Printing," *Scribner's* 19 (April 1880): 860–74 and 20 (May 1880): 34–45; "The Printing of Wood-Engravings," *Print-Collectors' Quarterly* 1 (July 1911): 365–79.

11. Frank Luther Mott, in *A History of American Magazines* (Cambridge: Harvard University Press, 1938–68), 3:501, says seventy thousand, but Century Company's own tallies suggest the smaller figure. Rodman Gilder Papers, Manuscripts and Archives Division, NYPL.

12. *Quarterly Illustrator* 1 (December 1893): 293.

13. TLD, "John Gutenberg," *Scribner's* 12 (May 1876): 73–85; "The First Editor," *Scribner's* 22 (October 1881): 889–98; "A Printer's Paradise," *Century* 36 (June 1888): 225–45; "On the Printing of the Century," *Century* 30 (September 1885): 808–9; "The Printing of 'The Century,'" *Century* 41 (November 1890): 87–99; "The 'Century's Printer' on the 'Century's Type,'" *Century* 51 (March 1896): 794–96.

14. Choate.

15. TLD to TBD, 1 September 1867, DeV Memorabilia, GC.

16. TBD to Henry Lewis Bullen, 20 January 1917, DeV Papers, CU.

17. Author's interview with Charles Adcock De Vinne, great-grandson of Theodore Low De Vinne, 8 July 1981, New Haven, Conn.

18. "Theodore L. De Vinne & Co. – Late Francis Hart & Co., A Notable New York Printing House," *Paper World* 6 (March 1883): 3.

19. TLD, *Manual of Printing Office Practice* (New York: Theodore L. De Vinne & Co., 1883), 8.

20. Peter Lyon, *Success Story: The Life and Times of S. S. McClure* (New York: Charles Scribner's Sons, 1963), 46–49; Samuel S. McClure, *My Autobiography* (New York: Frederick A. Stokes Co., 1914), 158–167.

21. Grolier Club, Records, 1884–1984.

22. In Comparato's study of the Hoe company, he offered this comparison of the family's generations: "Richard, Robert [II], and Peter Hoe [sons of the founder] had found the world so full of physical wonders that they were unimpressed by the subtleties of parlor and ballroom. They were indeed welcome at

many social functions, but they always seemed to prefer less ostentatious companionship. . . . The dilettantish Robert Hoe III [son of Robert II] called attention to family affluence and wealth as had no other family individual. His impeccable education and club affiliations were at last useful; his creation of the Grolier Club a masterful social, snobbish balm to remove any final traces of grease and grime." Frank E. Comparato, *Chronicles of Genius and Folly: R. Hoe & Company and the Printing Press as a Service to Democracy* (Culver City, Calif.: Labyrinthos, 1979), 654, 655.

23. *Art Age* 1 (May 1884): 114.

24. In 1885 the circulation was announced editorially as 250,000. NYPL's Rodman Gilder papers contain a tally of circulation by year from 1871 through 1913. It gives the highest figure as 216,959 for the year 1886–87, but it is not clear whether this is subscriptions, net paid circulation, or some other measure. As John Tebbel pointed out in *The American Magazine: A Compact History* (New York: Hawthorn Books, 1969), 197, before 1914 and the advent of auditing procedures by the Audit Bureau of Circulations, "There was little honesty in making circulation claims."

25. Plan #203 of 1885, "New Buildings Docket Ledger," Department of Buildings, New York City.

26. "A Noted Printer and a Notable Printing Establishment: The De Vinne Press," *Paper World* 14 (January 1887): 3.

27. Harmon H. Goldstone and Martha Dalrymple, *History Preserved: A Guide to New York City Landmarks and Historic Districts* (New York: Simon & Schuster, 1974), 144; Talbot Hamlin, "A Brief Guide for the Historical Bus Tour arranged by the Society of Architectural Historians 27 January 1952," [unpublished?] cited on an undated Historic American Buildings Survey Inventory form in files of the New York City Landmarks Preservation Commission; Lewis Mumford, "Architecture: Beautiful and Beloved," *New York Times Magazine*, sec. 6, pt. 2 (1 February 1953): 22; Paul Goldberger, *The City Observed, New York* (New York: Random House, 1979), 67; Francis Morrone, *The Architectural Guidebook to New York City* (Salt Lake City: Gibbs Smith, 1994), 92; Sarah Bradford Landau and Carl W. Condit, *Rise of the New York Skyscraper, 1865–1913* (New Haven, Yale University Press, 1996), 143; Andrew Dolkart, *Guide to New York City Landmarks: New York City Landmarks Preservation Commission*, 2nd ed. (New York: John Wiley & Sons, 1998), 50; Norval White and Elliot Willensky, *AIA Guide to New York City*, 4th ed. (New York: Crown, 2000), 161; Christopher Gray, *New York Times*, Real Estate Section (13 April 2003): 7.

28. "The De Vinne Press, New York," *British and Colonial Printer and Stationer & Booksellers' Circular* 16 (3 February 1887): 1–3, 6–7.

29. TLD, "The Printing of 'The Century,'" 92.

30. *Sanitary Engineer*, 13 (13 May 1886): 561.

31. Equivalent to $3,894,938 in 2003. John J. McCusker, "Comparing the

Purchasing Power of Money in the United States (or Colonies) from 1665 to 2003." Economic History Services, 2004, http://www.eh.net/hmit/ppowerusd/.

32. On a rotary press, the printing surface (type or plate locked onto the cylinder) actually rotates onto the paper rather than lying on a flat bed, awaiting the paper. "Web" means that the paper is on a continuous roll and not in sheets that have to be fed to the press.

33. TLD, "The Printing of 'The Century,'" 94.

CHAPTER 6

1. An entry in the 1928 Grolier Club catalogue for its De Vinne exhibit (p. 22) says, "Drawing in colors of the device of The De Vinne Press designed by George Babb, who used as a motif the terra cotta cartouche at the left of the entrance of The De Vinne Press building."

2. TLD to Henry Lewis Bullen, 5 December 1910, printed in *Inland Printer* 84 (October 1929): 77.

3. Bothwell Scrapbook, GC.

4. TLD to Gilder, 24 January 1886, Richard Watson Gilder Papers, Manuscripts and Archives Division, NYPL.

5. TLD to Ellsworth, 11 November 1887, and to the editors of *Century*, 19 November 1890, Century Company Records, Manuscripts and Archives Division, NYPL.

6. "A Noted Printer and a Notable Printing Establishment: The De Vinne Press," *Paper World* 14 (January 1887): 5.

7. $1,000,000 in 1890 was worth $20,189,357 in 2003. John J. McCusker, "Comparing the Purchasing Power of Money in the United States (or Colonies) from 1665 to 2003." Economic History Services, 2004, http://www.eh.net/hmit/ppowerusd/.

8. Arthur John, *The Best Years of the Century* (Urbana: University of Illinois Press, 1981), 135–136.

9. *O'Neill v. Morse* 385 Mich. 130, 147, 188 N.W. 2d 785, 794 (1971) (Black, J., dissenting).

10. Sidney I. Landau, *Dictionaries: The Art and Craft of Lexicography* (New York: Charles Scribner's Sons, 1984), 72, 109.

11. http://www.global-language.com/century

12. TLD, "Cooperation," *Century* 90 (July 1886): 404.

13. TLD, "Printing as a Profession for Young Men," *St. Louis Stationer* 2 (February 1890): 69, 71; reprinted from the St. Louis *Republic*.

14. "Noted Printer," *Paper World*, 4–5.

15. George Abbott Stevens, *New York Typographical Union No. 6: Study of a Modern Trade Union and its Predecessors* (Albany: New York State Department of Labor, 1913), 317.

16. TLD to W. W. Ellsworth, 11 November 1887, Century Company Records, Manuscripts and Archives Division, NYPL.

17. Typothetae Minutes, 3:81, 84, 87, Typothetae Papers, Rare Book and Manuscript Library, Columbia University.

18. Robert Underwood Johnson, *Remembered Yesterdays*, (Boston: Little, Brown, 1925), 29–30.

19. Brander Matthews, "The Grolier Club," *Century* 39 (November 1889): 87.

20. Authors Club, *The First Book of the Authors Club: Liber Scriptorum* (New York: The Club, 1893).

21. Duffield Osborne, *The Authors Club: An Historical Sketch* (New York: The Club, 1913); Arthur Bartlee Maurice, "Literary Clubland," *Bookman* 21 (July 1905): 499–506.

22. The Aldine Club, *Constitution, Rules, Officers, Members* (New York: The Club, 1892); William W. Ellsworth, *A Golden Age of Authors* (Boston: Houghton, Mifflin, 1919), 245; Matthews, "The Grolier Club," 86.

23. Moses King, *King's Views of New York 1896–1915 and Brooklyn 1905* (New York: Arno Press, 1980), reprint variously paginated, final page.

24. Years 1880–96, "New Buildings Docket Ledger," Department of Buildings, New York City.

25. $40,000 in 1889 was equivalent to $793,023 in 2003. McCusker, "Comparing the Purchasing Power."

26. TLD, speech before the United Typothetae of America, *American Bookmaker* 15 (September 1892): 92.

27. TLD, "Changed Conditions in the Printing Trade," *Printer and Bookmaker* 29 (December 1899): 185–86.

28. Leaflet, 27 December 1900, Bothwell Scrapbook, GC, quoted in *Inland Printer* 26 (February 1901): 785.

29. Notice to employees dated 11 April 1891, Bothwell Scrapbook, GC; and unidentified newspaper clipping, ca. April 1892, DeV Papers, CU.

30. Envelope, so marked in De Vinne's hand, DeV Papers, CU.

31. Henry Lewis Bullen, "Theodore Low De Vinne, Printer," *American Bulletin* 3 (April 1914): 8.

32. "The De Vinne Press Adopts Profit-Sharing," *Inland Printer* 9 (June 1892): 766–69.

33. He gave the date as 1850. Actually, the first book printed in the resurrected type was the 1844 *Diary of Lady Willoughby*, a fact he included in his *Plain Printing Types* in 1900. In fact, Whittingham had used Caslon capitals on title pages for Pickering from 1840. A. F. Johnson, *Type Designs: Their History and Development*, 3rd ed. (London: Deutsch, 1966), 80.

34. Brackets are the "filling in" of the corners created by the main strokes and their serifs (perpendicular finishing strokes).

---

35. TLD, "The 'Century's Printer' on the 'Century's type,'" *Century* 51 (March 1896): 796.

36. Carl Purington Rollins, "Theodore Low De Vinne," *Signature*, n.s. 10 (1950): 9.

37. *Types of the De Vinne Press*, (New York: De Vinne Press, 1907), 198.

38. The American Type Founders Company, established in 1892, was an amalgamation of some twenty type foundries.

39. Stanley Morison, *The Typographic Book, 1450–1935* (London: E. Benn, 1963), 55.

40. James Moran, *Stanley Morison: His Typographic Achievement* (New York: Hastings House, 1971), 26.

41. Michael Koenig, "De Vinne and the De Vinne Press," *Library Quarterly* 41 (January 1971): 10.

42. Virginia Smith, "Longevity and Legibility: Two Types from the De Vinne Press and How They Have Fared," *Printing History* 8.1, no.15 (1986): 13–21.

43. Paul Shaw, "The Century Family," *Fine Print* 7.4 (October 1981): 144.

44. For a detailed discussion of the Century family of typefaces in metal, see Mac McGrew, *American Metal Typefaces of the Twentieth Century*, 2nd ed. (New Castle, Del.: Oak Knoll, 1993), 76–81.

45. For background on the technical developments leading up to successful photo-mechanical illustrations, see David Pankow, "Dungeons and Dragon's Blood: The Development of Late 19th and Early 20th Century Platemaking Processes," *Printing History* 10.1, no. 19 (1988): 21–35.

46. Ellic Howe, "From Bewick to the Halftone: A Survey of Illustration Processes During the Nineteenth Century," *Typography* 3 (Summer 1937): 23.

47. TLD, "Color Printing in 1866," *Inland Printer* 26 (October 1900): 49.

48. Bamber Gascoigne, *How to Identify Prints*, (New York: Thames and Hudson, 1986), glossary, p. 205. The Meisenbach process, patented in 1882, is discussed by Howe in "From Bewick to the Half-Tone," 22.

49. Alexander W. Drake, letter to the editor, *New York Times* (19 February 1914): 8.

50. For an explanation of the collotype process, see Gascoigne, *How to Identify*, section 40.

51. John Tebbel, *The American Magazine: A Compact History* (New York: Hawthorn, 1970), 202.

52. TLD, "The Printing of William Morris," *Book Buyer* 13 (January 1897): 923.

53. U.S. Bureau of the Census. *Census of Manufactures for 1900*, vol. 9, pt. 3, p. 1100.

54. U.S. Patent 634259, granted 3 October 1899.

55. Both processes used light-sensitized gelatin. Edward could not have been the Edward Hale Bierstadt who was treasurer of the Grolier Club and who died

in 1896, more than a year before the patent application was filed. Nor was he Edward Hale Bierstadt, the author, who was born in 1891.

56. *Wickers v. McKee,* 29 Appeal Cases D.C. 4 (1907).

57. William Dana Orcutt, *The Kingdom of Books* (Boston: Little, Brown, 1927), 170.

58. Drake, *New York Times.*

59. Charles M. Gage, "The Origin of Coated or Enameled Book Paper," *Paper Trade Journal* 48 (3 July 1919): 28, 30.

60. Frank E. Comparato, *Chronicles of Genius and Folly: R. Hoe & Company and the Printing Press as a Service to "Democracy* (Culver City, Calif.: Labyrinthos, 1979), 527.

61. TLD, "Attractiveness in Books," *Independent* 57 (15 December 1904): 1377; Samuel C. Chew, *Fruit Among the Leaves* (New York: Appleton-Century-Crofts, 1950), 74.

62. TLD, "Masculine Printing," United Typothetae of America, *Proceedings of the Fifth Annual Meeting,* 1891, 143–44.

63. Stephen O. Saxe has pointed out to the author that there was a copy in the New York State Library in 1858 and that Joel Munsell listed a copy in his catalogue of books for sale in 1868.

64. Typothetae Minutes 4:66, 68–69, 109.

65. TLD to J. W. Phinney, 12 July 1891 and 4 January 1892, DeV Papers, AAS.

66. Morris's assistant, Sidney Cockerell, labeled it "Short account of the Press written by W.M. for one of De Vinne's books on Printing. An electro was sent to Mr. De Vinne. . . ." From a scrapbook in the British Library, quoted by William S. Peterson, *The Ideal Book: Essays and Lectures on the Arts of the Book by William Morris* (Berkeley: University of California Press, 1982), 77.

67. Susan Otis Thompson, *American Book Design and William Morris* (New York: Bowker, 1977), 37, n. 23.

68. TLD, "Masculine Printing," 143. Susan Thompson (ibid.) has noted (pp. 30–31) that this was the first mention of Morris in the *American Bookmaker.*

69. TLD, *The Practice of Typography . . . Plain Printing Types,* "proof edition," (1894), 207–8. Grolier Club.

70. TLD, *The Practice of Typography: A Treatise on the Process of Type-Making, the Point System, the Names, Sizes, Styles and Prices of Plain Printing Types* (New York: Century Co., 1900), 206–8.

71. Ibid., 361.

72. Ibid., 362.

73. TLD, "A Book That Won the Grand Prize," *New York Times Saturday Review of Books* (27 October 1900): 736.

74. TLD, "Printing of William Morris," 920; "Typographical Effect," *Independent* 55 (19 November 1903): 2723; Yale College Club speech, p. 30, typescript, DeV Collection, CU.

75. TLD, Yale College Club speech, 8.

76. TLD, *The Practice of Typography: Modern Methods of Book Composition, a Treatise on Type-Setting by Hand and by Machine, and on the Proper Arrangement and Imposition of Pages* (New York: Century Co., 1904), 105, 125; "Typographical Effect," 2724.

77. TLD, *The Practice of Typography: A Treatise on Title-Pages, with Numerous Illustrations in Facsimile, and Some Observations on the Early and Recent Printing of Books* (New York: Century Co., 1902), 390.

78. TLD, "Printing of William Morris," 921; TLD, *Treatise on Title-Pages*, 401.

79. TLD, *Treatise on Title-Pages*, 398, 400.

80. TLD, "A New Edition of the 'Inferno,'" *New York Times Saturday Review of Books* (16 May 1903): 338.

81. This gives credence to Rauri McLean's suggestion that in *Title-Pages As Seen by a Printer* De Vinne ignored such English contemporaries as Ricketts and Pissarro because he disapproved of their work. *Victorian Book Design* (New York: Oxford University Press, 1963), 168.

82. TLD, *Treatise on Title-Pages*, 390; TLD, "Printing of William Morris," 923; Nikolaus Pevsner, *Pioneers of Modern Design: From William Morris to Walter Gropius*, 3d ed. (Baltimore: Penguin Books, 1965), 24.

83. TLD to Ralph Fletcher Seymour quoted in Seymour's *Some Went This Way* (Chicago: R. F. Seymour, 1945), 120.

84. Lawrence C. Wroth, "Printing in the Mauve Decade," *New York Herald Tribune Books* (8 February 1942): 18.

85. TLD to Phinney, 30 March, 6 April, 5 May, 16 June, 19 September, and 8 October 1898, DeV Papers, AAS.

86. TLD to Robert Hoe III, 1 September 1898, GC Publications.

87. Fitz Roy Carrington, "Private and Special Presses: II. Notes on Some Book Clubs and on Printing in America," *Book Buyer* n.s. 23 (September 1901): 97.

88. William Dana Orcutt, "The Art of the Book in America" in Charles Holme, ed., *The Art of the Book*, special number of *Studio* for 1914, 260.

89. Mark H. Liddell to Bothwell, 28 November 1902, quoted in the Grolier Club's *Catalogue of Work of the De Vinne Press*, 76–77.

90. TLD, *Notable Printers of Italy During the Fifteenth Century* (New York: Grolier Club, 1910), 88.

91. McGrew, *American Metal*, 269.

92. Frank E. Hopkins, *The De Vinne and Marion Presses* (Meriden, Conn.: Columbiad Club, 1936), 40.

93. De Vinne felt it necessary to emphasize that no member of the De Vinne Press was responsible for the design. *Types of the De Vinne Press* (1907), 273.

94. J. A. St. John to TLD, 19 November 1890, DeV Papers, CU.

95. TLD, *Plain Printing Types*, 287–89 (emphasis added).

96. TLD, *Treatise on Title-Pages*, 260.

97. McGrew, *American Metal*, 118–121.

98. Peter Beilenson, *The Story of Frederic W. Goudy* (Mount Vernon, N.Y.: Walpole Printing Office, 1939), 18.

99. H. L. Bullen, "Discursions of a Retired Printer," *Inland Printer* 39 (June 1907): 354.

100. Hopkins, *De Vinne and Marion Presses*, 39.

101. TLD to J. W. Phinney, 19 December 1894, DeV Papers, AAS.

102. Ray Nash, *Printing As an Art: A History of the Society of Printers* (Cambridge: Harvard University Press, 1955), 30–31.

103. Thomas A. Larremore and Amy Hopkins Larremore, *The Marion Press: A Survey and a Check-List . . .* (Jamaica, N.Y.: Queens Borough Public Library, 1943), 85. The Larremores quoted from several unique documents in their possession. These documents were not part of the collection on Hopkins and his work that they subsequently donated to the Queensborough Public Library, and their whereabouts are unknown to this writer.

104. Ibid.

105. Ibid.

106. John Pierpont Morgan Papers, ARC 1196, Archives of The Pierpont Morgan Library, New York.

107. Lesley Armstrong Northup, "The '1892 Revision' of the Book of Common Prayer of the Episcopal Church" (Ph.D. diss., Catholic University of America, 1991).

108. The De Vinne Press would also be one of the printers of small-format prayer books for personal use: for instance, in 1896 a 32mo and a 48mo edition for T. Nelson & Son. See David N. Griffiths, comp., *The Bibliography of the Book of Common Prayer 1549–1999* (London: British Library and New Castle, Del.: Oak Knoll, 2002), 423. There also exists at least one offprint of a 32-page part of the text in folio format; the library at St. Thomas Church, New York, has a splendidly bound copy of *The Litany or General Supplication* presented in memory of the St. Thomas rector, the Rev. W. F. Morgan (d. 1888) by his daughters.

109. Daniel Berkeley Updike, *On the Decoration of the Limited Edition of the Standard Prayer Book of MDCCCXCII* (New York: De Vinne Press, 1893), reprinted in William S. Peterson, ed., *The Well-Made Book: Essays and Lectures by Daniel Berkeley Updike* (West New York, N.J.: Mark Batty, 2002), 283–88.

110. _____, *Notes on the Merrymount Press and its Work* (Cambridge: Harvard University Press, 1934), 10.

111. Updike quoted in Larremore and Larremore, *Marion Press*, 170.

112. Updike, *Notes*, 9.

113. E.g., regarding whether or not to "nickel" the plate when red ink – that may or may not have contained vermilion – was being used. TLD to DBU, 3 March 1898, Providence Public Library.

114. Updike, *Notes*, 15.

115. Letter of 18 February 1940 cited in Larremore and Larremore, *Marion Press*, 171.

116. Charles H. Cochrane, "De Vinne as I Knew Him," *Inland Printer* 73 (July 1924): 560.

117. TLD to Beverly Chew, 10 July 1893, GC Publications.

118. TLD to Gilder, 22 January 1897, Richard Watson Gilder Papers, Manuscripts and Archives Division, NYPL.

119. New York *Herald* (28 December 1899): 11.

120. TLD to Bullen, 5 December 1910, printed in *Inland Printer* 84 (October 1929): 77.

CHAPTER 7

1. *Columbia University Quarterly*, 3 (September 1901): 322–23.

2. *British and Colonial Stationer* 49 (1 August 1901): 7.

3. New York *Herald* (26 August 1901): 4.

4. New York *Herald* (2 February 1902): 7 ff.

5. TLD, "Printing in the Nineteenth Century," New York *Evening Post* (12 January 1901): 8–9; excerpted as "Perfecting the Press," *Current Literature* 30 (May 1901):533–35; reprinted in *The Nineteenth Century: A Review of Progress* (New York: G. P. Putnam's Sons, 1901) and in *Scientific American*, Supplement No. 1380 (14 June 1902): 22121–22.

6. Stanley Morison, *The Typographic Book, 1450–1935* (London: E. Benn, 1963), 55.

7. Someone, probably at the De Vinne Press, compiled a list of thirty-one influential people and their words of praise for *Correct Composition*. DeV Papers, CU.

8. *Pritchard v. Liggett & Myers Tobacco Co.*, 350 F. 2d 479, 490 n. 6 (3d Cir. 1965) (Freeman, J., concurring).

9. William Dana Orcutt "The Title-Page, A Study of Mr. De Vinne's Recent Volume," *Bibliographer* 29 (January 1903): 17–33; George French, *American Printer* 39 (December 1904): 291; George French, *American Printer* 35 (December 1902): 369; George French, *Literary Collector* 9 (March 1905): 101–6.

10. Carl Purington Rollins, "Theodore Low De Vinne," *Signature*, n.s. 10 (1950): 20.

11. Lawrence C. Wroth, "Corpus Typographicum: A Review of English and American Printers' Manuals," *Dolphin* no. 2 (1935): 157–70.

12. *Literary Collector* 9 (March 1905): 101.

13. TLD to Bullen 24 October 1913, published in *Inland Printer* 84 (January 1930): 69.

14. DeV Papers, CU.

15. Ibid.

16. Ibid.

CHAPTER 8

1. New York *Herald* (2 February 1902): 7; TLD to Ruth S. Granniss, 3 May 1905, 5 May 1905, and 5 June 1905, GC Publications.

2. TLD to Henry Watson Kent, Club Librarian, 6 October 1904, GC Publications.

3. TLD to Granniss, 26 December 1907, GC Publications.

4. *Styles of Types for Books and Advertisements Now in Service at the De Vinne Press* (New York: De Vinne Press, 1905), 20.

5. TLD to G. H. Boughton, 11 May and 8 June 1904, GC Publications.

6. In the Grolier Club's *Catalogue of Works of the De Vinne Press* (New York, 1929), p. 60, the process would be called "half-tone," but the technique was apparently the Benday process by which areas of mechanical tone could be added to relief plates by photographic methods and printed in colored inks, as desired. See Bamber Gascoigne, *How to Identify Prints* (New York: Thames and Hudson, 1986), sections 63b and 63c.

7. TLD to Granniss, 28 December 1908, GC Publications.

8. Carl P. Rollins, "Typographic Adventures of the Past: I. The Jade Book," *New Colophon* 2 (September 1949): 294–303.

9. TLD to Robert Hoe III, 27 August 1898, GC Publications.

10. TLD, "Logic, Law and the Union Label," *American Printer*, 33 (October 1901): 123.

11. For details see the author's essay, "Master Printers Organize," in Stuart W. Bruchey, ed., *Small Business in American Life* (New York: Columbia University Press, 1980), 185–86.

12. *Publishers' Weekly* 69 (13 January 1906): 47.

13. Typothetae Minutes, 8:63, 70, Typothetae Papers, Rare Book and Manuscript Library, Columbia University.

14. TLD to Ruth Granniss, 9 January 1906, 12 January 1906, 18 January 1906, and 10 February 1906, GC Publications.

15. New York Typographical Union No. 6, Book Arts Ephemera, Rare Book and Manuscript Library, Columbia University.

16. TLD to Granniss, 3 April 1907, GC Publications.

CHAPTER 9

1. TLD to Granniss, 8 February, 18 November, and 28 December 1908, GC Publications.

2. TLD to Beverly Chew, 3 March 1909, GC Publications.

3. James Bothwell to TLD, 22 July 1908, GC Publications.

4. TLD to Chew, 3 March 1909, GC Publications.

5. Theodore Brockbank De Vinne to Chew, 1 July 1914, GC Publications.

6. TLD to Bullen, 5 December 1910, quoted in *Inland Printer* 84 (October 1929): 77.

7. Bullen to Beatrice Warde, 14 February 1927, Beatrice Warde Correspondence, Typographical Library Manuscripts, Rare Book and Manuscript Collection, Columbia University.

8. Brander Matthews, "The Grolier Club," *Century* 39 (November 1889): 91.

9. TLD, "The Printing of Wood-Engravings," *Print-Collectors' Quarterly* 1 (July 1911): 365–78; DeV Papers, CU.

10. Samuel C. Chew, *Fruit Among the Leaves*, (New York: Appleton-Century-Crofts, 1950), 122–23.

11. Ibid., 119; Arthur John, *The Best Years of the Century*, (Urbana: University of Illinois Press, 1981), 234–36, 239.

12. Frank Luther Mott, *A History of American Magazines*, (Cambridge: Harvard University Press, 1938–68), 3:477; Robert Underwood Johnson, *Remembered Yesterdays*, (Boston: Little, Brown, 1925), 138 ff.

13. Rodman Gilder Papers, NYPL.

14. Equivalent to $2,490,977 in 2003. John J. McCusker, "Comparing the Purchasing Power of Money in the United States (or Colonies) from 1665 to 2003." Economic History Services, 2004, http://www.eh.net/hmit/ppowerusd/.

15. Rodman Gilder Papers, NYPL.

16. DeV Papers, CU.

17. Bothwell Scrapbook, GC.

18. Choate. Equivalent to $272,729 in 2003. McCusker, "Comparing the Purchasing Power."

19. TLD to J. W. Phinney, 15 April 1911, DeV Papers, AAS.

20. A replica was accepted by the Metropolitan Museum of Art for its collection, and a gilded copy plus a large bronze model went to the Grolier Club. H. L. Bullen, "How Theodore Low De Vinne Became America's Most Famous Printer," *Inland Printer*, 69 (July 1922): 518; Bullen, *Inland Printer* 83 (August 1929): 104; Council Minutes, 5:212, Grolier Club.

21. Council Minutes, 8:302, 10:54, 57, 59, Grolier Club.

22. "Resolution," Boston Typothetae Board of Trade, reprinted in *Theodore Low De Vinne, Printer* (New York: privately printed at the De Vinne Press, 1915), 49.

1. Choate.

2. *Publishers' Weekly* 87 (29 May 1915): 1661. Equivalent to $26,695,175 in 2003. John J. McCusker, "Comparing the Purchasing Power of Money in the United States (or Colonies) from 1665 to 2003." Economic History Services, 2004, http://www.eh.net/hmit/ppowerusd/.

3. Council Minutes, 8:81, 85, Grolier Club. Minutes should be interpreted circumspectly when – like these – they give only the final decision with no indication of what debate may have preceded it.

4. The copy of the auction catalogue owned by Stephen O. Saxe has the annotation "withdrawn for family" in the margin next to this item.

5. Samuel C. Chew, *Fruit Among the Leaves* (New York: Appleton-Century-Crofts, 1950), 125. According to Frank Luther Mott's *History of American Magazines* (Cambridge: Harvard University Press, 1938–68), 3:479, in 1930, with circulation below twenty thousand, ownership of *Century* was transferred to Forum Publishing Company, resulting in *Forum Combined with the Century Magazine* until it was taken over by *Current History*. In 1931 Century sold *St. Nicholas* to the American Educational Press of Columbus, Ohio.

6. He turned in 1024 shares of stock in the corporation plus $58,500 in exchange for 670 shares of preferred stock that were to pay a dividend of 5 percent a year out of net earnings before dividends were declared on common stock. The preferred stocks were redeemable at the rate of $110 per share. Choate.

7. *New York Times* (12 October 1926): 27.

8. For an account of the ill-fated Club Bindery, see Martin Antonetti, "The Club Bindery and Its Later Incarnations," *Gazette of the Grolier Club* n.s. 47 (1995–1996): 83–102.

9. In the "unopened" entry of his *ABC for Book-Collectors*, 3rd ed., rev. (London: Mercury, 1961), John Carter says that only philistines confuse this term with "uncut."

10. Quoted in Alexander S. Lawson, *A Printer's Almanac* (Philadelphia: North American Publishing Co., 1966), 9.

11. Pierce Butler, "A Typographical Library: The John M. Wing Foundation of the Newberry Library," *Papers of the Bibliographical Society of America* 15.2 (1921): 86.

12. One is at the Grolier Club, and one is in the private collection of Stephen O. Saxe.

13. He had written to Bullen, "One of [the Club's] last ventures was a collection of Whistler's etchings, which now sells for $100 a copy. I do not disparage Whistler, but I think that the device he used as a remarque, a butterfly, is characteristic of the man as an elegant trifler." TLD to Bullen, 5 December 1910, DeV Papers, CU.

14. Equivalent to $229,233 in 2003. McCusker, "Comparing the Purchasing Power."

15. *Catalogue of the Books in the Library of the Typothetae of the City of New York* (De Vinne Press, 1896), 176 pp.

16. Courtesy of Martin Hutner.

17. Frederick Melcher to Ruth Granniss, 11 October 1928, Committee on Public Exhibitions records, Grolier Club.

18. David Walker Mallison, "Henry Lewis Bullen and the Typographic Library and Museum of the American Type Founders Company" (D.L.S. diss., Columbia University, 1976), 85.

19. Henry Lewis Bullen, "Summary of the Contents of the Industrial Graphic Arts Library and Museum of the American Type Founders Company, Jersey City, NJ" [1933] 23 leaves, Book Arts Collection, Rare Book and Manuscript Library, Columbia University.

20. Unidentified clipping, Bothwell Scrapbook, GC.

21. *New York Times* (23 December 1922): 4.

22. *New York Times* (30 December 1922): 12; *Ledger*, Columbia, Ga. (2 January 1923).

23. D. B. Updike, *Literary Review* of the New York *Evening Post* (20 January 1923): 406.

24. *New York Times* (25 December): 12; Updike, *Literary Review*; Bullen, *New York Times*, sect. 2 (14 January 1923): 6.

25. U.S., Bureau of the Census, *Eighth Census of the United States, 1860: Manufactures*, cxxxiii, 383 and *Preliminary Report*, 174; A. F. Hinrichs, *The Printing Industry in New York and Its Environs* (New York: Regional Plans of New York and Its Environs, 1924), 15; Leonard A. Drake, *Trends in the New York Printing Industry* (New York: Columbia University Press, 1940), 4–5, 99–101.

26. *Brooklyn Daily Eagle* editorial (26 December 1922): 6.

27. *New York Tribune* (7 January 1923): 4.

28. Equivalent to $1,618,118 in 2003. McCusker, "Comparing the Purchasing Power."

29. Deeds filed in the New York City Register's office.

30. Incorporation records are on file at the New York County Clerk's Office.

31. Bothwell to Granniss, 20 March 1923, GC Publications.

32. How the colleagues obtained it is a mystery. If the date on the brass plate is to be trusted, De Vinne received the gift two years before his visit that resulted in enthusiastic writings about the museum.

33. Harry T. Peters to Ruth Granniss, 9 October 1928, Committee on Public Exhibitions records, Grolier Club.

34. The club's rolls at this point contained 523 members, of whom 220 lived

outside New York City and its environs.

35. Alfred E. Ommen, "To Theodore Low De Vinne Printers Pay Deep Homage," *Printing* 46 (22 December 1928): 16.

36. The Hall of Fame had been initiated in 1900 when New York University invited the public to submit names of great Americans. Those selected by the university's senate were memorialized by bronze busts in the curving colonnade designed by Stanford White for NYU's University Heights campus in the Bronx. Theodore Morello, ed., *The Hall of Fame for Great Americans at New York University: Official Handbook* (New York: New York University Press, 1967).

37. *Merit Machine Mfg. Corp. v. De Vinne-Hallenbeck Co.*, 227 A.D. 296, 237 N.Y.S. 472 (1st Dep't 1929); *De Vinne-Hallenbeck Co. v. Autoyre Co.*, 113 Conn. 97, 154 Atl. 170 (1931).

38. Equivalent to $9,824,286 in 2003. McCusker, "Comparing the Purchasing Power."

39. L. A. Drake, *Trends*, 97.

40. D. B. Updike, *Literary Review*.

CHAPTER 11

1. D. B. Updike, *Literary Review* of the New York *Evening Post* (20 January 1923): 406.

2. The former, a benevolent society organized in 1785, was open to "any mechanic or tradesman of good character." In later years it sponsored lectures and scholarships to trades schools and maintained an "apprentices' library." (General Society of Mechanics and Tradesmen of the City of New York, *Annual Reports*, 100 (1886).) The New York Typographical Society, founded in 1809 as a "protective and benevolent" association, represented workers in wage, apprenticeship, and other matters until 1818. Then, in order to obtain incorporation, it yielded to demands from the New York State Legislature that it cease trade regulation activities and become solely a benevolent organization. (George Abbott Stevens, *New York Typographical Union No. 6: Study of a Modern Trade Union and its Predecessors* (Albany: New York State Department of Labor, 1913), 41–104.)

3. Alexander Drake, letter to the editor, *New York Times* (19 February 1914).

4. Robert Underwood Johnson, in *Theodore Low De Vinne, Printer* (New York: privately printed at the De Vinne Press, 1915), 26.

5. Alfred E. Ommen, "To Theodore Low De Vinne Printers Pay Deep Homage," *Printing* 46 (22 December 1928): 15.

6. Camille De Vèze, "A Tale of Two Foremen," *American Printer* 72 (5 July 1921): 60.

7. Bothwell Scrapbook, GC.

8. This and all other quotes from Frank Hopkins are from his *De Vinne and*

Marion Presses (Meriden, Conn.: Columbiad Club, 1936). See especially pp. 11–12, 13–14, 23, 34, and 42.

9. Henry Lewis Bullen, "Recruiting the Army of Printers," *Master Printer* 8 (March 1911): 139.

10. DeV Photographs, GC.

11. De Vèze, "Two Foremen."

12. *Typothetae Bulletin* 28 (3 December 1928): 1.

13. Carl Purington Rollins, "Theodore Low De Vinne," *Signature*, n.s. 10 (1950): 13.

14. H. L. Bullen, "Theodore Low De Vinne, Printer," *American Bulletin* 3 (April 1914): 8, and "How Theodore Low De Vinne Became America's Most Famous Printer," *Inland Printer*, 69 (July 1922): 519.

15. New York *World* (17 February 1914): 2.

16. Ira Brainerd, "Theodore Low De Vinne: The Printer, the Author, the Man," *Printing Art* 35 (May 1920): 205, 206; De Vèze quoted in Bullen, "TLD, Printer," 8; John Clyde Oswald, "Reminiscences of De Vinne – Master Craftsman," *Typothetae Bulletin* 28 (24 December 1928): 360.

17. TLD to Hamilton Wright Mabie and Beverly Chew, 23 May 1910, GC Publications.

18. TLD to Bullen, 24 October 1913, published in *Inland Printer* 84 (January 1930): 69; TLD to Bullen, 1 August 1911, DeV Papers, CU.

19. Unidentified clipping in DeV Papers, CU; Oswald, "Reminiscences of De Vinne," 360.

20. *Century* 88 (May 1914): 151.

21. The beret was given to the Grolier Club in March 1986 by great-grandson Charles Adcock De Vinne and the family.

22. TLD to Seth Low, 22 July 1896, Seth Low Papers, Rare Book and Manuscript Library, Columbia University.

23. Gregory Weinstein, *The Ardent Eighties* (New York: International Press, 1929), 35.

24. Ira H. Brainerd, "De Vinne, the Immortal," *Printing* 46 (8 December 1928): 17.

25. H. L. Bullen, "How TLD Became America's Most Famous Printer," 520.

26. *Century* 88 (May 1914): 152.

27. TLD to Thomas E. Donnelley, 19 December 1893, quoted in *Typothetae Bulletin* 18 (24 December 1928): 362.

28. Ira H. Brainerd, "Theodore Low De Vinne and the Century Company," *Typothetae Bulletin*, 28 (24 December 1928): 363.

29. Rollins, "TLD," *Signature*, 11.

30. Robert Underwood Johnson, *Remembered Yesterdays*, (Boston: Little, Brown, 1925), 110.

31. William W. Ellsworth, *A Golden Age of Authors*, (Boston: Houghton, Mifflin, 1919), 200.

32. Brainerd, "TLD and the Century Co.," 363–64; R. U. Johnson in *TLD, Printer*, 29; "Our Printer," *Century* 62 (September 1901): 794–95.

33. Brainerd, "TLD and the Century Co." 364; Hopkins, *De Vinne and Marion Presses*, 20.

34. TLD, "The Printer's Art," *Printer and Bookmaker* 29 (October 1899): 91.

35. George French, letter to the editor of the *Dial* 56 (16 March 1914): 236; Frances B. Greene, "De Vinne – A Permanent Influence in Development of Industry," *Typothetae Bulletin* 28 (24 December 1928): 356.

36. Richard Watson Gilder, editorial, *Century* 41 (November 1890): 87–99, 148.

37. However, he suggested that Henry Lewis Bullen write it, as his own "day of writing or authorship seem[ed] to be over." TLD to Bullen, 1 August 1911, DeV Papers, CU.

38. George French, letter to *Dial*, 236; "Theodore L. De Vinne & Co. – Late Francis Hart & Co., a Notable New York Printing House," *Paper World* 6 (March 1883): 2.

39. TLD, "American Printing," in Chauncey Mitchell Depew, ed., *1795–1895: One Hundred Years of American Commerce* (New York: D. O. Haynes & Co., 1895), 1:318.

40. TLD, address to Electrical Engineers, 9 February 1903, typescript, DeV Papers, CU.

41. TLD to J. W. Phinney, 31 December 1894, DeV Papers, AAS.

42. TLD to J. W. Finney, 28 May 1891, DeV Papers, AAS.

43. TLD, "The Linotype as I Have Found It," [New York, c. 1909. Listed in previous De Vinne bibliographies. Unconfirmed.]

44. TLD, *The Practice of Typography: Modern Methods of Book Composition, A Treatise on Type-Setting by Hand and by Machine, and on the Proper Arrangement and Imposition of Pages* (New York: Century Co., 1904), 96.

45. TLD, Yale College Club speech, p. 5, typescript, De V Collection, CU; "Do Machines Hurt a Trade?" *Manufacturer and Builder* 21 (June 1889): 138; "Printing Sixty Years Ago," in Columbia Typographical Union, *Third Year Book* (Washington, D.C.: 1901), 33.

46. TLD, "Machinery in Printing," *American Bookmaker* 19 (September 1894): 67.

47. Howard Mumford Jones, *The Age of Energy* (New York: Viking Press, 1971), 16.

48. Irene Tichenor, "Master Printers Organize," in Stuart W. Bruchey, ed., *Small Business in American Life* (New York: Columbia University Press, 1980), 118–19.

49. Susan Otis Thompson, *American Book Design and William Morris* (New York: Bowker, 1977), xiii.

50. TLD, *The Practice of Typography: A Treatise on Title-Pages, with Numerous Illustrations in Facsimile, and Some Observations on the Early and Recent Printing of Books*. (New York: Century Co., 1902), note on p. 198.

51. TLD to G. P. Holden, 6 September 1911, DeV Papers, CU.

52. TLD, "Some History of Taste in Typography," *Inland Printer* 27 (May 1901): 191.

53. TLD to R. U. Johnson, 8 November 1907, DeV Papers, CU.

54. TLD, speech before the National Editorial Association, *National Journalist*, undated clipping, DeV Papers, CU.

55. TLD, *Modern Methods*, 167–70, 109.

56. TLD, "Typography in Advertisements," *Printers' Ink* 4 (7 January 1891): 3.

57. TLD, "Some History of Taste in Typography," 191.

58. TLD, "Do You Know the Letters?" in *Liber Scriptorum* (New York: Authors Club, 1893), 192.

59. TLD, "The Mazarin Bible," *Printers' Circular* 8 (September 1873): 233–35.

60. TLD, "Masculine Printing," United Typothetae of America, *Proceedings of the Fifth Annual Meeting*, 1891, 140.

61. TLD, "Mediæval Printing," *Printer* 5 (April 1864): 66.

62. While the capitals were based on actual Roman inscriptions, original lower-case "roman" types were based on letterforms of Renaissance manuscripts written with a broad-nibbed pen and held at a natural writing slant of about a 45-degree angle, creating gradual, mild variation between thick and thin strokes. In the resulting type, the thick strokes have a diagonal stress counterclockwise from the vertical. In the eighteenth century, the stress changed from diagonal to vertical but the mild variation between thick and thin was retained. Roman types designed in the late eighteenth and early nineteenth century departed from calligraphic models of these "old-style" types and imitated the delicacy of engraving, making an abrupt change from thick to thin within each letter and reducing the thin strokes of the letters and their serifs to hairlines, giving a distinctly vertical appearance. Firmin Didot (1764–1836) in France and Giambattista Bodoni (1740–1813) in Italy brought "modern" types to their logical extreme.

63. TLD, "The Old and the New," in *Book-lovers Almanac for 1896* (New York: Duprat & Co., © 1895), 47.

64. TLD, *The Practice of Typography: A Treatise on the Process of Type-Making, the Point System, the Names, Sizes, Styles and Prices of Plain Printing Types* (New York: Century Co., 1900), 253.

65. TLD, *Historic Printing Types* (New York: Grolier Club, 1886), 73.

66. TLD, untitled article, *Printers' Miscellany* (July 1859): [4].

67. Beatrice Warde, "Type Faces, Old and New," *The Library* 16 (September 1935): 121–43.

68. TLD, *Historic Printing Types*, 73. For further discussion of Scotch-face, see James Mosley, "'Scotch Roman': What It Is & How It Got Its Name," *Ampersand* 17 (Autumn–Winter 1998): 2–11 and Alastair Johnson, "Scotch and Water," *Print* 52 (September–October 1998): 48, 50, 330.

69. Curiously, among the 145 pages are three of an ornamented face with curlicues that he patently opposed, as well as two pages of "German" face, and one of Greek.

70. Daniel Berkeley Updike, *Printing Types, Their History, Forms, and Use: A Study in Survivals* (Cambridge, Mass.: Harvard University Press, 1922), 2:193.

71. Martin Hutner, *The Merrymount Press: An Exhibition on the Occasion of the 100th Anniversary of the Founding of the Press* (Cambridge, Mass.: Houghton Library, Harvard University and New York: Grolier Club, 1993), 75.

72. Updike, *Literary Review*.

73. TLD, speech to the National Editorial Association.

74. There were plenty of precedents for this style. Perhaps, for example, he was thinking of Caleb Stower's *The Printer's Grammar*, (London, 1787).

75. TLD, *Title-Pages As Seen by a Printer* (New York: Grolier Club, 1901), 312 and 313; *Treatise on Title-Pages*, 216–217.

76. TLD to Edmund Clarence Steadman, 17 December 1887, DeV Papers, CU.

77. Joseph Blumenthal, *The Printed Book in America* (Boston: David R. Godine, 1977), 31.

78. TLD, *Printers' Price List* (New York: Francis Hart, 1871), pp. 403–4.

79. TLD to James Bothwell, 17 July 1902, printed in Grolier Club, *Catalogue of Work of the De Vinne*, 76.

80. TLD, National Editorial Association speech, 389.

81. Hopkins, *De Vinne and Marion Presses*, 39.

82. TLD, "The Printer's Province," *Printing Art* 5 (May 1905): 131.

83. Ibid., 130.

84. TLD, "The Printer's Art," 91; *Theodore Low De Vinne, Printer*, 2; "A Perfect Specimen of American Bookmaking," clipping identified as "Tribune, August 8," DeV Papers, CU.

85. Stanley Morison, *Four Centuries of Fine Printing* (New York: Farrar, Straus & Co., 1949), 11.

86. TLD, National Editorial Association speech, 388.

87. Charles T. Jacobi, "Influence in America of the Chiswick Press, with Notes on American Typographers," *American Printer* 80 (20 January 1925): 18–19.

88. This was explicit, for example, in *Title-Pages As Seen by a Printer*, pp. 237–41.

89. Arthur Warren, *Charles Whittinghams, Printers* (New York: Grolier Club, 1896), 15–16.

90. TLD, "Masculine Printing," 141; TLD to Robert Underwood Johnson, 8 November 1907, DeV Papers, CU.

91. TLD, Yale College Club speech, 1.

92. William Dana Orcutt, "American Low-Cost Volumes," *Times Literary Supplement*, Printing Number (13 October 1927): 60.

93. Robert D. Harlan, *John Henry Nash: The Biography of a Career* (Berkeley and Los Angeles: University of California Press, 1970), 14.

94. Updike, "The Essentials of a Well-Made Book," a 1940 lecture, reprinted in Peterson, *Well-Made Book*, 39–40.

95. Stanley Morison, "Recollections and Perspectives" in *Updike: American Printer and His Merrymount Press* (New York: American Institute of Graphic Arts, 1947), 56–66.

96. Printer's note in TLD, *The Old and the New: A Friendly Dispute between Juvenis and Senex* (Marlborough, N.Y.: The Village Press, 1933), unpaged.

97. Stanley Morison, *The Typographic Book, 1450–1935* (London: E. Benn, 1963), 55; James Moran, *Stanley Morison: His Typographic Achievement* (New York: Hastings House, 1971), 106.

98. Gregg Anderson, "Hand-Book for an Exhibition," in *Updike: American Printer and his Merrymount Press* (New York: American Institute of Graphic Arts, 1947), 69.

99. Walter Gilliss to H. H. Chambers of the *New York Times*, 16 February 1924, GC Publications.

100. John Russell Taylor, *The Art Nouveau Book in Britain* (Edinburgh: Paul Harris, 1980, c. 1966), 153–54.

101. TLD, "Mediæval Printing," 65–67.

102. Ralph Green, *A Check List of American Nineteenth Century Type Specimen Books* (Chicago, 1951); Rollo Silver, *Typefounding in America, 1787–1825* (Charlottesville: University Press of Virginia, 1965), 24.

103. George Parker Winship, "The Literature of Printing," *Dolphin* 3 (1938): 476.

104. E. C. Bigmore and C. W. H. Wyman, comps., *A Bibliography of Printing*, 3vols. (London: Bernard Quaritch, 1880–86), 1:390.

105. See Blades's "Literary Ghosts," *Caslon's Circular* no. 31 (Winter Season, 1883): [1–2]; and *On the Present Aspect of the Question – Who Was the Inventor of Printing?* (London: privately printed, 1887), especially p. 3.

106. Brainerd, "TLD, Printer, Author, Man," 204.

107. Now in the private collection of G. Thomas Tanselle.

108. TLD to J. W. Phinney, 17 April, 27 October, and 19 December 1894, DeV Papers, AAS.

109. TLD to Brander Matthews, 15 November 1902, Brander Matthews Papers,

Rare Book and Manuscript Library, Columbia University. The changes from one "edition" to the next were relatively minor; in bibliographic terms they are considered different *printings*.

110. TLD, "William Caxton," *Printers' Circular* 7 (October 1872?): 321.

111. See Bullen's "Collectanea Typographica" column in *Inland Printer* 83–84 (August 1929–April 1930).

112. The Grolier Club's De Vinne exhibit catalogue, *Catalogue of Works of the De Vinne Press* (New York, 1929), said the bookplate was "designed and engraved" by French (p. 27). I am grateful to Mark D. Tomasko for suspecting and verifying that the catalogue entry is in error.

113. G. Thomas Tanselle, "A Rationale of Collecting," *Studies in Bibliography* 51 (1998): 1–25.

114. Ira Hutchinson Brainerd, address at exhibit opening, Grolier Club, *Catalogue of the Work of the De Vinne Press*, 12.

Chapter 12

1. U.S., Bureau of the Census, *Twelfth Census of the United States, 1900*, vol. 8, *Manufacturers*, pt. 2, *States and Territories* (Washington, D.C., 1902).

2. Attribution to De Vinne: Otto Fuhrmann, *Gutenberg and the Strasbourg Documents of 1439* (New York: Press of the Woolly Whale, 1940), 103. The saying is recorded as being an inscription above the door of Laurens Coster's house in Haarlem in 1540. William Francis Henry King, *Classical and Foreign Quotations* (London: Whitaker and Sons, 1887), 48.

3. D. B. Updike, *Literary Review* of the New York *Evening Post* (20 January 1923): 406; John Clyde Oswald, *Publishers' Weekly* 114 (1 December 1928): 2291; Will Ransom to Thomas A. Larremore, 25 March 1941, quoted in Thomas A. Larremore and Amy Hopkins Larremore, *The Marion Press, A Survey and a Check-List* . . . Jamaica, N.Y.: Queens Borough Public Library, 1943), 67; Susan Otis Thompson, *American Book Design and William Morris* (New York: Bowker, 1977), 154.

4. William Dana Orcutt, "The Art of the Book in America" in Charles Holme, ed., *The Art of the Book*, special number of *Studio* for 1914, 259.

5. In "Printing Should Be Invisible" (© 1932), Beatrice Warde used wine goblets as a metaphor for the function of printing: a true wine connoisseur would choose to drink from a crystal-clear goblet rather than an ornate one of solid gold. Reprinted in Paul Bennett, ed., *Books and Printing: A Treasury for Typophiles* (Cleveland: World Publishing Co., 1951), 109–14.

6. Brander Matthews, "The Grolier Club," *Century* 39 (November 1889): 95.

7. Carl Purington Rollins, "Theodore Low De Vinne," *Signature* n.s., 10 (1950): 20–21.

SELECTIVE BIBLIOGRAPHY OF SOURCES

MANUSCRIPT AND ARCHIVAL SOURCES

American Antiquarian Society
> Theodore Low De Vinne Papers

Choate Rosemary Hall, Andrew Mellon Library
> De Vinne Papers

Columbia University, Rare Book and Manuscript Library
> Theodore Low De Vinne Papers
> Typothetae Papers

Grolier Club
> Club archives
> Theodore Low De Vinne Memorabilia Collection, 1850–1914
> Theodore Low De Vinne Photograph and Memorabilia
> Collection, 1897–1924

New York City Government
> City Register (real estate deeds and mortgages)
> New Buildings Docket Ledger, Department of Buildings

New York Public Library, Astor, Lenox and Tilden Foundations
> Century Company Records
> Richard Watson Gilder Papers
> Rodman Gilder Papers

BOOKS AND ARTICLES

Antonetti, Martin. "The Club Bindery and Its Later Incarnations." *Gazette of the Grolier Club* n.s. 47 (1995–1996): 83–102.

Baker, Elizabeth Faulkner. *Printers and Technology: A History of the International Printing Pressmen and Assistants' Union.* New York: Columbia University Press, 1957.

Barnett, George Ernest. *The Printers: A Study of American Trade Unionism.* Cambridge, Mass.: American Economic Association, 1909.

Blades, William. *On the Present Aspect of the Question – Who Was the Inventor of Printing?* London: privately printed, 1887.

Blumenthal, Joseph. *The Printed Book in America.* Boston: David R. Godine, 1977.

Brainerd, Ira H. "De Vinne, the Immortal." *Printing* 46 (8 December 1928): 16–17, 32.

_____. "Theodore Low De Vinne: The Printer, the Author, the Man." *Printing Art* 35 (May 1920): 201–7.

Selective Bibliography

Bullen, Henry Lewis. "Collectanea Typographica" column. *Inland Printer* 83–84 (August 1929–April 1930).

_____. "How Theodore Low De Vinne Became America's Most Famous Printer." *Inland Printer* 69 (July 1922): 515–20.

_____. "Theodore Low De Vinne, Printer." *American Bulletin* 3 (April 1914): 5–8.

Carrington, Fitz Roy. "Private and Special Presses: II. Notes on Some Book Clubs and on Printing in America." *Book Buyer* n.s. 23 (September 1901): 96–100; (October 1901): 215–18.

Century Company. *Two Score and Five: Quality*. New York: Century Co., 1915.

Chew, Samuel C. *Fruit Among the Leaves*. New York: Appleton-Century-Crofts, 1950.

Cochrane, Charles H. "De Vinne as I Knew Him." *Inland Printer* 73 (July 1924): 560.

Comparato, Frank E. *Chronicles of Genius and Folly: R. Hoe & Company and the Printing Press as a Service to Democracy*. Culver City, Calif.: Labyrinthos, 1979.

Delaware Art Museum. *The Golden Age of American Illustration, 1880-1914* [catalogue of an exhibition September 14–October 15, 1972]. Wilmington: Delaware Art Museum, 1972.

De Maré, Eric. *The Victorian Wood-Block Illustrators*. London: Gordon Fraser, 1980.

Drake, Leonard A. *Trends in the New York Printing Industry*. New York: Columbia University Press, 1940.

Ellsworth, William W. *A Golden Age of Authors*. Boston: Houghton, Mifflin, 1919.

French, George. "The Work of the De Vinne Press." *American Printer* 32 (July 1901): [4 unnumbered pages] between 356 and 357.

Gage, Charles M. "The Origin of Coated or Enameled Book Paper." *Paper Trade Journal* 48 (3 July 1919): 28, 30.

Gascoigne, Bamber. *How to Identify Prints*. New York: Thames and Hudson, 1986.

Griffiths, David N., comp. *The Bibliography of the Book of Common Prayer 1549-1999*. London: British Library; New Castle, Del.: Oak Knoll, 2002.

Grolier Club. *Catalogue of Work of the De Vinne Press*. New York: Grolier Club, 1929.

Gustafson, W. Eric, "Printing and Publishing." Max Hall, ed. *Made In New York: Case Studies in Metropolitan Manufacturing*. Cambridge: Harvard University Press, 1959, 135–239, 341–54.

Harlan, Robert D. *John Henry Nash: The Biography of a Career*. Berkeley and Los Angeles: University of California Press, 1970.

Hinrichs, A. F. *The Printing Industry in New York and Its Environs.* New York: Regional Plans of New York and Its Environs, 1924.

Hopkins, Frank E. *The De Vinne and Marion Presses.* Meriden, Conn.: Columbiad Club, 1936.

Howe, Ellic. "From Bewick to the Halftone: A Survey of Illustration Processes During the Nineteenth Century." *Typography* 3 (Summer 1937): 19–23.

Hutner, Martin. *The Merrymount Press: An Exhibition on the Occasion of the 100th Anniversary of the Founding of the Press.* Cambridge: Houghton Library, Harvard University and New York: Grolier Club, 1993.

Jacobi, Charles T. "Influence in America of the Chiswick Press, with Notes on American Typographers." *American Printer* 80 (20 January 1925): 18–19.

John, Arthur. *The Best Years of the Century: Richard Watson Gilder, Scribner's Monthly, and the Century Magazine, 1870–1909.* Urbana: University of Illinois Press, 1981.

Johnson, A. F. *Type Designs: Their History and Development.* 3rd ed. London: Deutsch, 1967.

Johnson, Alastair, "Scotch and Water." *Print* 52 (September–October 1998): 48, 50, 330.

Johnson, Robert Underwood. *Remembered Yesterdays.* Boston: Little, Brown, 1925.

Kelly, R. Gordon. *Mother Was a Lady: Self and Society in Selected American Children's Periodicals, 1865–1890.* Westport, Conn.: Greenwood Press, 1974.

Koenig, Michael. "Theodore Low De Vinne: His Contributions to the Art of Printing." Master's thesis, University of Chicago Graduate Library School, 1968.

_____ . "De Vinne and the De Vinne Press." *Library Quarterly* 41 (January 1971): 1–24.

_____ . "Theodore Low De Vinne." *DLB* 187 (1997): 67–72.

Landau, Sarah Bradford. "The Row House of New York's West Side." *Journal of the Society of Architectural Historians* 34 (March 1975): 19–36.

Larremore, Thomas A. and Amy Hopkins Larremore. *The Marion Press: A Survey and a Check-List.* Jamaica. N.Y.: Queens Borough Public Library, 1943.

Linton, William James. "Art in Engraving on Wood." *Atlantic Monthly* 43 (June 1879): 705–15.

_____ . *The History of Wood-Engraving in America.* Boston: Estes & Lauriat, 1882.

Lipset, Seymour Martin, Martin A. Trow, and James S. Coleman. *Union Democracy: The Internal Politics of the International Typographical Union.* Glencoe, Ill.: Free Press, 1956.

Selective Bibliography

Lockwood, Charles. *Bricks and Brownstones: The New York Row House, 1783–1929, An Architectural and Social History.* New York: McGraw-Hill, 1972.

———. *Manhattan Moves Uptown: An Illustrated History.* Boston: Houghton Mifflin, 1976.

Mallison, David Walker. "Henry Lewis Bullen and the Typographic Library and Museum of the American Type Founders Company." D.L.S. diss., Columbia University, 1976.

Matthews, Brander. "The Grolier Club." *Century Magazine* 39 (November 1889): 86–97.

Maurice, Arthur Bartlee. "Literary Clubland." *Bookman* 21 (July 1905): 497–513.

McCusker, John J. "Comparing the Purchasing Power of Money in the United States (or Colonies) from 1665 to 2002." Economic History Series, 2003. http://www.eh.net/hmit/ppowerusd/.

McGrew, Mac. *American Metal Typefaces of the Twentieth Century.* 2nd ed. New Castle, Del.: Oak Knoll, 1993.

McLean, Rauri. *Victorian Book Design.* New York: Oxford University Press, 1963.

A Memorial of Joanna Augusta De Vinne. New York: printed for family friends only, 1888.

A Memorial of the Reverend Daniel De Vinne. New York: printed for the family, 1883.

Moran, James. *Stanley Morison: His Typographic Achievement.* New York: Hastings House, 1971.

Morgan, Charlotte. *The Origin and History of the Employing Printers' Association.* New York: Columbia University Press, 1930.

Morison, Stanley. *Four Centuries of Fine Printing.* New York: Farrar, Straus & Co., 1949.

———. *The Typographic Book, 1450–1935.* London: E. Benn, 1963.

Mosley, James. "'Scotch Roman': What It Is and How It Got Its Name." *Ampersand* 17 (Autumn–Winter 1998): 2–11.

Mott, Frank Luther. *A History of American Magazines.* 5 vols. Cambridge: Harvard University Press, 1938–68.

Northup, Lesley Armstrong. "The '1892 Revision' of the Book of Common Prayer of the Episcopal Church." Ph.D. diss., Catholic University of America, 1991.

"A Noted Printer and a Notable Printing Establishment: The De Vinne Press." *Paper World* 14 (January 1887): 1–6.

Ommen, Alfred E. "To Theodore Low De Vinne Printers Pay Deep Homage." *Printing* 46 (22 December 1928): 14–16, 18.

Orcutt, William Dana. "American Low-Cost Volumes." *Times Literary Supplement*, printing number (13 October 1927): 56, 58–60, 62.

———. "The Art of the Book in America." In *The Art of the Book*, edited by Charles Holme, 259–63. Special number of *Studio*, for 1914.

———. *The Kingdom of Books*. Boston: Little, Brown, 1927.

Oswald, John Clyde. "A Great American Printer." *Publishers' Weekly* 114 (1 December 1928): 2289–95.

Pankow, David. "Dungeons and Dragon's Blood: The Development of Late Nineteenth and Early Twentieth Century Platemaking Processes." *Printing History* 10.1, no. 19 (1988): 21–35.

Peterson, William S., ed. *The Ideal Book: Essays and Lectures on the Arts of the Book by William Morris*. Berkeley: University of California Press, 1982.

———. *The Well-Made Book: Essays and Lectures by Daniel Berkeley Updike*. West New York, N.J.: Mark Batty, 2002.

Powell, Leona M. *The History of the United Typothetae of America*. Chicago: University of Chicago Press, 1926.

Rogers, Daniel T. *The Work Ethic in Industrial America, 1850–1920*. Chicago: University of Chicago Press, 1968.

Rollins, Carl Purington. "Theodore Low De Vinne." *Signature* n.s. 10 (1950): 3–21.

———. "Typographic Adventures of the Past: I. The Jade Book." *New Colophon* 2 (September 1949): 294–303.

Shaw, Paul. "The Century Family." *Fine Print* 7.4 (October 1981): 144.

Smith, Virginia. "Longevity and Legibility: Two Types from the De Vinne Press and How They Have Fared." *Printing History*. 8.1, no. 15 (1986) 13–21.

Stevens, George Abbott. *New York Typographical Union No. 6: Study of a Modern Trade Union and Its Predecessors*. Albany: New York State Department of Labor, 1913.

Sturgis, Russell. "The City House: The East and South." *Scribner's Magazine* 7 (June 1890): 707–9, 712.

Tebbel, John. *A History of Book Publishing in the United States*. 4 vols. New York: Bowker, 1972–1981.

———. *The American Magazine: A Compact History*. New York: Hawthorn Books, 1969.

"Theodore L. De Vinne & Co. – Late Francis Hart & Co., a Notable New York Printing House." *Paper World* 6 (March 1883): 1–3.

Theodore Low De Vinne, Printer. New York: privately printed, 1915.

Thompson, Susan Otis. *American Book Design and William Morris*. New York: Bowker, 1977.

Tomsich, John. *A Genteel Endeavor: American Culture and Politics in the Gilded Age*. Stanford: Stanford University Press, 1971.

Tooker, L. Frank. *The Joys and Tribulations of an Editor.* New York: Century Co., 1924.

Tracy, George A., comp. *History of the Typographical Union, Its Beginnings, Progress, and Development* . . . . Indianapolis: International Typographical Union, 1913.

Typothetae Bulletin 28 (24 December 1928) [issue devoted to De Vinne].

Updike, Daniel Berkeley. *Literary Review* of the New York *Evening Post* (20 January 1923): 406.

_____ . *Notes on the Merrymount Press and Its Work.* Cambridge: Harvard University Press, 1934.

_____ . *Printing Types, Their History, Forms, and Use: A Study in Survivals.* 2 vols. Cambridge: Harvard University Press, 1922.

Updike: American Printer and His Merrymount Press. New York: American Institute of Graphic Arts, 1947.

Warde, Beatrice. "Type Faces, Old and New." *Library* 16 (September 1935): 121–43.

"The Warehouse and the Factory in Architecture." *Architectural Record* 15 (January 1904): 1–17; (February 1904): 122–33.

Way, W. Irving. "Theodore L. De Vinne, the Scholar Printer." *Inland Printer* 23 (April 1899): 33–37.

Weinstein, Gregory. *The Ardent Eighties.* New York: International Press, 1929.

Winship, George Parker. "The Literature of Printing." *Dolphin* 3 (1938): 471–91.

Wroth, Lawrence C. "Corpus Typographicum: A Review of English and American Printers' Manuals." *Dolphin* no. 2 (1935): 157–70.

_____ . "Printing in the Mauve Decade." *New York Herald Tribune Books* (8 February 1942): 18.

Ziff, Larzer. *The American 1890s: Life and Times of a Lost Generation.* New York: Viking Press, 1966.

INDEX

Index

Index

Index

Index

Index

SET IN MILLER TYPES
DRAWN BY MATTHEW CARTER
BASED ON SCOTTISH TYPES OF
THE NINETEENTH CENTURY

———————

Book design & typography
by Jerry Kelly